CATCHING
THE SKY

CATCHING THE SKY

TWO BROTHERS, ONE FAMILY, AND OUR DREAM TO FLY

COLTEN MOORE

WITH KEITH O'BRIEN

37INK

—

ATRIA

NEW YORK   LONDON   TORONTO   SYDNEY   NEW DELHI

ATRIA PAPERBACK   37INK

An Imprint of Simon & Schuster, Inc.
1230 Avenue of the Americas
New York, NY 10020

First 37 INK/Atria Paperback edition February 2017

37INK / **ATRIA** PAPERBACK and colophon are trademarks of
Simon & Schuster, Inc.

For information about special discounts for bulk purchases,
please contact Simon & Schuster Special Sales at 1-866-506-1949
or business@simonandschuster.com.

The Simon & Schuster Speakers Bureau can bring authors to your
live event. For more information or to book an event contact the
Simon & Schuster Speakers Bureau at 1-866-248-3049
or visit our website at www.simonspeakers.com.

Interior design by Paul Dippolito

Manufactured in the United States of America

10   9   8   7   6   5   4   3   2   1

Library of Congress Control Number: 2015044662

ISBN 978-1-5011-1724-4
ISBN 978-1-5011-1725-1 (pbk)
ISBN 978-1-5011-1726-8 (ebook)

For my mother, my father, and Caleb

But why, some say, the moon? Why choose this as our goal? And they may well ask why climb the highest mountain? Why, 35 years ago, fly the Atlantic? Why does Rice play Texas?

—President John F. Kennedy, giving his
famous "moon" speech at Rice University
in Houston, Texas, September 1962

CONTENTS

PART III: THE MOUNTAINTOP

AUTHOR'S NOTE

PEOPLE ALWAYS want to know why I take the risks that I do.

"Am I afraid?" they ask—when really, what they mean is, "Am I crazy?" When I set out to write this book, I wanted to answer these questions by not only telling my personal story but also by placing that story in the broader context of American risk-taking, of men and women, pursuing sports, on the edge. To do that, I needed to work with an accomplished reporter and author—and it was clear that Keith O'Brien was the right choice. This is my story, my brother's story, and my family's narrative. But hopefully, in the end, it's more than just that. Am I afraid? All the time. Am I crazy? Aren't we all?

AUTHOR'S NOTE

CATCHING
THE SKY

PROLOGUE

THE STORM moved in at nightfall, spitting snow from the sky. I wasn't concerned about it and, of course, neither was my brother. Caleb never worried about anything: not what people thought of him; not the backflips he was about to do on a quarter-ton snowmobile three stories up in the air on national television; and certainly not a little storm closing in on the mountain. By Colorado standards, the storm was nothing—just a little snow, with some ice and low visibility later, maybe. But who cared? This was Aspen, ESPN's Winter X Games, our one chance every year to prove we were the most talented freestyle snowmobilers alive—the best at flipping the machines. Of course there would be snow. There was supposed to be snow. And, anyway, it just added to the ambiance—the whole feeling that this was big, that there was magic in the cold winter night. The snow, falling from the heavens, seemed to sparkle in the lights on the mountain.

I looked at Caleb, sitting atop his black-and-red two-cylinder snowmobile emblazoned with a gold star and his beloved No. 31. He looked ready—his usual self—and that put me at ease. His practice runs in recent days had been shaky at times. In the weeks before we arrived in Aspen, Caleb had crashed all too often as he honed his tricks for the competition—uncharacteristic tumbles that left his body bruised and his back aching. While Caleb didn't seem to dwell on his mistakes, I certainly did, rolling them over in my mind. But then, that was me—the younger brother, always stewing in silence. Did I have what it took? Could I really do this? We were from the panhandle of Texas, where hills are hard to find and snowstorms about as likely as a stampede of dinosaurs. Did we really belong on this mountain with Canadians and Minnesotans, guys who had been riding sleds all their lives? In recent years, I had worried about that a lot. And so, yes, I had noted Caleb's crashes in the days before Aspen. I could see my brother was pushing himself, pushing the edge of what was possible, anything to win his first gold medal at the X Games.

But that afternoon in our final practice runs on the course in Aspen, Caleb had been perfect, nailing down his seventy-five-second routine of flips and jumps. He was dialed in and he knew it, flashing his country-boy smile to the cameras and predicting a big night. "It's going to happen," he said as the sun went down and the cold began to set in.

Now everything was in place: the riders, the television trucks, the crowd. Fifteen thousand people had gathered on the mountain to watch. A million more were viewing at home. And ESPN's broadcast was ready from Aspen, about to go live to the world. "We're at two minutes right now," a producer informed us, standing in the snow at the start of the course.

"Two minutes," he said again.

A hush fell over the riders. Even the producer wouldn't speak much anymore, flashing hand signals instead to let us know that it was time.

One minute to go.

Thirty seconds.

Five, four, three, two, one . . .

Caleb straddled his sled and revved his engine, pulling on the throttle. He was alone on the course—the first of eight finalists to go for the night.

• • •

THE ANNOUNCERS were almost giddy as the competition got started. "The infamous Moore brothers," the play-by-play man called us on television, as ESPN's cameras panned to my brother wearing his goggles and helmet. "Caleb has been throwing down in practice," the TV commentator added. "He's got the big tricks. But I'm really hoping he can smooth out that run."

My brother looked square into the camera as he pulled away, stood up on his sled, popped a wheelie in the snow, and acknowledged the crowd with a raised fist and a flick of his finger—classic Caleb, always the showman. Then he turned, hit the throttle, kicked up a cloud of snow, and peeled off toward the first ramp, whipping through the flurries falling from the sky. He landed his first jump just fine, flying some ninety feet through the air, as he let go of the handlebars, held on momentarily with his feet, and then grabbed the bars once again. But it wasn't exactly perfect. The nose of his sled came in a little high, causing it to slam into the snow as the back treads touched down again—a fact the announcers pointed out to everyone watching at home. He had stomped out the landing, but still. *"A little tentative start there for Caleb Moore."*

Tentative was the last thing Caleb ever was—on that day or any other. The word most people used to describe him was fearless. He'd first proven it racing and jumping ATVs on backcountry dirt racks in rural Texas and, later, on this very mountain in Aspen, on a snowmobile. But there was certainly reason to be tentative—for Caleb, for me, for all of us—if you let your mind go there. We'd all been injured riding, snapping bones and suffering countless concussions. No one could say exactly how many. It's not like we always went to a doctor. Even if my parents demanded that we go get checked out at a hospital, we'd ignore them at times, especially Caleb, once he turned eighteen. He wanted nothing to do with doctors, nurses, or paramedics—anyone who might keep him from riding, from being free. Once, while practicing for an ATV freestyle show in Amarillo, the engine on his four-wheeler bogged out and died—in midair—two stories up. He jumped off the floating hunk of metal and slammed down onto the hard floor of the empty arena, injuring his back. For months afterward, Caleb ached, struggling to walk or sit at times. Chiropractors became his best friends. But he refused to see a doctor, fearing he'd be told to stay off the machines. It was only later we learned that he had cracked a bone in his back that day in Amarillo—a serious injury that would have sidelined just about anyone, in any sport. Not Caleb, though. He rode like that for months. "I'm fine," he'd say, rubbing his lower back. "I've got this."

Part of the toughness was practical. If we didn't ride, we didn't get paid. This was our job. It wasn't like we had extra money sitting around at home to finance a few weeks of doing nothing, with our father working as a truck driver and our mother employed as a school librarian. You couldn't let the injuries get to you—physically or mentally. Or that was it. You were done. No more riding for you. Still, we struggled at times to come to terms with the risks we were taking in flight—especially when we saw, with our own eyes, how even a simple mistake, something so small, could ruin a life, destroy entire families in an instant, and set into motion a horrifying chain of events. There's your friend, under-rotating his quad in the air and slamming into the ground. There's his blood in the dirt—too much of it—and people screaming, lots of screaming. There's the medical helicopter landing in the pasture by your house. And there's your mother—*our* mother—at the kitchen window, shaking with fear, refusing to come outside, unwilling to face what we had done.

She hadn't chosen this: our sport, our lives. The only way she got through it was by praying—and that she did all the time. At home. When we were on the road. And certainly before the X Games, our biggest event of the year. Just before the snow started falling that night in Aspen, our mother gathered everyone around inside our trailer. We held hands. We fell silent. And, with our heads bowed, she began to pray.

"God, please watch over these riders, all the riders, and keep them safe. Help them have successful runs," she said. And then, she added one final wish. "I'm just going to come right out and say it, God. I'm asking for your favor. We want our boys to win."

"Amen."

Caleb and I began to pack up, grab our things. It was time to ride. My mother always liked to hug us one last time. She needed that moment of closeness between mother and son, before we left. But being up first, Caleb felt pressed for time. Amid the flurry of well-wishers and back-slappers, people seeing us off, my brother slipped out the door of the trailer, crunching across the snow in his riding boots. It would be a minute before my mother realized he was gone, too late to say good-bye.

• • •

IF HIS first jump was tentative, Caleb's next few were perfect—huge tricks that thrilled the crowd, the announcers, and also our sponsors watching at the end of the course. B. C. Vaught, our manager, was standing right next to them, nodding, as Caleb nailed not one but two blackflips, as well as a body varial that left him dangling off the edge of his sled in midair, high above the hard, frozen ground.

"Holy cow!" one sponsor exclaimed.

"That was awesome," said another.

B.C. wasn't always the most relaxed presence at an event. Sometimes, our goateed manager would scream out of fear about what we were doing—so much so that it became a running joke among us on the road. "Calm down, old man," Caleb would have to tell him.

But not tonight. Watching Caleb, B.C. felt good—as good as he'd ever felt at the X Games. "He's riding unbelievably well," our jittery manager informed our sponsors while keeping his eyes locked on Caleb's sled. I felt sure my brother was headed for a great first run, gold-medal contention easily. And up on the hill, my parents did, too, waving Texas flags in the night.

"Under thirty seconds left for Caleb Moore," the announcer declared. Plenty of time to hit the last ramp on the course for one final stunt—a trick called the tsunami indy flip. To do it, you need every second you've got. Right off the ramp, you need to pull for the flip, fully committing to it. Then, when the sled is upside down and you're hanging underneath it, dangling off the handlebars, you kick your legs out to the side and whip the snowmobile back around. It's one of the most difficult tricks out there—because, with your body dangling so far away from the sled, there's no time to recover from even the smallest mistake. In the parlance of freestyle, it was a KOD flip, a kiss of death, a big finish for Caleb, and sure to please the judges. We all figured he would nail it; he had executed such flips countless times before. But as soon as he went airborne and pulled for the flip, tugging his 450-pound machine in the sky, it was clear there was a problem.

"Under-rotated," one announcer declared.

"Coming up a little bit short," said the other.

My brother, now hanging beneath his sled, kicked his legs and pulled on the throttle, but he couldn't get it all the way around. The ski tips on the front of the snowmobile clipped the snow coming back down. The crowd groaned. Caleb rocketed face-first into the ground, sliding across the snow. The snowmobile flipped end over end and then hit Caleb, spearing him right in the chest with the nose of the machine. "Just pummeled him," one announcer sighed on national television. The tsunami had gone horribly wrong. His body bounced, flipped over, and then spun to a rest. He was faceup, on his back, with his arms and legs spread wide, like a snow angel on the mountain.

I ran to him. B.C. ran to him. My father jumped a barricade holding back the fans and ran to him, too. Caleb was unconscious. When he came to, about thirty seconds later, the medical staff started asking questions.

Do you know your name?

Caleb Moore, he replied.

Do you know where you are?

Aspen. The X Games.

Do you know what happened?

Caleb was speaking as if through a fog, like he had just awakened from a long sleep. But he knew exactly what had happened. As far as he was concerned, he had squandered his shot at a gold medal—again. "I had a perfect run going," he complained to our father as he lay there in the snow. "And then I had to go and ruin it on that one last jump."

After a long while, and still more questions, Caleb sat up, peeled himself off the ground, and began to make his way to the medical tent nearby for further evaluation. He was shaky on his feet. To get to the tent, he'd need to hold on to my father's arm. But he was walking on his own and claiming to be okay.

"Does anything hurt?" my father kept asking.

"Not really," Caleb would reply.

I scampered back to my own snowmobile, with B.C. in my ear. "Your brother's fine," he told me, trying to get me to focus on what I still had to do. "He walked to the medical tent," B.C. continued. "He's in good hands. . . . You need to start thinking about your run. . . . Remember why you're here."

It was the stuff a good manager should have been saying. But I wasn't listening. B.C. was talking right through me. I was thinking about Caleb, my eyes cast down at the snow. The event would go on. The riders, including me, would still ride. And, of course, there was the crowd, still cheering. Yet something didn't feel right. It's like I already knew.

In the medical tent, off camera and out of sight, my brother was collapsing. In the ambulance, he'd need to be sedated. And at the hospital in Aspen, his blood pressure would begin to fluctuate, then fall, until it was clear Caleb needed help—a different hospital, a heart surgeon, a complicated procedure to save his life. He needed to get out of Aspen. But now we were battling weather, time, and Caleb's broken body. His heart was racing, too fast.

155 beats a minute.

162 beats a minute.

177 beats a minute.

Outside the snow kept falling: through the darkness, on the road, swirling past the ambulance taking Caleb away, and stirring up thoughts inside me.

Without my brother, I was nothing.

THE FLATLANDS

It is a region almost as vast and trackless as the ocean—a land where no man, either savaged or civilized, permanently abides; it spreads forth into a treeless desolate waste of uninhabited solitude, which has always been, and must continue, uninhabited forever; even the savages dare not venture to cross it except at two or three places, where they know water can be found.

—Capt. Randolph B. Marcy, upon visiting Texas, in 1849

Part I

THE FLATLANDS

COME AND GET IT

WE WERE broke again—this is the story they told us—we were broke and this time it was serious. My parents had no money for Christmas. No money to buy us new toys. The bill collectors were calling— all the time now, especially during dinner. They were coming for everything—the car, the house, the new store-bought furniture inside—and my mother was worried.

She looked around our home on the outskirts of Fort Worth with a growing sense of disgust and shame. The house itself wasn't much: a modest, three-bedroom ranch with new siding we shouldn't have bought and a patio out back we rarely used for entertaining, tucked into the suburban sprawl near the airport. Inside, my parents, living on credit cards and dreams, had overdone it. In our quest to be big-city people living notable lives—look at the encyclopedias on the shelves, check out the king-size waterbed in the master bedroom, or kick back on our new floral-pattern couch set in the living room—we had almost assured ourselves that we'd remain what exactly we were: country folks, trying too hard.

"When can I expect payment?" the bill collector asked on the phone.

"I don't know," my mother replied, being honest. Everything had been fine when my father still had his job hauling dirt and heavy equipment from construction sites. But he'd been out of work for months. And my mother, a second-grade teacher with a college education, was underemployed, working temp jobs, doing data entry

11

and other tedious, mind-numbing tasks inside cubicle-walled ware-houses. "We're trying," she told the faceless and increasingly impa-tient creditors on the phone. "Hey, now. Listen," she'd say. "I can't even buy groceries, let alone pay your bill."

It got to the point where my parents unplugged the phone at night, not wanting to take the creditors' calls. As it was, their mes-sages were stacked up on the answering machine on the bookshelf near the kitchen, the red light blinking to remind my parents just how much they had failed, just how far they had fallen. They were three hundred miles from home with two small boys, a stack of un-paid bills, and dwindling options. By the end of the year, we were so far behind on the minivan payments that the bank was threatening to come and take the Chevy Astro right out of our driveway, there in the heart of suburban Texas.

"Just come and get it," my mother told them finally, beaten down by months of stalling, and finding some relief—and even power—in letting go.

Shortly after the New Year, my parents saw a lawyer, just some guy out of the phone book, and declared bankruptcy—a plan of last resort that my father had long resisted. We'll be fine, he had told my mother for months. They would find a way to make it work. Always had before. Would again now. Bankruptcy, to my father, felt like a fancy word for quitting—a legal loophole that made failure permis-sible to weak souls who didn't have the strength of character that he had.

"I wasn't raised that way," he told my mother.

"It's okay," she assured him.

Anyway, they had no other choice. They sold off the furniture. Lost the house. Soon enough, the repo man came for the van. For a while, the only car we had was a 1965 Chevy pickup truck that my father intended to fix up one of these days—when he had the money.

It was dark green and rusted and so beat-up even my grandfather didn't want to be seen with it, as he helped us pack, watched us say good-bye to the old house, and then drove us north, up the highway, back home to the panhandle of Texas, and a town called Wheeler, with my father following along in the Chevy.

"Don't drive so close to me," my grandfather joked, speaking to my father over crackling CB radios as we rumbled north. "I don't want people to think you're with me."

FULL-BLOODED

IN WHEELER, my grandfather had a reputation to keep. As a land-holder, sure. And a cattleman, yes. But mostly just as a man. Grand-dad was the surviving patriarch of nearly a century of Moores in Wheeler. The cowboy hats he wore—straw in the summer and felt in the winter—were not for show. And neither was the brown leather belt around his waist branded with the letters that spelled our name: M-O-O-R-E. The hats kept the hot Texas sun off his head and the belt held up his pants as he drove around the county checking on his cattle—fifteen hundred head at times. Life, for him, was simple that way. Boiled down. Everything had its purpose. The shotgun on the dashboard of his pickup was for shooting quail, if he happened upon them, because quail were good eating. The rifle on the floorboards was for killing coyotes, if he spotted them in his fields, because coy-otes were a menace to his livestock. His bare hands were for killing wasps; he'd squish them with his fingers. And evenings in Wheeler were for glasses of Crown Royal and my grandmother, a kind-hearted woman everyone in town called Butch.

They say cowboys, by definition, are bronzed and wiry, the sort of lonesome travelers who look like they could live in the saddle for days, fortified only by beans and bacon. But my grandfather, father, and Caleb fell into a different stock of plainsmen: broad-chested and strong-armed; thick, though not exactly heavy; and big, though not exactly large. They were just somehow substantial—solid men with twinkling eyes, wide brows, and angular jaw lines, carved as if from a ridge. There was nothing wiry about them. And that, to me, always seemed more like the true definition of a cowboy. To make it here, in Wheeler, to eke out an existence on these high arid plains, required something substantial of a man. Anything less and you'd leave town—or simply never come in the first place. It's not like you just happen upon Wheeler, population 1,592, ninety miles east of Amarillo, fifteen miles west of the Oklahoma state line, north of Shamrock and south of Briscoe and close to just about nothing else.

We rolled into town in my father's old Chevy, broke and busted, looking like Tom Joad's lost cousins from Texas, all belt buckles and brims. My mother was embarrassed before we even stepped out of the truck. But my father didn't care. He was already thinking about rebuilding. The bankruptcy hadn't been his choice; he didn't like to discuss it. And coming back home to Wheeler hadn't been his plan. Fine, he'd admit that—at least to my mother. But he wasn't going to sulk about it. Whining didn't suit him. Instead, he got a job. Using family connections, my father got hired at a feedlot, off Highway 152 west of town, grading cattle pens, filling holes with dirt, and shoveling cow manure all day. It was not a great job.

The good news was, he was working again and had an income. Also, he didn't have to shovel the manure by hand. Instead, he operated a motor grader that rumbled past the rows of cattle pens, pushing the manure off the concrete slabs where the cattle ate all day and where the feces piled up. Loaders would then move in behind my father and form still bigger piles of crap until there was enough to haul away and sell to farmers as fertilizer. This was the job, this was how we started over, and everyone, including my father, was happy to have the work. The bad news was, he came home smelling of the feedlot, of the cows—of manure most of all. My mother would force him to strip off his clothes outside every night in a yard that was more dirt than grass. Perhaps most troubling of all, even more so than the manure, was that the job didn't pay much, not enough, at least, for us to rent a good house.

The place we got was near the town cemetery. It was another ranch, only smaller this time and down a dirt road, perched on a small ridge, and surrounded by alfalfa fields and someone else's cattle. And even this—this old farmhouse, without even so much as a dishwasher—had to be negotiated. My father promised to tear down a dilapidated barn on the property—hard labor in exchange for the rent we didn't have.

The barn came down and, in time, my parents even managed to buy a dishwasher; the landlord let us deduct the cost of the new kitchen appliance from our rent. Still, my mother hated the house: the sprayed-on stucco exterior; the hand-me-down furniture inside, gifts from friends and family to replace what we had lost; and, above all, the isolation amid the cows in the fields, isolation that gave my mother too much time to second-guess all the mistakes they had made.

Even in the best of times, it can get lonely in Wheeler. In a single feedlot in town, there are more cattle than there are people in the whole county—or the next five counties combined, for that matter. Cows, overall, outnumber people by about fifteen to one, making actual humans far more scarce than livestock. And that lonesome feeling only gets amplified after nightfall, in the silence and all-consuming darkness of the plains. There are no streetlights in most places, no neighbors, and no city glow in the distance. It's just you and the other animals out there, making their presence known. We heard them not long after we moved into the farmhouse by the cemetery: the creatures, unseen and mysterious, howling in the night.

"Listen," my mother said. "Hear that?"

We were sitting on the couch and I turned, wide-eyed, first to my mother and then to the window, pressing my face against the glass.

"Hear the coyotes?" my mother said.

"Coyotes," I nodded, repeating my mother's words with a certain awe. We were alone—this was true. You could feel it. But like generations of other Wheeler residents who had come before us, Caleb and I were not afraid.

．　．　．

MY FATHER'S job at the feedlot didn't last long; my mother's general dissatisfaction with our lives did. It was more than just the house. Actually, it was everything: the house, the loneliness, the shame of the bankruptcy. It clung to all of us, like a bad smell, but especially to my mother. She had convinced my father that they weren't failures for having gone bankrupt—a clearheaded argument she had made many times back in suburban Fort Worth before the foreclosure proceedings. But now that we had retreated back home to Wheeler, my mother was the one who couldn't shake it off.

Whether it was true or not, she believed people in town were whispering about us: the Moores who had failed, the fancy ones who had left for the big city, only to come back broke and eating frozen dinners around a hand-me-down dining room table in that house by the cemetery. Trips into town were especially hard on her. Waiting in line at the post office, running errands around the square, or buying groceries inside the Thriftway on East Oklahoma Avenue, my mother was sure she could feel the stares of the locals as Caleb and I followed along, all smiles, oblivious. There's Michele Moore. Yeah, that's the one. Over there. You didn't hear? They're back, all right. Living in Cecil's place out by the cemetery. Hear they lost everything. *Bankrupt.* Can't make their rent.

My parents' wedding, just a few years earlier, had been a big country to-do, with rented metal folding chairs and a trellis, set up in my grandfather's yard down the dirt road south of town. My grandmother had seen to the flowers: roses and mums and daisies, every one of them yellow, to match the yellow bows on the patio, the yellow icing on the four-layer wedding cake, and the yellow napkins, personalized, of course: Michele & Wade. My mother's dress was homemade, sewn by her hardworking mother in less than six weeks, and my father's tuxedo was clean and crisp, an eye-blistering white—so bright in the late summer sunshine, with its matching white bow tie, you could have spotted him all the way from Lubbock.

Everything about the wedding was small-town perfect. Here was the state champion fullback, No. 35 in your program, marrying the Wheeler High School cheerleader—*Go Mustangs!*—the homecoming court princess, third runner-up most beautiful, according to the class of '84, and number four in her class of twenty-two kids. An honors graduate, my mother. She had come late to Wheeler, only moving here in high school, with her father, and she had gone to college, Texas Wesleyan, on a scholarship. A real catch. Uncle Stanley was the preacher. Uncle Todd was the best man. Aunt Beverly and Uncle Jerry had forged the wedding bands. And the party—fueled by ice chests full of Coors—raged long into the panhandle night.

The newlyweds, not wanting to miss out on all the fun, delayed their honeymoon in San Antonio by a day and spent their first night as a married couple sleeping in my father's childhood bedroom, in the back of my grandparents' farmhouse. But the next morning, they were off in my father's pickup, my mother smiling in the passenger seat. She was young and married and sure of one thing: They would never live in Wheeler again. And yet, here we were, just a few years later, back home, in the Thriftway. Cleanup on aisle five. We were a mess.

My father and mother never argued; they aren't prone to shouting. But for a while after we moved back to Wheeler, they stopped talking. My mother was depressed and anxious, and my father was helpless to change it.

"What's wrong?" he'd ask.

"I don't know," she'd reply.

Well, that doesn't give me much to work with, my father would say. And she'd agree with him. She understood his frustration. Yet still, she couldn't explain the deep sadness inside her. It wasn't Wheeler, exactly. It was a good enough place to live, but she had no kin left in the county, outside of us. Her father had moved on, left Wheeler. She felt alone. For my mother, it was somehow *everything*.

My father shook his head. They had a truck. He had a job—no matter how bad it was. They had the farmhouse by the cemetery and even cobbled together eight hundred dollars to buy a second car: a real beater, rusting and shedding silver paint everywhere. Their newly acquired Oldsmobile '98, with its maroon interior, had seen better days. But still, it was a second car, a step in the right direction. As my father saw it, life could be worse, much worse. And my mother understood that, too. Of course it could be worse, she conceded. Yet knowing that still didn't help.

I just don't feel it, my mother said.

Feel what? my father asked.

Everything, she told him. She was numb, distant.

Briefly, there was talk of leaving and of divorce. It wasn't a good option; they both knew that. My father refused to even discuss it. "We have kids," he told my mother. "That's not right. That's not the way it's supposed to be." If he had learned one thing in all his years in Wheeler, it was this: A Moore boy never gave up. If he got knocked down, he got back up again. He took his licks and kept fighting. An old plains- man once said there were three kinds of pioneers on the panhandle: quarter-breeds, half-breeds, and full-blooded men—a comment not about cowboys and Indians, but about the character of the people in this country, regardless of race. That last stock—"the full-blooded," the plainsman noted—were tough men who endured the elements, took great risks, and "rode into battle with splendid abandon." And one thing was certain: A Moore boy was expected to be full-blooded. There would be no divorce. No quitting. My father shot down anyone who suggested that he cut the tie and let my mother go.

"I ain't done yet," he told them.

THE HARDEST
KIND OF LIFE

THE FIRST of the full-blooded plainsmen—my ancestors—showed up on the Texas Panhandle in the 1850s. Within twenty years, Wheeler had become something of a destination, a place where American dreams could come true, and most certainly would, if you had the grit to survive the Indian raids and the gunfights, the droughts and the sandstorms, the isolation and the wolves and the arbitrary swings of fortune, born of lawlessness.

They came for the buffalo, at first, turning killing into a science. A small crew of well-armed men could slaughter as many as a thousand buffalo on the panhandle in just a few weeks' time, earning as much as $2.50 per hide—a lot of money. They'd go out in the morning, usually, with a rifle, a strong horse, and two belts of ammunition—say, eighty rounds—riding downwind of an unsuspecting herd and then approaching on foot from about three hundred yards away. What happened next was simple. A hunter would take aim at a buffalo's lungs—shooting for a spot just behind the fore-shoulder—and fire a single shot. The sound of the whistling ball would often startle the herd and incite a stampede. So the hunter's next shot wouldn't be at them, but ahead of them, trying to turn the buffalo back. And then he'd do it again and again, working with surgical precision—until the herd was churning with chaos, milling in circles, and consumed with the scent of its own blood spilling onto the sandy ground. "By this time," local hunter Emanuel Dubbs explained years later, with a killer's cold analysis, "their attention would be entirely distracted and the hunter could shoot them at his leisure."

Dubbs, an Ohio native and Union soldier, came west to Wheeler in 1871, after losing everything in a fire—a classic pioneer tale. And he wasn't alone. Just about everybody could find a place to fit in on the panhandle. Along with early, well-meaning settlers like Dubbs came others: desperadoes and outlaws, gamblers and prostitutes, horse thieves and cowhands and rustlers. By the 1880s, Wheeler boasted 512 residents, almost twice as many as the next-largest county on the entire Texas Panhandle. And with these settlers, this collection of dreamers and fools, came some semblance of civilization in Wheeler County's biggest town, Mobeetie. There was a post office, a jail, and a courthouse; a blacksmith shop, a brothel, and two hotels. There were two large mercantile stores, a smattering of shacks, and, of course, saloons—seven or eight of them—frequented by gun-toting gamblers, runaway pool hall girls, and gritty frontier characters named Butcher Knife Bill and Frogmouth Annie, Diamond Girl, and The Kid.

Lawmen did their best to maintain order, handing out fines for what they deemed to be unacceptable behavior. Drunkenness, saloon fighting, and using obscene language with a woman? That would cost you three dollars. Displaying a gun to the terror of bystanders? That was five. Gamblers faced steep fines up to twenty-five dollars. And women who chose to expose themselves on the street could pay as much as fifteen. And yet, it didn't matter. The fighting, the terror, the drinking, and the gambling continued, unabated. There were a lot of ways to die in Wheeler.

Cross a gambler. Cheat—get shot in the chest from across the table. Cuss the wrong man. Steal his horse or his woman—get shot through the jaw. Dying men asked pale-faced bystanders to drag them outside saloons and pull off their boots, so that they might die a more respectable death—slow and agonizing, but somehow more respectable—dying on the street, looking up at the big Texas sky. Others went fast, cut down by bullets meant for someone else. And still others never saw it coming. In 1879, according to records at the courthouse, J. N. Morris struck another man, J. S. Wheeler, in the head with a wooden club while he slept, fracturing his skull and killing him. Red Holly went down right inside a saloon, shot dead with a pistol. And Jack Tanner just disappeared, leaving his mother—a petite woman from Missouri—to search for him from Texas to Montana for years to come. She was sure something terrible had happened to him; Jack, a good son, had been so dedicated about writing letters home. And she was right: He'd been shot after stumbling upon another person's crime. Old Jack Tanner had learned that a butcher was slaughtering other people's cattle to increase profits. And to protect himself, the rogue butcher had no choice but to kill Tanner and bury his bones. It would be years before a sheriff, using a plow, found his remains, and by then no one in Wheeler knew how to contact his poor mother, still searching somewhere out there for her son.

These were just the ways you could die in town. The countryside, by comparison, was far more dangerous. If there wasn't enough water—if it hadn't rained or you were simply too dumb to find a source—you could die and often did. Thirst could gut men from the inside, rendering them haggard, thin, and even unrecognizable, if they had gone too long without drinking. Droughts killed crops and cattle. Angry sandstorms moved in—blotting out the sun—as did clouds of grasshoppers, devouring whatever crops had survived. At times it was so dry, cowboys said, they could ride three hundred miles without finding so much as a puddle. Animals went insane—"wild for water," it was said—and friends turned on each other, fighting and killing, their throats full of dust.

And yet, the opposite was also a problem. If there was too much water, panhandle rivers swelled up, sometimes in a flash, uprooting cottonwood trees, sweeping away cattle by the hundreds, and drowning men who were ignorant of the dangers. Wagons overturned in high currents—there were no bridges—and everything would be gone, all the supplies, all the food. You'd bury the dead in graves on the riverbank—or just leave the corpses to bake in the sun, wrapped up in old buffalo hides. Everyone knew the stakes.

There were almost no hospitals or doctors. In 1880, there was just one civilian physician on the entire panhandle—and what he didn't know could have flooded the Red River. If you got typhoid fever, you'd die. If you got mountain fever, you might die, too. Bullet wounds got infected and gangrene set in. Amputations almost never went well. So pioneers treated themselves. Snakeroot for diarrhea. Boiled button willow for the chills and coal oil for rattlesnake bites. You'd put the oil in a bucket, soak the bite, and hope for the best. Or slice open the bite wound, pack it full of salt, and, again, hope for the best.

Bathing wasn't common; flies were. Pioneers, and specifically buffalo hunters, were said to be "dirty, greasy, and the toughest-looking men" anyone had ever seen. And yet in a violent thunderstorm, alone out there on the plains with lightning cracking all around, they'd break down, praying and singing:

> *Jesus loves me—this I know,*
> *For the Bible tells me so . . .*

Because they knew there was no taming this land. No defeating it. And there were no guarantees, either—no promises in this country that everything would be okay in the end. It was, said pioneer Tom Burgess, "the hardest kind of life." You could only hope to survive the hardships, like the angry twister that finally leveled Mobeetie in the spring of 1898.

By the time it was over, just about everything the pioneers had built was gone, blown away, like so much dust. Boards ripped away from houses. Adobe walls collapsed. The Palmer baby died. The Masterson baby, just six weeks old, died, too. Seven lost in all. Mobeetie and in some ways the entire county were never the same again. The population dipped. The county seat moved from Mobeetie to the town of Wheeler, ten miles away. Not long after that, my ancestors—the Moores—decided yes, absolutely, Wheeler was the ticket. Wheeler, Texas, was the place for us. J. C. Moore, my great-great-grandfather, was especially certain of it. He packed up his family of nine, hitched up the wagons, and headed to the panhandle—across the Clear Fork River and the Brazos—bound for a hot, flat stretch of American nothing: Wheeler, my home.

It was a surefire plan, a can't-fail proposition. Like those old newspaper advertisements that had lured the original pioneers to these lands in the first place, there was great confidence in the idea. This was going to work.

"Good Bye," the ads said. "We're going to Texas."

HONKY-TONK
SAVIOR

THE PREACHER sensed my father's pain. The man, a family friend, wore a cowboy hat and boots and a concerned look on his clean-shaven face. He didn't know what was happening at home with my mother. Couldn't say for sure, but he felt something was wrong. And one day, down at the feedlot, he pulled my father aside amid the dust and the manure and the cattle pens to ask him a question.

"You doing all right?" the preacher inquired.

My father hesitated, looking away.

A full-blooded Texan did not seek help from another man—preacher or otherwise. A full-blooded man solved his own problems, did his own work, saved his own marriage, and spoke nothing about it. These were the rules—unwritten perhaps, but rules nonetheless. Things had changed in Wheeler in the century since the Moores had arrived, but not by much. If a twister came through, you rebuilt your own house. If your family needed protecting, you got your own gun. Panhandle settlers were—in the description of the *Amarillo Daily News*—"the fighting kind." "Sturdiness, ruggedness, fortitude and courage were bred into the plainsman," the newspaper once declared. "He lived a hard life, fought bitter fights; he civilized the plains and made it prosperous."

My father was living in a different era—with pickup trucks instead of wagons and tractors instead of horse-drawn plows—but he wasn't all that different from those who came before him. He was a fighter, born of fighters, and he certainly wasn't inclined to talk to any preacher, even if he was a family friend, about deep personal problems. But sitting in the pickup truck that day, cowboy to cowboy in the unrelenting heat, my father made a decision. For once in his full-blooded life, he was reaching out for help.

No, he told the preacher, plainly. He wasn't right at all. Things were rough at home. Had never been worse, he confided to the preacher. My father—consumed with worry and losing weight as a result—was honest: He was lost. He and my mother had two boys to care for, obligations to keep, and dreams like everyone else. They just wanted to live a good life, a better life. But they were lost. They were losing it all, it seemed, and my father said he didn't know what to do.

The preacher nodded, listening from behind the wheel of his pickup. He understood. Life was hard out here—he got that. But we weren't alone. Maybe, he said, we'd benefit by paying a visit down at the church.

. . .

IT WAS a honky-tonk, really. And before that a skating rink. Or maybe I have that backward. Maybe it was a honky-tonk first and a skating rink later. Either way, it was a long, flat warehouse, with a banked metal rooftop and corrugated metal walls. Not much of a church, at least in the traditional altar-and-steeple sort of way. From the outside, driving past the building, south of Wheeler, on the two-lane highway to Shamrock, it looked more like a storage facility than anything else.

But inside, on Wednesdays and Sundays, all day sometimes, people prayed, baptizing the newly saved in a water trough made for horses. Right away, inside the walls of the old honky-tonk, my parents felt at home, felt welcome. My mother could almost feel her anxiety and depression washing away. Here, even right up by the highway, she found peace. We were a family once again. My parents held hands and became church leaders. Caleb and I learned the Bible—memorizing verses in exchange for badges and colored bracelets: black for sin, white for purity, red for the blood Jesus shed. We were like Boy Scouts, only for God. And we were good at it, competitive with each other to get the verses right—even if we didn't always understand the full weight of what we were saying. *Ephesians 2:8–9*: "For by grace are ye saved . . ." *John 5:24*: "Verily, verily, I say unto you, He that heareth my word, and believeth on him that sent me, hath everlasting life . . ." And yea, verily, on it went, with Corinthians and Romans, Proverbs and Psalms. We learned verses about those who went to heaven—"They shall hunger no more"—and those who missed out on that boat and found themselves somewhere else. "Whoever was not found written into the book of life was cast into the lake of fire."

My parents can't find the badges we earned for our Bible work, although they're sure they kept them somewhere, boxed up and safe. "I would never throw those away," my mother told us. But everyone in my family always looked back on that time with fondness. My parents got counseling, the help they needed, and found their footing as a couple. Caleb and I made friends in Wheeler. My father escaped the feedlot for a better job—doing road maintenance for the county—and we saved enough money to rent a better house, in town, where my father used steel pipes to build the largest jungle gym you'd ever seen. There were turtle races on the Fourth of July, a city pool for swimming in the summer, birthday parties at my grandparents' house with balloons and cake, and soon another move—this time to a small town near Abilene.

My father had landed work as a prison guard. If he wanted the job—which he did, the money and benefits were good—we needed to move. I was five years old when we left Wheeler; Caleb was seven. But this small town on the panhandle would always be home to us. My mother even came to believe there was magic in the dust of Wheeler County. She'd seen it with her own eyes one day while we were still living in the old farmhouse near the cemetery.

She was alone with Caleb and me that morning. We were playing with trucks in the dirt, just being boys. I was still young. After a while, she took me into the house for a nap, leaving Caleb to play by himself outside for a few minutes. When she returned a short while later, my brother was gone. He was four years old—and he was just gone. She checked around the house—no sign of Caleb. She walked out to the shed—no sign of Caleb. Calm initially, my mother now began to worry—half angry, half afraid.

"Caleb?" she shouted.

"Mommy!" he answered finally. "Here I am."

My mother looked up for the first time, squinting into the sun. And there was Caleb, on the rooftop of the house. Higher than the roof, actually. While she had been inside, my brother had climbed up a television antenna that ran up the side of the house—a ten- to twelve-foot climb in all—over the eaves. My mother was afraid. What if Caleb fell? If he did, he was sure to get hurt. Or what if my mother had to climb the antenna to retrieve him? What then? There was, of course, no way to reach my father. No cell phones. No neighbors. There was a boy on a roof and a mother on the ground—and a problem to be solved.

My mother asked Caleb if he thought he could come back down on his own. And Caleb nodded. He was smiling. This was easy for him, my mother thought, as she watched Caleb shimmy down the antenna, hand over small hand, until his feet touched the ground again, sneakers in the dirt—proud.

Look at me, Mama. Look what I did.

My mother scooped Caleb up in her arms, furious. Relieved and thankful, but also angry. What was he doing up there? Didn't he realize he could get hurt? There was to be no more climbing things, my mother declared. It was too dangerous; we could fall. For a while, this was a rule in our house.

COW PALACE

CALEB HAD big plans: push the trampoline under the fifty-foot pecan trees in the backyard, so that if you leaped off the lowest branches of the tree you could hit the middle of it, the sweet spot, and really catch some air. Or set up the trampoline over some sprinklers in the yard, so that the surface would get slick and extra bouncy—and, again, if you hit it just right, you could really catch some air. From the moment Caleb laid eyes on our new home near Abilene, he saw its unlocked potential. All we needed to do was get up into those trees and then jump onto the trampoline. The possibilities were endless. It was going to be something, he said. A real show. By second grade, he was doing backflips.

"You can do it, too," Caleb told me.

"I can't," I replied.

"You gotta at least try."

"No, I don't," I said. "I can't do it."

"Yeah, you can," Caleb assured me. "Just trust me."

The new home was just off Interstate 20 in a small town called Clyde. It was a real Texas spread, with that trampoline in the yard, a massive rope swing hanging from an oak tree out back, and ten acres of pastureland for us to explore on bicycles and go-carts. Caleb and I couldn't have been happier about the land outside. But the house, on the inside, needed work. It had no front door, no toilet, no bathtub, and no shower. The local high school kids—burnouts, bored and with too much time on their hands—had converted the home into a Saturday-night beer-drinking hangout. The "Cow Palace," they dubbed it, spray-painting the name across an interior wall. And that wasn't even the craziest discovery. There was evidence that other creatures had been hanging out, too. My father found animal scat upstairs, most likely from raccoons.

It wasn't surprising, really. The house was basically an abandoned structure, left behind on the western prairie to rot in the sand and the sun. But it was cheap—this was the key. We could afford the house. After everything that had happened to us, my parents were mindful of saving money, especially my mother. There would be no Nike sneakers for us, no Hollister hoodies, and no American Eagle shirts, either—the name brands other kids were fond of wearing. On the rare occasions when we did go to a mall, my mother directed us to the sales rack, shepherding Caleb and me past the things we really wanted. "A twenty-dollar shirt?" she told me once. "Really, Colten?" We were regulars at Goodwill stores and at home in the generic aisle at the supermarket. No Lucky Charms for us. We could make do with the store-brand imitations that came in clear bags, not boxes. Even Lunchables—the prepacked, cellophane-wrapped packages of crackers, deli meat, and cheese—were out of reach for us. "We can make our own," my mother said. "It's just meat and crackers. We can buy crackers. We can cut up meat."

It was the new frugality, the way we had to live. All of us, even my mother—my mother, perhaps, most of all. In Wheeler, she had lost the diamond out of her engagement ring while digging around inside a file cabinet at school. Unable to afford a new gem, she replaced it with cubic zirconium. My mother didn't like it any more than the rest of us. But she was going to enforce the new order—someone had to do it. And the house in Clyde was just the latest example of how our lives had changed. My parents installed a front door and a new toilet before we moved in. These were deemed *necessary* amenities. And they painted over the "Cow Palace" graffiti in the living room. The place needed to be livable.

Other things we could do without—at least for a while. For the first several weeks in Clyde, we had no bathtub and no shower. Instead, we bathed outside, lathering up beneath a garden hose my father connected to the kitchen sink, ran out the window, and then hooked to the eave of the house. The water temperature was easy enough to adjust. All you had to do was fiddle with the knobs at the sink. Although there was a paved road out front, this was still the country. We had plenty of privacy, my father assured us. "Cars would have to stop in just the right spot to see you showering," my father said. Anyway, the weather was still warm and the arrangement just temporary. If we were worried about it, we could shower fast.

At night, lying in our bunk beds upstairs, we could hear our parents whispering about money at times, running the numbers. We didn't know everything, but we knew enough: that money was important, that we never seemed to have enough of it, and that if you wanted to bathe inside—if you wanted a real shower like everyone else—you had to work for it.

"When I get older," Caleb told me one night inside that house, "I don't ever want to worry about money."

"I don't want to, either," I replied.

Still, we seemed to have just enough for everything we truly needed: diving lessons for Caleb at the swimming pool in Abilene, karate classes for both of us, and our go-cart—a small three-horsepower machine that Caleb and I drove every day after school, doing doughnuts in the sand on the backside of our property. Caleb taught me—and anyone else who came over—how to do the best doughnuts and, also, how to do backflips on the trampoline in the yard. It was about getting a good bounce, he said. You needed distance between your body and the surface of the trampoline, obviously. But mostly, Caleb instructed me, it was about fully committing to the flip—about letting go and believing your body would come back around. Don't freak out, he told me. If you freak out midflip, and try to abort, you won't make it.

I nodded. I set my feet and bounced. I freaked out, midflip, just like he told me not to do, and then landed square on my head and neck with a terrible crunch, rolling over to one side.

"You all right?" Caleb asked.

"I don't know," I groaned, my voice weak and little.

For days, I thought I must have broken something in my neck—it hurt that badly. But soon I was back on the trampoline. "You're fine," Caleb told me. Nothing ever seemed to hurt him—not even the time he fell from our rope swing in the backyard, landing on his back from two stories up in the air. My father had been pushing the swing that day, really trying to launch him—Caleb always begged my father to push him higher—when the loop at the bottom of the rope came undone. With nothing to hold his weight, Caleb lost his grip on the rope, let go at the highest point—a mistake—soared through the air while my father and I watched, horrified, and then landed with an awful thud in the grass. My father, panicked, scooped up Caleb's little body and ran him inside to my mother, shouting. In his mind, Caleb was dead. Caleb wasn't breathing. He'd really messed up this time, my father had, pushing the rope so hard. Someone call a doctor. It was that kind of panic.

But Caleb was fine. Had the wind knocked out of him. That was all. The next day, he was back outside, dreaming up new ways to take flight. These dreams would often come to us at night, while we were sleeping, and they were always the same. We were flying. We were soaring. We were catching the sky.

"I flew again last night," Caleb told me in the morning after these dreams, sleepy-eyed at the kitchen table over the bags of generic cereal.

I would nod. I understood him.

"Me, too," I told my brother. I had the same dreams.

•   •   •

IN EARLY 1998, my father finally caught a break. A friend from the trucking industry back in Fort Worth was going out on his own. He needed a business partner. Maybe my father would want to join him.

Caleb was ten, I was eight, and my parents were willing to take the risk. If they were going to make another move, now seemed like a good time for it. They had saved some money. And Caleb was a few years away from high school, when moving would be harder. My father relocated first, renting a room in a small boarding house outside Dallas to save money. The place was filled with drifters, drunks, and other cash-strapped laborers. At night sometimes, tenants, blind on cheap beer, would mistake my father's door for the bathroom and bang on it incessantly, demanding to be let in so that they could relieve themselves—not an ideal living situation. But the trucking business proved successful. Dallas and Fort Worth were growing, new subdivisions popping up everywhere. Trucks were needed to haul dirt and bulldozers across town—work my father knew well—and in June, after school let out, he sent for us. He was moving out of the boarding house and we were leaving our home in Clyde, saying good-bye to the Cow Palace. "Would you believe it?" my brother wrote around that time in a hardbound journal he had started keeping. "We moved again."

Our new home was an apartment in a complex in exurban Denton, forty miles north of Dallas—and this, too, wouldn't last. The apartment itself was fine, a cheap two-bedroom place, nothing fancy, but certainly good enough for a while. It was the neighbors who proved problematic. The kids who lived there had the run of the place, and their games were different from ours. Gone were the trampoline, the go-cart, and the ramps we built for our bicycles. Our new playmates liked to divide up into teams, gather up rocks, and throw them at each other. The goal: hit the other team, as hard as possible.

I should have left the other boys to play by themselves—I knew the game was a bad idea—but I didn't. One day, when my brother wasn't around, I listened to the older kids, joining the ill-advised rock-throwing game. At best, I was an easy mark, short for my age and bone-thin. At worst, I appeared awkward, with a head that seemed too large for my small body. Either way, I was no match for the city kids, who gathered up their rocks with glee.

The game started and I began to bob and weave, dodging the incoming fire. The other kids knew the game, sure, but they had terrible aim. I had played baseball in Clyde. I could throw a ball, so I could throw a rock. I reared back and let one fly, pegging another boy right in the mouth.

There was screaming, maybe some blood. It was hard to say. The kid disappeared. The game ended. I walked back home to the apartments and right into an ambush. My victim was waiting for me there with reinforcements: his older brother and two other bigger boys, high school kids, ready to exact revenge. I tried to run. I didn't get far. The kid's older brother, the enforcer, grabbed me and held me. I struggled, but had nowhere to go.

"Hit him!" the kid told his younger brother.

I blinked back tears, screaming and crying.

"Hit him!" the enforcer told his brother again. The rock I had thrown had chipped the boy's tooth—real damage. I had what was coming to me, the older brother kept saying. "If you don't hit him, I will."

I somehow squirmed away and got home, locking the door behind me, but still crying, inconsolable. These boys were coming to get me, I told my parents. Yet it was the injured boy's mother who showed up first, knocking at our door with righteous anger. She wanted to speak to my parents. She wanted them to pay for the damage I had done. Didn't they see how I had chipped her son's tooth? That was uncalled for.

"That was the game," my father said, correcting her.

The boy's mother kept after him, still arguing. But my father was unbending on this point. The rules of the game—as stupid as they were—had been agreed to by everyone, he told the woman. Throw rocks and dodge rocks. That was it. That was the game. Her son should have dodged faster, my father said, or he shouldn't have played in the first place.

She left angry, vowing this wasn't over. I stopped crying and calmed down. But not really. Sooner or later, I believed, the older boys would get their revenge. They would come for me, I told my parents, still trembling. My parents agreed. They were worried, too. Within a few days, they made a decision to break the lease on the apartment, take the financial hit, and move yet again—to Krum, Texas, ten miles farther north, but still close enough to Dallas, so my father could keep working. My mother had a job as a school librarian there. Caleb and I were already enrolled in the town's schools, thanks to my mother's employment.

Krum was it, the next—and, we hoped, the last—stop.

TROPHIES

MY FATHER rolled down the gravel driveway, proud of his purchase, just tickled. Behind his pickup, he was towing a trailer loaded down with three Honda ATVs: a yellow 400EX for him, a red 250EX for Caleb, and another red one for me. My father had draped a tarp over his cargo. He wanted the quads to be a surprise when he arrived at our house in Krum. But Caleb and I knew what my father had on the trailer before his truck even rolled to a stop. The tarp hadn't covered everything. We spied the tires on the quads, and we could also see my father's smile—a big self-satisfied grin. The only question we had was: when? When could we start riding the new ATVs?

We had been driving go-carts for years, first in Clyde and then in Krum. We started small—with the three-horsepower cart—but soon graduated to the faster, five-horsepower model and began racing each other. A friend had carved a flat dirt track on his property where we'd square off—wheel-to-wheel, jockeying for position, like miniature NASCAR drivers. Other times, we'd go swerving through trees, playing follow the leader. The go-carts maxed out at about 20 mph—and the ones we owned had other limitations. They didn't have roll cages or seatbelts. But we had friends with carts that did. And Caleb borrowed them every chance he got. He had figured out a way to make the vehicles do things the manufacturer hadn't intended. If he turned hard one way, then just as hard back the other way—and then hit the brakes—he could make the carts flip, somersaulting on their roll cages while he just laughed, strapped inside the cage, safe, at least mostly. He pulled the trick so often that our friend's father soon had a new job: rewelding the battered cages onto the dented carts.

The new Honda quads my father had purchased were not to be used for such things. He envisioned relaxing weekend rides on trails in the woods. The quads, as he saw them, offered us a chance to bond as a family: Caleb and I chugging up ahead while he followed along, my mother on the seat behind him, her arms wrapped around his waist. That kind of thing. But his plans for family bonding backfired before we had even pulled the tarp off the new ATVs in the driveway. My mother was furious. He hadn't cleared the purchase with her. My father had gone off and spent fifteen thousand dollars on three ATVs and had failed to mention anything about it to my mother.

His trucking business was doing well. The risk he had taken in leaving the steady prison job in Clyde had paid dividends. But the business wasn't doing *that* well. It wasn't like we had fifteen thousand dollars sitting around in a bank account. My father had financed the quad purchase and my mother just could not believe it. She was speechless. While Caleb and I whooped and hollered about the new gas-powered toys in the driveway, she eyed my father, her arms folded across her chest, quiet.

Later, he'd come asking for forgiveness. A husband should consult his wife about major life purchases. Yes, he understood that. Could she please forgive him? There was no way to get rid of the quads now. Like it or not, we owned them.

•   •   •

AT FIRST, we used the machines as my father had expected. We would ride on weekends as a family on nearby ranches and trails designed specifically for ATVs. Pay ten dollars and you could ride all day. But puttering along was never our speed and soon we were pushing the limits of what was possible on the four-wheelers, testing their mechanical boundaries.

Caleb, thirteen now, crashed one of the very first times he ever saddled up, going too fast over flatlands that suddenly dipped into a washout, a small gully. My brother never saw it coming—and both he and the quad went flying. "You can't do that," my father told him, livid, when he caught up to Caleb. We couldn't go racing across terrain we didn't know. "You don't know what's there," my father said. The wreck scared me; I didn't want to crash. But it didn't worry my brother. He rode up steep hills—and flipped, end over end, somehow escaping serious injury. When we finally found a flat strip of grass— about one hundred yards wide and a quarter-mile long—just below a lake on one of these weekend warrior ranches, my brother was the first to line up his little red four-wheeler, ready for real racing. "Let's go," he told me. On the strip by the lake, with the throttle pinned on our machines, going full out, we could hit almost 50 mph.

The strip was popular among riders, a gathering spot where we could challenge each other. One day when we were out there, Caleb and I noticed something unusual. One of the other riders had numbers on his quad, professional decals. Caleb just had to ask. "Hey," he said, with a nod to the man's four-wheeler. "What's up with the numbers?"

The story the rider told us next changed everything. There was this place, he said, a place not far from here, where quad riders of all ages could race. It was a real dirt track, this place, with ramps and landings, rules and competition. Riders came from all over north Texas to be there. Wednesdays were for practice, Fridays were for racing. Ten dollars would get you in the door. Twenty-five dollars got you in the race—and the winners took home trophies, real hardware. Plastic gold, the man said.

Trophies.

Caleb and I could hardly believe it. At Krum Intermediate School, where Caleb was in sixth grade and I was in fifth, neither of us were considered athletes. Nor were we particularly cool—or uncool. We were floaters, drifting from clique to clique and trying on new identities like jackets off a rack in a store. Choir kid. Band member. Trumpeter. Basketball player. Nothing stuck. For one thing, we were too small for team sports—especially me. Kids called me Little Amigo, Little Bud, or Shorty. I was no athlete. I played on the middle school basketball team, yes. But that was going nowhere. Most games, you could find the Moore brothers on the bench, spectators in our own adolescent lives. Now, there was talk of trophies and this racetrack—in Weatherford, Texas, was it? We needed to go, Caleb told my father. Like soon. When? When could we go?

. . .

WEATHERFORD WAS sixty miles from Krum, down the back roads—west on 380 and south on 114. We headed out there the following Wednesday evening, towing our quads behind my father's pickup and bouncing with excitement. The day in school, for us, had been a total waste. We could only think about one thing: riding. And what the track would look like. And how big the ramps would be. And if there would be crowds. Seeing the course—aglow on the plains under massive light stands—only made me more nervous. Trail riding this was not. The sculpted dirt jumps and landings in Weatherford were far bigger than anything we'd hit before—and there was a real kicker at the end: a point-to-point tabletop jump, maybe sixty feet long.

Caleb bounded out of my father's pickup, ready to go. But our first night there was a total bust. Track officials took one look at us in our blue jeans and tennis shoes and turned us away. We needed professional motocross boots to ride here. Real gear, they told us, shaking their heads at the greenhorns from Krum. We had been reduced to spectators once again. But the following week we were back, properly outfitted this time—after my father spent still more money to buy us the right gear—and soon we had a new routine. Practice on Wednesday night. Race on Friday night. Bring home trophies.

I was fast, streaking past other kids in my little quad, emblazoned with a new number: 21. Caleb was faster—and bold. He had chosen the No. 31, reversing the digits in 13, reversing, he said, bad luck. Nothing scared him—and he proved it first on that tabletop jump in Weatherford. I didn't want anything to do with that jump—and neither did most adults. The conservative approach was to hit the first ramp, land, ride across the tabletop, wheels on the ground, and then hit the second ramp—easy. But the faster, and more dangerous, approach was to hit the first ramp and soar all the way to the next ramp, some sixty or seventy feet in the air. And that typically required a modified quad or at least a quad with a larger engine. Caleb did it on his little Honda, a machine built for kids. All you had to do, Caleb said, was pin it—go full throttle. "That's all it takes." And then he repeated the feat at other Texas tracks we soon discovered—in towns like Euless, Nocona, and Caddo Mills. Sometimes, just to make it more interesting, Caleb would hit the ramps extra hard and then let go with his legs in midair, stretching out like Superman—a little flair, for the people who were watching.

Not every rider appreciated the showmanship, thinking Caleb reckless, too flashy. Others came out to practice, just to see him, hoping to learn by watching. He was starting to get a reputation as The Next Big Thing—at least out here, in rural Texas. But it was Caleb who walked around pumping others for information, peppering the older riders with questions that he hoped would give him an advantage on the track.

"What kind of shocks do you use?"

"How fast do you hit that jump?"

"What gear are you in?"

I just tried to keep up—and not crash. I wasn't always successful. In January 2002, when I was twelve years old, we packed up one morning, piled into my father's pickup, and drove an hour west to Jacksboro for a cross-country quad race. Organizers there had set up a long, winding track through some trees. Motorcycles were to go first—and there were too many of them. The event took all day. By the time officials were ready for the quads, the sun was starting to set. Darkness would surely fall before we finished the course in the trees. So race officials decided that the four-wheelers would race, all together, in a large pasture instead. Three laps around, in a big circle—an unorthodox plan that stirred some debate. By a vote of hands, one official finally asked, who still wants to race?

My family voted yes. Most riders did. We had waited all day for this moment. But the plan made me nervous—all these four-wheelers running together at dusk, like a herd of motorized wildebeests—and it only got worse once we started. The quads racing through the pasture-turned-ad-hoc-racetrack kicked up a cloud of dust no one had anticipated. Visibility was terrible. Officials at the finish line threw up the checkered flag after just one lap, realizing they had a serious safety problem on their hands. I never made it that far. Going outside the other riders to escape the dust cloud, my quad hit a dip in the earth and the next thing I knew I was on the ground—tossed over my handlebars at more than 40 mph. By the time my father got to me, I couldn't feel anything below my waist.

"I'm sorry!" I screamed, panicked.

"It's all right," he told me, calm.

"I'm sorry!" I kept screaming. "I'm sorry!"

"It's not your fault," my father replied. I didn't need to keep apologizing, he told me. I hadn't done anything wrong.

For a moment, I relaxed. Then I turned to my next concern. My legs. I couldn't feel them. What had happened? Was I paralyzed? Was it worse?

"Am I going to die?" I asked my father, still panicked.

"No." He shook his head. "You're not."

Both my femurs had snapped in the crash. One leg was lying across the other at an impossible, freakish angle, crooked at midthigh, which made the extent of my injury clear. It was a real mess. I would live, my father assured me, alarmed yet still calm. I just needed to get to an emergency room. "We're going to get you fixed," he said.

A helicopter evacuated me to a hospital in Fort Worth—I demanded that my father be allowed to fly with me. My mother met us there. She was calm, too. And for the next six weeks she rarely left my side. My mother bathed me and helped me go to the bathroom. To make sure I didn't fall behind at school, she stayed home from work and gave me my lessons: math, science, and English, whatever needed to be covered. Unable to move, with surgically implanted rods supporting my shattered femurs, I needed her for everything. And she was there.

It would have been easy at this point for her to question my choice of activities. Other people certainly did. In the waiting room at the hospital the day of my crash, worried relatives whispered about the decisions we were making. The consensus was: It was time to sell the four-wheelers. No more racing, no more riding. But my mother never brought it up. In all the time we spent together after the crash—those long days recovering inside the house in Krum, with my bed moved into the living room so I wouldn't have to take the stairs—she never questioned the racing or told me it was over. As much as the sport worried her, she understood: I rode four-wheelers now. This was who I was, who we were, what we did. After years of searching, I had finally discovered myself—and others had, too. I was no longer just Little Amigo, Little Bud, or Shorty—the small boy not big enough to play. I was Colten Moore, the racer, who had broken his legs while riding. Hadn't you heard? I was the talk of Krum

Intermediate. Everyone at school hoped I was all right and told me as much in the letters they sent home with my mother.

From the seventh-grade boys basketball team. *"We miss you."* From the keyboarding teacher, Mrs. Carr. *"Did you know we all miss you?"* Brandi said it wasn't the same in English without me. *"Come back as soon as you can."* Robyn said she hoped we could be friends and sent along her phone number. *"You can call to chat."* Meagan wrote me twice; she was just that concerned. *"I mean, it's not every day that someone breaks their pelvis and both legs."* And the boys at school wrote me, too. *"You think you'll ever race again? Knowing you, you'll probably try."* I was tough. *"Get better, so you can race and beat 'em all."* I was notable. *"I will pray for you."* I mattered.

"Get well soon."

"Get well, racer."

"PS—Don't get back on the four-wheeler for a while."

I loved the newfound camaraderie. Still, it hurt not to be out there on my quad, red and fast, riding with Caleb. And my father knew it. He could see that I was aching inside, strapped into leg braces and sitting in a wheelchair.

"You want to ride?" he asked me one day while my mother was out.

"Yeah," I told him.

He picked me up, carried me outside to my quad, and set me down gently in the seat. And for a few minutes, I drove around the yard in circles—slow, methodical circles, careful not to fall.

"Don't tell your mama," my father said.

COLLEGE MONEY

CALEB HAD it all figured out. We needed to go national. In just a few years' time, we had collected pretty much every trophy you could win on the local racing circuit—the Texas Quad Racing Association, or the TQRA. First place, Mosier Valley, 2001. First place, Mosier Valley, 2003. Second place, Blaster Class. Second place, Texas Motor Speedway. TQRA, first place, winter. TQRA, first place, summer. In every season, on every track, we had won—until those trophies, the plastic gold, filled our bedrooms and spilled out into the garage. My legs had healed; the surgically implanted rods in my femurs had held. We were ready. Caleb kept saying it: We had to go national.

Quad racing, by then, was no longer just a backwoods pastime, staged on cattle ranches, in farmers' pastures, or on remote grass strips like the one we had first discovered near our home. It was a real sport—with rules, requirements, certified racing bodies, and established tracks for competition. A kid who was interested—and good enough to compete—usually worked his way up the ranks, like a minor league baseball player, proving his worth on local and regional tracks before squaring off against national competition. But most of all, going national required one thing: money, a serious investment.

My parents wanted to talk about it, calling a meeting around the kitchen table in the fall of 2004. Caleb was starting his junior year of high school then; I was one year behind him. We weren't little kids anymore, my parents said, so we needed to understand a few things.

If we did this, they explained, if we raced on the national circuit, everyone would have to sacrifice.

"It's going to cost a lot of money," my father said plainly.

"We'd be spending your college money now," my mother added.

Caleb and I didn't care. College, to us, seemed like an abstract idea—a notion in the clouds, a thing that people did, though we weren't totally sure why. Racing was tangible. We could feel it, touch it. And we honestly believed it would take us somewhere. Even my mother—the school-district librarian in Krum and our family's only college graduate—agreed with that. This wasn't just a lark, she believed, but the beginning of something—a career and maybe more. She had witnessed Caleb's acrobatic achievements as a toddler, climbing to the rooftop of our house in Wheeler. Now, with the wild racing, throttle pinned, she had confirmation. It felt meant to be. We were different. We were going somewhere. That's the case she made to the high school principal, anyway, when she met with him that fall to inform him that Caleb and I were going to be missing a lot of school that year after Christmas.

The national racing season began in January. Preparations needed to be made and supplies purchased. My father bought a used semi-truck cab. Cost: eight thousand dollars. Next he picked up an enclosed trailer to haul our ATVs, which cost twenty thousand dollars. And then he began organizing the parents of other riders we'd met on the TQRA circuit. We were going national, he informed them, and they could join us, if they liked. Together the families could split the gas money—another significant cost. A half dozen other kids signed up. In early January—with parents riding in the truck cab and kids piled up inside the plywood-paneled living quarters of the trailer—we headed west to California for our first national event at the famous Glen Helen Raceway in the dusty foothills of the San Bernardino Mountains. While all the other kids in Krum were in school, we were traveling and racing—though, at first, not that well.

Our best finish at Glen Helen was ninth place. We improved a few weeks later, closer to home in Lake Whitney, Texas, where Caleb finished fourth. But early on, mediocre finishes—seventh place in Macon, Georgia; ninth place in London, Kentucky; eleventh place in Gilmer, Texas—were commonplace for us. The problem wasn't ability; it was equipment. Many kids on the national circuit already had sponsors—companies that effectively paid them to ride, financing better gear and faster quads. Most machines had been modified with after-market improvements to increase speed, smooth out landings, and provide more agility in tight turns. They installed high-end sport shocks for twenty-five hundred dollars and new suspensions for another twenty-five hundred—or more. Pistons would be swapped out and motors polished. A well-polished motor increased horsepower. New tires helped, too. No one at nationals raced on stock tires. Stock machines—the quads you got off the dealership floor—were sure losers.

Yet somehow, even that first year, Caleb won. First place, New Berlin, New York. First place, Gainesville, Florida. First place, Mt. Morris, Pennsylvania. We had no money to make great modifications to our quads, no sponsors to hook us up, and no luxuries on the road. We slept in the forty-foot trailer or in tents right next to it, camping out at the track. "Redneck racers," my father called us, with a glimmer in his eye. To him, the term was a compliment. We were the know-nothing nobodies, getting the most out of what we had and somehow beating kids riding superior machines. A race at an outdoor track in Greenville, Texas, around that time showed why.

Caleb and about ten other riders straddled their machines at the starting line, staring down one of those massive tabletop jumps, which, to make it even more difficult, led directly into another double jump. "All you gotta do is come around that turn," Caleb told me, "and pin it." This was his strategy—everyone else knew it. Hit the throttle and go—flat out. Since the other riders on the starting line refused to take such risks, they came up with a plan to stop him. Get the lead out of the gate. Take the middle line and block Caleb, forcing him to the edge where the track was half mud and half dirt, and he wouldn't be able to hit the ramp as hard as he wanted.

When the race began, Thomas Brown, a friend and fellow rider, did exactly that. Thomas had Caleb totally blocked going into the tabletop, hugging the middle line, just like he had planned. But Caleb, working on the edge, went for it anyway, pinning the throttle on his No. 31 quad. He knuckled the first landing—coming up short and bouncing hard on the top of the dirt landing. The impact knocked his legs off the four-wheeler and sent his body flying. But to Thomas's amazement, Caleb hung on, hands gripping the handlebars, and then, somehow, he managed to hit the second jump, too. The race had just started, and it was over. Caleb was gone.

Moves like these made people notice my brother, remember him, and, at times, fear him on the track. One family—with money, sponsors, and expensive, modified, after-market machines—even lodged an official complaint against Caleb's driving at one point. Said their boys, two brothers, wouldn't ride, if Caleb Moore was riding.

"Tell them they can go home," my father informed the race organizer.

Caleb—never fond of backstabbing, gossipmongering, or drama—decided to take a different approach. He addressed the issue directly with the privileged boys on their perfect quads. He walked right up to them the day before the race. He wanted to clear the air.

"Is there a problem?" Caleb asked.

No, the boys replied. Nope. Sure wasn't.

Caleb smiled and beat them both the next day.

• • •

THE SEASON of nationals left a mark on all of us. My parents were
back in debt, swimming in credit card bills. Six months on the road
not only depleted our college money; it tore a gaping hole in the safety
net my mother had worked so hard to stitch together since the bankruptcy. If we wanted to do nationals again next year, my parents informed us, Caleb and I were on our own.

Then there was the matter of school. After months of traveling—
tonight Danville, Virginia; tomorrow Blountville, Tennessee—returning
to high school in Krum full-time seemed like the worst kind of purga-
tory for us. Staring down his senior year, Caleb worked to graduate six
months early. He planned to get out in December, just before the national season began again. But as school started that fall, I was just a
junior, one year behind Caleb, which meant I still had two years of high
school left. And that was way too long to be away from riding. More important, it was too long to be apart from my brother. I asked my parents if I could graduate early, too, and my parents considered it. Said I
could try. We had certain rules in our house by that point. If we didn't
do our chores, we weren't riding. If we blew off school, we weren't riding.
"Grades go down?" my father would say. "You ain't riding."

Now I had even more motivation to study. To get ahead, I took
classes that entire summer and put myself on pace to graduate
in May 2006, six months after Caleb and one year before the rest
of my classmates. In my mind, I was going to be gone before the
final guitar chords of "Free Bird"—the official song of the class of
2006—had faded away in the hot Texas night. I was out of there.
By the end of that summer, Caleb and I had still more reasons to
leave. Fresh off our first taste of real success on the national tour,
we got news of a different event being held in the rolling, black-dirt
prairie not far from our home. A one-armed quad rider with land

just north of Plano, Texas, was organizing a freestyle show—Quad Zombie, he called it. There were going to be ramps, and girls, and big air—riders from all over the country would be throwing down tricks on their ATVs.

Caleb and I just had to go. We had become junkies of the *Huevos* movies—films that former quad racer Wes Miller had started shooting about a decade earlier. The movies—*Huevos Grandes*, *Huevos 2*, *Huevos 3*, and so on—were basically the same every time. They were montages of dudes—fearless American dudes—attempting the most ridiculous stunts they could think of while riding their quads. There was no plot in these features, no narrative arc, and no chance for an Oscar for Miller. But his *Huevos* series won lots of Xtremey Awards for best quad video—and they made a lot of money, too. At his peak, Miller, a California native, was selling as many as fifty thousand DVDs—*per film*—and making four-wheelers cool. "When it comes to ATV action sports video entertainment," an editor at *Quad Magazine* once wrote, "no one has done as much to drive the field to such heights as Wes Miller and his company H-Bomb Films."

We could spend hours watching his movies, Caleb and I, and often did, analyzing the films from my parents' living room in Krum, as if we were Siskel and freaking Ebert, with ball caps turned around backward. Miller, to us, was a god—and so were the quad riders who appeared in his films: Jimmy Elza and Doug Gust, Dana Creech and Jon Guetter. We wanted to be like them: soaring, doing heelclickers and supermen, in flight—in the movies. That could be us, Caleb would say. We could do it, I'd agree. And now, with this Quad Zombie event being organized near Plano, we had our shot. We had to be there. But my father didn't approve.

No way, he told us, initially.

For months, he had denied our desire to jump our quads off steel ramps. No Wes Miller action for us. No way to channel our

inner Jimmy Elza or Jon Guetter. Frankly, freestyle scared my father. Seemed dangerous to him. "We need to keep racing," he told us.
"That's our thing."

Just before the event near Plano, however, my father gave in to our
demands. Caleb was about to turn eighteen in August; he could make
his own decisions now. And if Caleb was going, I had to be there, too.
We had one day to practice on the steel ramps before the Saturday-
night event. We had no experience with these ramps and, really,
no idea what we were doing. None of it mattered. I finished first in
the amateur class and Caleb grabbed the headlines. One writer declared him "the newfound talent in Texas." "We were all in awe as we
watched Caleb," he noted. My brother hadn't won; he had finished second. Unlike me, Caleb had entered the pro class, competing against
professionals and pulling off moves no one had ever seen before on a
quad—and no one there would ever forget.

Riders still spin stories about it, even today, recounting the legend
of Caleb Moore with the hushed, solemn tone one might use when
telling a ghost story around a campfire—only this was true. We had
seen it: how Caleb had let go of the handlebars with both hands while
in midair; how he had trusted the machine to fly, let go with his legs,
too, and floated away, back to the seat; how he grabbed on with both
hands, slapping the gas tank, and then, before it was too late, found
his way back to the handlebars, completing the holy man grab; and
how everyone came running, grabbing video cameras—*could he do
it again?*—and shaking my brother by the shoulders in the hardtack
hills of Texas. Any lunatic could jump a quad off a ramp. What my
brother had just done was different. He had flown separate and apart
from the machine, letting go, yet still in control—of the machine, of
his body, of the trajectory, everything. As far as we were concerned,
he was like Orville Wright on wheels.

A California film crew was there—led in part by Jon Guetter, the erstwhile star of Miller's *Huevos* movies, now making his own DVDs with his brothers, Dan and Derek. And they, too, couldn't believe what they had seen. There were maybe five guys in the world who could even try a holy man on a four-wheeler. But none of them had. None of them could do it. And the next day the Guetters paid us a couple hundred dollars to film our best tricks. Then they asked if we could travel with them that summer. And off we went: to Minnesota and Illinois. County fairs, mostly, nothing big. There was no such thing as freestyle ATVs at the time. No official sport and no money in it, either. We got paid almost nothing to ride with the Guetters. But still. This was big. We weren't on the couch anymore, analyzing the videos—fast-forward, rewind, repeat, discuss. We were in the videos, my brother especially. Miller, the Guetters, and now Caleb were inventing the sport and often taking great risks to make it happen.

Just weeks after he graduated from high school, Caleb drove with a friend to Caineville, Utah—a sixteen-hour all-night haul fueled by energy drinks, candy, and sunflower seeds. The Guetters were filming a new DVD out there and wanted my brother to appear in it, along with several other riders. Caleb earned his usual fee—gas money— and wrecked his quad on the very first day, bending an A-arm, part of the front suspension, and scraping up his torso on the hard, rocky terrain. The Guetters thought he was finished for the week, but Caleb twisted the mangled A-arm back into shape as best he could and told them he was good to ride. He wasn't going to miss out on this: canyon jumps and wild ravines. There were no steel ramps out here. The goal was to find natural rock formations for jumping. This would make good television.

There were plenty of sites to choose from, but early in the week the crew found one place that stuck in their minds: a small canyon framed on either side by twenty-foot rock walls, a naturally formed ramp and landing, just sitting there, waiting to be jumped. The distance between the two walls was about eighty feet—no one could say for certain—and as soon as the Guetters saw it they decided it was too dangerous to even attempt. The nearest hospital was about five hours away. It just wasn't worth it. Obviously, it would be an epic shot, the Guetters said. But after a few days in Utah, they already had epic footage, plenty of it. You don't have to do this, they told the riders. And the riders agreed. They all balked at the canyon jump. Except my brother.

"Guess it's now up to me," Caleb said.

The sun was shining. His face was ablaze with youth. He went out and started raking the rocks on the approach, trying to flatten out the ground as best he could. "Gotta step it up," he said, turning to the rolling cameras. "Always gotta push harder than everybody else. Gotta see what we can get—whether it be a really good crash or a sweet jump."

Derek Guetter—the youngest of the Guetter brothers—began to worry about the possibility of a crash. "A really good crash," he said. A strong wind had kicked up, making it even harder to determine the distance, what gear Caleb should have his four-wheeler in, or how fast he should be going on the approach. There was no way to practice it. Again, the Guetters told him he didn't have to do this. "There are so many things that could go wrong," Derek said. But Caleb wasn't listening. He raked the ramp and made a couple of practice approaches, just gauging his speed.

"You think I'm going fast enough?" he asked. "Too fast?"

No one really knew.

The Guetters set up three cameras, including one to capture a crash, if that happened. They had to be prepared for everything. Then Caleb saddled up for the stunt, slipped his helmet over his head, hit on the throttle, and went for it.

From the far side of the canyon, from the landing site, all anyone could hear was the engine—Caleb's engine whining in the Utah desert. No one could see him. Then, as he cleared the rocky lip off the natural ramp, they spotted him for the first time: Caleb flying, wheels spinning, so high, too high.

"Oh, my God," one rider whispered.

Everyone was afraid. Derek Guetter—himself an accomplished freestyle rider who never shied away from taking chances—would later say it was one of the scariest moments of his life. Silence fell on the canyon. The only sounds were the wind and Caleb's engine and then screaming—wild screaming.

"Oh, my . . ."

"Holy Toledo!"

"That was sick!"

Caleb nailed the jump on his first try and all the other riders mobbed him, hugging my brother and shouting.

"You're a madman."

"Dude, that's the craziest thing I've ever seen."

"In my life."

"It was pretty hard," Caleb said. Scary for him, too, he admitted. "But I'll do it again."

"No, you're done," said Ben Bettis, a friend and fellow rider, standing next to my brother on the landing. "One is enough," he told Caleb. "I'm not going to go through that again."

•　•　•

CALEB DIDN'T listen, of course. He did the canyon jump a few more times that day, just to make sure the Guetters had the shot. And not long after that he started getting phone calls. Was Caleb available for a show? Was he free the weekend after next? How about October? Real money was in play now—a thousand dollars a weekend, more if he could do a backflip on his quad. Could he backflip? Such riders were in demand. Even Wes Miller—with his *Huevos* film crews and

his red-carpet parties and his awards, out in Los Angeles—was in
need of a rider who could flip. Miller's latest backflipping protégé—
a young Canadian named Christian Gagnon—had recently played
himself out of the job.

Christian was a member of Miller's Bomb Squad riding team and
a rising star in the extreme motorsports industry. Just that spring, he
had become, by our count, only the second person to ever backflip a
quad, achieving the feat in California in March with Miller's cameras
rolling. The Quebec native, speaking broken English, quickly proved
he could repeat the stunt, doing it at events in Costa Rica, Oregon,
and California. Christian was officially a hero now, a quad-riding pioneer, a name worthy of the marquee. And then came the show in England in late October.

Christian never felt good about the flip that day. For the first time,
he'd be doing it off a different ramp—not the one he'd been using all
these months. And to him, this British ramp didn't look right. "Too
steep," Christian thought when he first saw it. He could have done a
practice flip—at least one. Later, he'd think about that—a lot. Maybe
he should have done a practice flip. But the crowd was big, people
were waiting, and despite his concerns, he thought he could do it.
He'd be fine. Christian was *Huevos* material, after all—he had *huevos*.
He didn't do the flip until the show, and that's when he learned he had
been right about that ramp. It *was* too steep.

Christian lost his grip on the handlebars as he flipped upside
down. The quad stopped rotating, and to save himself, Christian
bailed out, trying to push the floating four-wheeler away from him.
"But in the air," he recalled later, "it's hard to push a quad." Especially when you're upside down. And scared. And about to crash into
a metal landing in front of thousands of people on a beach at sunset
in England, thousands of miles from home. Christian landed first and
the ATV landed on top of him, crushing one leg.

The crowd gasped. Doctors feared for a while they might need to amputate Christian's leg at the knee to save him—a possibility that Christian didn't totally understand, given his lack of English and the fog of painkillers. Either way, he was out. No more flipping for the great Christian Gagnon, at least for a while. Which was too bad. Quite a shame, said a promoter calling Wes Miller's office that fall. He was concerned because Christian was supposed to be flipping at his monster truck show in Montreal at the end of November. Did Miller have another guy who could do the job?

Benjamin Charles Vaught—better known as B.C.—carefully considered the promoter's question on the phone. He was thirty-six years old and had no freestyle riding experience whatsoever. The Southern California native was a former ambulance driver who had found success as a drummer in a heavy-metal band called (hed)PE. He had signed his first record deal a decade earlier and had traveled the world with the band, playing the drums—not riding machines.

But B.C. grew up riding motorcycles, three-wheelers, and quads— recreationally, at least—in the California desert. He understood the allure of the machines and appreciated Wes Miller's *Huevos* DVDs. The pair had met when Miller wanted to use a (hed)PE song in one of his films. B.C. became friends with Wes, and then ultimately left the music industry to work for him. His job, among other things, was recruiting new riders. The drummer-turned-salesman knew how to talk to people, sell ideas, solve problems, and identify abilities in others. And B.C. had taken a liking to my brother, in particular. What he had noticed first of all was his demeanor. Caleb was serious, B.C. thought, all business. In a world that could be populated at times by spoiled-rotten rich kids burning daddy's money, hard-drinking hell-raisers itching for a fight, and tattooed misfits striking a pose for the world, Caleb seemed different—"a blue-collar boy," he called him, with some down-home Texas manners thrown in to make him even more likable. The first time B.C. ever spoke to Caleb, complimenting his jumps at a show in Minnesota, my brother called him sir. *"Thank you, sir."* B.C. liked that, found it impressive. This kid was respectful. But in the end, it was about the work—about the riding talent. And with Caleb there was no question about it. B.C. had already invited him to fill in, at times, on Miller's Bomb Squad. Caleb had traveled to France and England with the team; he was there on the beach when Gagnon crashed. Maybe he was the guy, B.C. thought. Maybe Caleb could replace Christian and do the backflip in Montreal.

"Do you want to do it?" B.C. asked my brother after getting off the phone with the promoter.

"Hell, yeah," Caleb replied.

B.C. expected this response from my brother—of course, Caleb would want to do it. So B.C. pressed him. *Could* he do it? He wasn't going to sign Caleb up for the flip in Montreal unless Caleb was certain he could perform the stunt without injuring himself, like Christian had. Everyone—perhaps B.C. most of all, given his lack of riding experience—was rattled by what they had witnessed in England. That couldn't happen again.

Of course, Caleb said. He understood. He could handle the gig.

"What's it pay?" he asked B.C.

"Five thousand dollars," B.C. replied.

Caleb could hardly believe it.

"Book that show, man," he said. *Five thousand dollars?* It was more money than Caleb had earned in his entire career to that point—and now he was going to make it in a single night? With one backflip? "Book it, B.C.," he said again. "I'm going to do it."

Then Caleb called my father to tell him the exciting news about the show in Montreal and the flip he was going to do and the money he was going to make.

"But you don't *know* how to backflip," my father said.

"I know that," Caleb replied.

"When's the show?" my father said.

"In late November," Caleb replied.

"This month?"

"Yep."

"Caleb, that's three weeks."

"Yep," he said again. "I need to learn to backflip."

YOU'RE NOT GOING
TO LIKE ME

THE ROAD to Helps, Michigan, begins in Green Bay, Wisconsin. From there, Helps is a straight shot, 130 miles due north: across the Menominee River, skirting the icy banks of Lake Michigan, through the tiny towns of Ingalls and Daggett, Powers and Carney, and still farther north, past the lumber yards and the doublewides, deep into the forested wilds of Michigan's remote Upper Peninsula.

Helps doesn't appear on many maps. The mailing address is actually Perronville. The closest real city is Escanaba, population 12,552, more than thirty miles east. But it was Helps my brother was seeking when he left Texas in early November 2006, towing his quad behind my father's pickup truck—a place called Helps and a man named Scott Murray. If Caleb was going to flip his four-wheeler in Montreal, if he was going to fulfill the commitment he made to B.C. and that promoter, he was going to need Murray's guidance. After my father, Murray was my brother's first phone call.

"Hey, this is Caleb Moore," he said, introducing himself on the line and, for once, a bit nervous. Caleb had met Scott only one time before, about a year earlier, through other riders, friends of friends. What if Murray didn't even remember him? Or what if he wasn't available? What if he couldn't help?

"Hey," Scott replied, welcoming my brother's unexpected call. He remembered the name, Caleb Moore. Even recognized Caleb's Texas accent. Caleb got right to the point. Told Scott about the promoter, and the show in Montreal, and how, despite the promises he'd made to B.C., he really had no idea what he was doing or how to get there in the short time he had to prepare.

"You think you can help me out?" Caleb asked.

"Absolutely," Scott replied.

Murray was a gifted motocross rider. But at this point, Caleb and I knew a lot of gifted riders. My brother's interest in Scott Murray had less to do with what he knew and more to do with what he had. On the backside of the forty acres he owned in Helps, Murray had built a massive foam pit, thirty-four feet wide by forty-eight feet long. The walls of the pit were six feet high and made from sheet metal. They were held together by cedar poles that Murray had cut by hand, and two-by-six oak planks he had salvaged from the old, abandoned saw-mill on his land. The key to everything was what Murray placed inside the rectangular contraption: roughly thirty-five hundred dollars' worth of scrap foam he had purchased from a mattress factory in Escanaba. It was one of the few foam pits in the country at the time, a place where riders like us could practice—and practice relatively safely. And Caleb was wondering if he could jump his quad again and again into that Escanaba mattress foam, so that he could learn to flip, without seriously injuring himself.

Of course, Scott replied. Caleb was welcome in Helps anytime.

That's the thing, Caleb told him on the phone. He needed to come right away. The Montreal show was in just a few weeks, Caleb informed Scott, and he had even less time than it seemed, because of an awards banquet he was supposed to be attending in November. Caleb had finished fifth on the national racing circuit that year and just couldn't miss the banquet.

"*Are you serious?*" Scott thought. In his mind now, Murray was running numbers—time left divided by what Caleb still had to learn,

multiplied by an unknown factor of fear and danger. "That means
you've got, like, eight days or something like that?" Scott told him.

"Yeah," Caleb answered.

"Well, you better get up here, then," Scott said. "You're not going
to like me by the time this is done."

·   ·   ·

SCOTT MURRAY was a lumberjack by trade. Like generations of
Murray men before him, he swung a saw in the great American north
woods, working beneath towering statues of maple and birch, spruce
and poplar. He got paid by the stick. Every piece of lumber that was
eight feet long by four inches wide was considered "a stick." And if
the log was thicker, it might count as two sticks or more. The going
rate, for a stick, was twenty or twenty-five cents. And a strong man,
working hard, could easily bring home five or six hundred sticks a
day, sometimes much more. There were tales of loggers who could
bring in a thousand sticks, a full load of pulp. Good money for the
Upper Peninsula—the best one could expect, anyway, working without a college education.

Supplies were important: gloves, helmets, goggles, padded chaps,
steel-toed boots, and chainsaws, most of all. Some men used Stihls or
Jonsereds; Murray favored Husqvarnas. His grandfather, a French Canadian by descent, had always used them, so Scott would, too, walking into those woods with a couple of Husqvarnas upon graduating
from high school in 1994. A small chainsaw could easily take down a
softwood tree, like a poplar. But for a maple, a hardwood, he'd need
something bigger. Either way, the work was hard and dangerous. Falling limbs—widow makers, the loggers called them—often took men
out, clipping them across the head as they worked facedown around
the trunk, knocking them unconscious, or killing them on the spot,
there in the woods. Trees could pinch saws, crack, and roll over un-

expectedly, injuring loggers. Saws could bounce back, clipping off fingers or worse. And then there was the problem of barbers' chairs. Trees could split in half, top to bottom, long ways down the trunk, and fall unexpectedly to one side as a logger was sawing. The half-fallen tree formed a sort of seat in the woods—a barber's chair. You didn't want to be underneath it when it fell, but sometimes it was hard to escape.

Murray dodged widow makers and barbers' chairs, took splinters in the eye, and chainsaws off his helmet. One time, his prized Husqvarna bounced off a tree trunk and sliced a quarter inch deep into the brim of his hardhat, maybe an inch away from his skull. Another time, Murray stabbed himself in the foot with a pickaroon, an axlike tool with a steel pick on the end, doing his best to crucify himself in the forest. On at least one occasion, he failed to dodge the widow maker in his path. It came straight down, like a wooden arrow, and failed to seriously injure him only because he turned at the last moment. The glancing blow to his neck left him bruised and bloodied, but alive.

Murray would return to the forest. He'd keep working—at least until his arrests for drunk driving. The second one led a judge to revoke his driver's license, which essentially marooned Murray on his property in Helps. With nowhere to go—unemployed, twenty-five years old, and stuck at home—he started thinking about what he really wanted to do with his life, which was riding motorcycles. In the 1990s, to help dull the boredom of living in Helps, Murray had hit the local motocross circuit, racing bikes in places like Denmark, Wisconsin, and Christmas, Michigan. Now, making a decision—a "conscious decision," he would say later—to improve his life, Murray refocused himself on the bikes, his first love. He built the foam pit. Learned some tricks. Managed to get some gigs—in Escanaba, at first, and then far away from Michigan, on the road, traveling, living the life he had imagined for himself.

He was afraid of nothing. Like me, Murray had crashed, broken his femur, and kept on riding. He was twenty-nine when Caleb called him—a veteran, ten years older than my brother. He understood how to backflip; he'd been flipping his motorcycle to dirt for more than a year and his quad into the foam for about six months. And, anyway, he had that foam pit. In short, Scott Murray was the perfect man to prepare Caleb for Montreal—even if Murray himself didn't believe he had enough time to teach his Texan apprentice how to flip. Not in eight days. As far as Murray was concerned, Caleb was making promises he probably couldn't keep. But he decided to be upbeat with my brother, stay positive. Murray figured there was no sense in telling Caleb he couldn't do it. "You're going to be living in that foam pit," he told him instead. "Going, going, going—and not stopping."

•   •   •

IT'S A mathematical equation, really—flipping. $L = I\omega$—where L is angular momentum, I is the moment of inertia, and ω is angular velocity. Physicist Michael Naughton, chairman of the department of physics at Boston College, once described it like this: Any mass in motion has velocity and, therefore, momentum. But an object that's rotating—like a flipping four-wheeler—has what's called angular momentum or *mvr*—mass, times velocity, times the radius, or the distance from the center of rotation. It also has angular velocity. The object—in this case the four-wheeler—is actually spinning, so ω is the change of angle, divided by the change in time. And finally, such an object has what's called a moment of inertia—mass times radius squared. In other words, the motion of any mass will be affected by how its weight is distributed around the axis of rotation.

These are, in the end, some of the most basic laws of physics. "Boiled down," Naughton said, "it's totally elementary." Sir Isaac Newton wrote about these forces as early as 1687, recording the basics in his landmark publication, *Principia*. "Everything I just discussed starts on page twelve," Naughton noted. "That makes it sound kind of simple." Within this alleged simplicity, there are layers of physical complications. The moment of inertia would be relatively easy to calculate, say, on a baseball—its weight distributed evenly around its center. But the mass of a four-wheeler hurtling through the air isn't uniformly distributed at all. There are bits of mass—handlebars, fenders, plastic, and metal—all over the place. "The moment of inertia is still mass times radius squared," Naughton said. "But you have to ask yourself: what radius?" Multiple calculations would need to be run to find, first, the center of mass on an ATV, and, later, its moment of inertia. And then there are other wrinkles: namely, torque. A rider on board, moving and changing position. Or the motor itself, revving faster or slowing down. These internal torques inevitably change the moment of inertia, which changes the angular momentum, which changes everything about a rotating object. If you reduce the radius, by altering your position on the quad, it will spin faster—like a figure skater pulling her arms in while spinning on the ice. If you increase the radius, it spins more slowly—like a skater stretching her arms out. "And so, if you want to see what's really going on when somebody's doing flips, don't just look at what the flip does. Look at what the body is doing, the person, changing their position, and what the motor is doing," Naughton said. "There are so many moving parts."

Despite all these complexities, the rider is in control of the flying machine—a control that, Naughton said, is learned intuitively, empirically, through experience, not from the equations themselves. Are you coming in nose heavy? Lean back more the next time. Are you over-rotating the machine? Maybe dial back the throttle on the ramp. "They're not thinking 'I should exert internal torque and change the moment of inertia.' But that's what they're doing," Naughton said. "A rider can learn how to control a four-wheeler."

· · ·

CALEB DIDN'T understand the physics. None of us did. We had left Sir Isaac Newton behind in our textbooks back in Krum. But my brother learned the most basic lesson shortly after arriving at Scott Murray's house in Michigan. There was a reason only a few people in the world had ever backflipped a quad: It was really hard—even when flipping into the relative safety of a foam pit. The machine was heavy—about four hundred pounds. The wheels were much smaller than those on a motorcycle, giving quad riders less centrifugal force to work with as they tried to get the ATV back around. And, in general, four-wheelers just felt huge—like a massive block of metal flying through the air. Angular momentum? $L = I\omega$? Forget about all that. There was no mathematical equation to describe the total absurdity of this idea. As Murray once said, "It feels like you're flipping a couch."

"Watch me on the ramp," Murray told Caleb to start, reeling off a few jumps on his own quad so my brother could see his body positioning and note the acceleration of his ATV on the face of the ramp. It was all about the face of the ramp. "That's where the magic happens," Murray said. Hit the ramp hard, then pull just as the machine takes flight, dropping your weight back, butt down and knees locked. These things were far more important than anything that happened afterward in midair. "You gotta get away from trying to make the thing flip while you're airborne," he said.

Caleb nodded. He understood. He had tried flipping at least two other times before—once into a foam pit and another time into a pond, so the water would soften the blow of the landing. He expected to have the flip figured out in no time. But his first day in Michigan couldn't have gone much worse.

He pulled too late and under-rotated the quad, nose-diving into the foam or landing upside down, on his head.

"Do it again," Murray told him.

He pulled too early, or went too fast, and over-rotated, landing butt-down, on his rear axle.

"Do it again," Murray said.

They worked together on the side, just going through the motions, like dancers practicing pirouettes in front of a mirror. "No," Murray told him. "You're bending your knees.... Don't bend your knees." And then they returned to the ramp—for still more crashes into the foam.

"I need to take a break," Caleb said finally.

"Nuh-uh," Murray said, shaking his head. "Do it again."

By the end of the day, Caleb's body was bruised and his quad bent out of shape. All those nosedives into the foam had knocked the front suspension out of whack. But it was his ego that seemed to be hurting most of all. That night, inside Murray's house, Caleb was unusually quiet, filled, for once, with doubt.

"What do we do now?" he asked.

Murray believed the problem was the ramp Caleb had brought with him to Michigan. They didn't seem to be getting enough lift out of it. So the next day they switched to a different ramp—and right away there was improvement. Caleb nailed a few in a row, then under-rotated. Nailed a couple more in a row, then over-rotated. He worked at it for a couple more days, briefly left to attend that awards banquet, and then returned, with me, to Murray's pit once again—with just a few days remaining to prepare for Montreal.

I could feel the tension as soon as we arrived. Caleb had no more time for mistakes. This much was clear. It was one thing to under-rotate or over-rotate into the foam. It was quite another to do the same thing while trying to land on dirt. "You need perfection," Murray told Caleb. The same approach every time. Muscle memory. Not thinking. Just doing. And, above all, not panicking in the middle of a flip. If there was a life lesson in the backflip, it was this. "At the end of the day, it's about commitment," Murray said. "You've got to lean back and commit."

Caleb was nervous—as nervous as I had ever seen him. Just a couple of weeks earlier, he had watched Christian Gagnon flip, then bail, throw the quad, crash, and seriously injure himself in front of that crowd in England. He had seen the damage a falling four-wheeler could do to a human body. And Christian had gotten off lucky. Doctors said he was going to keep his leg. It could have been worse. Caleb didn't talk about that, but we all knew it. And now here he was trying the same trick in the backwoods of northern Michigan—and running out of time. By the morning of his last day there, he didn't have a choice. He needed to leave the foam pit and try the flip on a less forgiving surface: dirt.

We measured off the distance between the ramp and the landing—sixty feet. We double-checked it and checked again. We rolled out some carpet on the ground to smooth out his approach. And then with me, Murray, and a few other riders watching, Caleb climbed aboard his quad and tore off toward the ramp, his engine echoing in the forest.

The flip—his very first flip to dirt—had no chance from the start. Caleb pulled as the quad left the ramp, but then immediately threw the machine away from him, jumping off like Christian had—not out of necessity, but out of fear. He was aborting in midair, abandoning ship. He landed on his feet (a good thing), twisting an ankle (a bad thing), while the machine landed on its back bumper, mangling its subframe, fenders, and exhaust system, before skittering off, a runaway quad, rumbling into a thicket of trees.

The twisted ankle hurt; it swelled up on Caleb right away. But the busted quad was the bigger problem. Caleb needed parts to replace what was broken, not only to keep practicing, but to go to Montreal—*if* he was still going to Montreal. After some discussion, Murray allowed Caleb to take the parts off his own quad—a brand-new Honda 450—to fix what Caleb had broken in the crash. But only if my brother made him a promise. "Don't do that again," Murray said.

This time, he wouldn't. This time, he committed. This time, the second time, the backflip was perfect. From ramp to dirt, Caleb was perfect. We celebrated on the landing—young men jumping and screaming in the woods. "Thank you," Caleb kept telling Murray. "Thank you so much for this." And then, within hours, we were gone, bound for Montreal in my father's pickup truck—with Murray's lessons in Caleb's head, his ramp on our trailer, and his parts on my brother's quad, promising to return everything to Michigan soon. All I remember about the trip was that it was cold and gray, and that when we saw the skyline of the city, and Le Stade Olympique, where Caleb would be flipping his quad, a hush fell upon us. The stadium was huge.

· · ·

MY FATHER'S truck disappeared during dinner. This was the first problem in Montreal. The second problem was that all of Caleb's riding gear—his helmet, gloves, boots, and clothes—was in the backseat at the time. It was the night before the show. My parents had flown north from Texas. B.C., Caleb's new manager who got him the gig, had flown in, too. We were all here, together. We were all nervous, together. And now we were standing in the parking lot, outside a Canadian-owned Japanese steakhouse where we had just eaten dinner, staring at an empty parking space in the dark.

"Dad?" Caleb said, calling to my father.

"What?"

"The pickup's gone."

"*What?*"

"It's not here."

We figured we had parked in a tow-away zone, country folks making mistakes in the big city. So we checked with the restaurant. They hadn't towed the truck. We checked with other businesses nearby. They hadn't towed the truck, either. That's when members of our dinner party—including some new friends from Canada who would be performing with Caleb in the monster truck show the next day—started asking questions.

"What were you driving?" one of the Canadians asked.

My father started ticking off the specs of his truck. "It's a four-wheel drive, Ford F350, four-door—"

"It's gone," the Canadian said, cutting my father off. "You don't see many of them up here." The Ford had been stolen, he guessed. "It's headed north," the Canadian said. "Somebody's got it, and it's headed north right now."

We called the police and filed a report—and then called the promoter. Caleb needed new gear, like now. The promoter said he'd take care of it and sent a girl to our hotel in the morning to take Caleb shopping at a nearby dealership. She was a beautiful woman, French speaking, who didn't know the first thing about riding gear, but she managed to get my brother anything he wanted, sweet-talking the dealers on the showroom floor as she told them the sob story of Caleb Moore, the Texan daredevil, who was risking his life tonight at the Stade, or whatever they called the giant concrete fortress of a stadium we had seen the day before. Surely, they could help Caleb out, the girl said. *Oui?* And they did.

My brother arrived at the stadium outfitted in new gear—free of charge—and ready to go. He didn't seem to be worried about the stolen truck, or the flip, or the vast expanse of polished concrete he would crash into if he botched his jump that night in the stadium. Even the odd formation of the jump itself didn't trouble him. Caleb was expected to land his quad on a mound of dirt, pushed into the side of an old, yellow school bus, parked horizontally to the ramp and adorned across the front with a single word: "Ecoliers." *Schoolchildren.*

My parents didn't like it—not any of it. Inside the stadium they took to pacing across the concrete floor that would surely injure my brother, or worse, if he crashed. My mother passed the time chain-smoking Virginia Slim 120s. A half-a-pack-a-day smoker at the time, she probably smoked that much just waiting for the show to start. Meanwhile, my father kept his distance. For days now, he had been putting on his best tough-guy, plainsman act, trying to conceal his worries from my brother by saying as little as possible.

"So you got it down?" he asked Caleb after we left Scott Murray's house.

"Yeah," my brother replied.

"Landed it to dirt?"

"Yeah," he said again.

"How many times?" my father asked.

"About six," Caleb said.

Six times? It didn't seem like enough to my father. *Just six flips to dirt after all those days in Michigan?* It felt like that number should have been higher—a lot higher—given the risks: the concrete floor and the weird bus landing, the crowds and the promoter, and, of course, Caleb's physical well-being. My father wanted to talk to Caleb about all of this, but he didn't want to plant seeds of doubt in Caleb's mind—even if there was plenty of reason to be doubtful. That would only make things worse. So, instead, at the stadium, my father came to me, venting his bottled-up panic while Caleb wasn't around.

"Listen, damn it," my father said, grabbing me and pulling me close to him. "Does he have it or not?"

I had been with Caleb in Michigan. I had seen him fail. I had seen him crash into Scott Murray's foam pit, under-rotating and over-rotating, for days at a time. I had seen him crash during his first back-flip to the dirt, and I had even seen him scared—my brother, afraid. But I'd also seen him nail it those half dozen times while Scott Murray and I looked on, cheering. So, yeah. I felt good. As good as one could expect. Anyway, there was no stopping Caleb now.

I looked my father in the eye.

"Yeah, Dad," I told him. "He's got it."

•   •   •

THERE ARE people who will never understand what motivated my brother to climb aboard his quad that night in Montreal. There are people, even, who would consider what he was about to do stupid, without merit, an idiot's mission with a ramp, an engine, and four wheels—a death wish, beneath the lights in Canada. But just as these critics don't understand us, we don't understand them.

We live today in a bubble-wrapped world, where playing at all usually means playing it safe. Put a helmet on your child—for everything. Don't let him walk to the school bus alone—ever. No running wild through the forest—we don't know what's out there. No digging in the dirt—we don't know what's in it. Wash your hands. Get out of that tree. You might fall. You might get hurt. Parents today want to control the outcome—or at least convince themselves that they can. It's like they want to keep the butterfly inside the cocoon for fear that it might fly away on the wind.

But the world wasn't built by people who chose to sit around inside their caves and thatched huts, afraid of the untamed world outside. It was made by those who strayed far, chasing big—and, often, dangerous—dreams. In their journals, early ocean explorers wrote of storms so violent that they'd be lost at sea for days, without hope or any chance of being rescued, in wooden ships taking on water. Boats sank and men died, slipping beneath the frothy waves, gone. But people kept sailing, returning to the water again and again until they finally found what they were seeking: treasure, dry land, the next island just beyond the horizon, or, in Christopher Columbus's case, a new world. Upon reaching the West Indies in October 1492, he reported the natives were so amazed at the sight of his ships and crew "that they asked us if we had come from heaven."

Early American settlers were similarly inclined to take chances—with smallpox, Indians, food shortages, and bears. On their epic expedition across the western frontier, Lewis and Clark reported grizzlies so large that they were almost impossible to kill. Lewis, for one, said he'd rather fight two Indians than one bear. Yet they kept going, deeper into the unknown wilderness. And other American pioneers soon followed—on foot at first and then in the skies. The Wright brothers? People dismissed them as silly dreamers. Chuck Yeager breaking the sound barrier in a rocket-propelled airplane? Skeptics thought he'd break up and die. And the astronauts? They were crazier still, signing up "for the privilege," one journalist wrote, "of strapping themselves to experimental equipment powered by explosives." This, too, would certainly kill them—and, also, fail miserably. As late as 1949, public opinion polls found that only 15 percent of Americans believed that humans would reach the moon by the end of the century.

What Caleb was about to attempt in Montreal—on a quad—wasn't exactly a moon landing or a flight in Kitty Hawk, North Carolina. Both of us would admit that. But just as these men before us wanted to fly, so did we. Just as they were willing to take chances, we were, too. This was our one shot, Caleb's shot. If he failed, we were all going back to Texas with nothing.

• • •

THE PROMOTER didn't want Caleb to do a practice flip. He might crash and injure himself or damage his quad. And that would be it.

No backflip in the Saturday-night monster truck show in Montreal, one less thrill for the fans at Le Stade Olympique. B.C. agreed with the promoter, though for a different reason. If Caleb was going to crash, B.C. thought, at least crash during the show. "At least then," B.C. said, "you'll get paid." But Caleb didn't listen. Remembering what had happened to Christian in England, he wanted one practice run. Needed it, really. He set up the ramp, took his red Honda out for a ride, went for the flip, and promptly crashed, over-rotating the machine and landing nose up.

Caleb skittered off the back of his four-wheeler and slid down the mound of dirt on the seat of the brand-new pants the woman had helped him acquire that morning. The quad rolled away, righting itself on its wheels. It was fine, undamaged, and Caleb had escaped injury, too, celebrating his failed attempt before he even skidded to a stop.

"I got it!" he shouted.

Despite the rough landing, he felt like the flip was a success. "I know what to do," he said. He and my father went over to the ramp, which was propped up with a few two-by-four boards to increase the pitch at takeoff. "Let's take one board out," Caleb said, "and I won't over-rotate."

He didn't want another practice run on the reconfigured ramp. "I don't need to hit again," he said. Unlike the rest of us, he didn't seem worried at all—about the ramp or anything else. He was calm—we all noticed it. Caleb was in control, barely nineteen, but somehow older than his age and ready for the moment. As night fell in Montreal, and fans began to fill the stadium, Caleb mugged for cameras, granted interviews, and sat on his quad, at ease with himself, until the announcer finally called his name.

The crowd was informed that this was for history, that Caleb was about to do something he had never tried before at a show, and that it was dangerous, a crazy stunt that Caleb Moore had no business trying. "He wants some love," the announcer boomed in his French-Canadian accent. *"C'mon! C'mon!"*

B.C., nervous and pacing on the stadium floor, pumped his fist to the crowd. Pyrotechnics fired flames into the air. The cameras in the stadium focused in on Caleb, beaming his helmeted image onto the massive jumbotron. And then, with everyone watching, he hit the gas, rumbling toward the ramp.

"Watch out!" the announcer shouted.

Caleb accelerated in the face of the ramp, as Murray had taught him, and pulled just as the wheels crossed over the lip. His weight was back, and his legs were straight, and he was committed—fully committed—bathed in the yellow lights of the stadium and flipping, three stories up in the air, end over end, one time around, while the crowd shrieked.

The landing was easy—it was like Caleb had done it a thousand times before—and the crowd roared in approval. Fireworks shot off and B.C. went running. We all went running, trying to catch Caleb, but he was gone, racing his quad back up the landing, to the top of the school bus, to celebrate.

He had claimed it. It was his. Like a mountain climber planting his flag on the summit, Caleb wanted to leave something to let everyone know he had been there. Before we packed up, left Montreal, and headed back home to Texas—a weeklong odyssey across North America—my brother left his mark in red spray paint, scrawling big block letters down the side of the yellow school bus. The letters spelled his name.

"CALEB MOORE."

SKETCHY

I MET her at a rider party in McKinney, about an hour east of Krum. There was beer for drinking, and a balcony for hanging out—and girls, including one named Ashley Hammons. She didn't care at all about riding. Ashley was from Van Alstyne—a tiny railroad town on the north Texas plains—and had never seen our races, much less our growing repertoire of freestyle moves. So the riding, the ATVs, didn't have anything to do with her interest in me. But she was definitely interested, trying to speak with me at the party. For her, that first night, it was almost a game. I was a mystery—and she was the one who was going to solve it. Who was this quiet kid at the card table? Could he even talk?

It was a fair question. While my brother spun stories and laughed and slapped people on the back—*Who needs another beer?*—I shrank in the face of conversation, a small kid, suddenly smaller. If Caleb was like my father—the proud cowboy regaling folks around the campfire on the Western range—I was more like my mother, channeling the role of the sidekick, quiet and reflective. Just as I liked to follow my brother in competition—letting him hit the ramps first and waiting for him to tell me what to do, to show me the way—I was content to let Caleb do the talking in almost any social situation.

But Ashley wasn't eyeing my brother. She kept trying to talk to me—at the party in McKinney and later at other parties that followed. Finally she wore me down. I couldn't help but be interested. Our first real date was at an Applebee's, chosen in part because it was halfway between Krum and Van Alstyne. Ashley showed up in a new outfit she had purchased at the Midway Mall in rural Sherman, specifically for our date. I picked up the tab at dinner, we said good-bye after dessert, and kissed outside in the Applebee's parking lot—two teenagers in the dark Texas night.

"Are you sure you want to do this?" I asked her.

Ashley's friends were skeptical—in part because I rarely summoned the courage to speak to them and in part for other reasons. Caleb and I were on the road a lot. "I'm always traveling," I told Ashley. Gone almost every weekend, racing or jumping somewhere. And Van Alstyne was an hour away from Krum. It wasn't like she could just come over and hang out with me every afternoon after she got out of school. But none of that mattered to Ashley.

"I want to give it a try," she told me.

Soon she was attending my races and freestyle events. I had a girl—and a pretty girl at that—cheering for me from atop trailers and truck beds. Still, she didn't totally understand what I was doing. Early on, during races, Ashley had trouble finding me out there amid the growling sea of machines. All the riders looked the same to her—once we put on our helmets. And, in general, the sport worried her. There were so many ways we could get injured, it seemed to her, and often did. That could be you, Ashley told me.

I just shrugged it off. I had to ignore the risks in order to keep up with Caleb. After the show in Montreal, he was no longer on the fringes of Wes Miller's Bomb Squad riding team; he was at the core of it—one of the daredevils that fans came out to see, the grand finale, the backflipping genius with *huevos*. Caleb had *huevos*. My brother was going to be in Miller's movies—this was certain. Miller was already filming him. B.C. was booking him shows. And Caleb was earning other perks, too: namely, new quads, free of charge, courtesy of Polaris, the Minnesota-based ATV manufacturer and one of the

Bomb Squad's corporate sponsors. When Polaris staged a multiday
dealer show in Tennessee in the summer of 2007—to unveil the company's new four-wheeler product line to its sales force—there was no
question Caleb would be there to entertain the crowd, jumping the
new quads to show what they could do. My presence was unlikely, but
my brother pushed for it anyway, telling B.C. that I could ride.

"He *can*?" B.C. asked Caleb, incredulous.

B.C. had met me for the first time months earlier at the show in
Montreal. I was seventeen, fresh out of high school, having graduated
early, and still small. "Small, but fast," I told people on the racetracks
from Texas to Pennsylvania—this was my mantra. Still, there was no
getting around it. I was definitely small. B.C. thought I looked like
a little boy—and told my brother as much. "Dude," he said, "he looks
like he's twelve years old."

The fact that I had probably uttered three words to B.C. in
Montreal—too shy to speak to the Los Angeles–based manager who
was helping Caleb—didn't help my cause. But Caleb vouched for me.
Yes, I could ride, he told B.C.

"As good as you can?" B.C. said, pressing him.

"He's going to be better than me," Caleb replied.

B.C. didn't buy it—even after he started watching me jump. Caleb's words sounded like bluster to him. And Wes Miller wasn't buying it, either. To Wes, I looked "sketchy"—that was the word he used.
I was sketchy. Every time I climbed on my quad, Wes got nervous.
The problem, they both agreed, was confidence. I didn't seem to have
any. On my four-wheeler at freestyle events, I looked unsure of myself,
they believed, following Caleb again and again on the side in practice,
to gauge his speed on the ramps, before I'd ever try the actual jump
myself. This worried them. B.C. thought the injuries I had suffered
early on—namely the broken femurs—had taken a toll on me. "That
wears on your soul," he said. Maybe that was my problem. Either way,

I didn't have *huevos*. Without Caleb, they were pretty sure I couldn't ride at all. And there was no way they were bringing me to their corporate sponsor's big event. B.C. was worried I would crash the new machines in front of the people who had built them.

"I don't want that happening in front of Polaris," B.C. told my brother.

"Please," Caleb said. He was begging now.

Caleb promised B.C. that he would work with me before the event. He made a slew of other promises, too—that I wouldn't crash, that I was ready, that I had *huevos*, they'd see. "Just give him a chance," Caleb said—and finally B.C. gave in, beaten down by Caleb's persistent arguments. I could come to Tennessee, but I had to make him a promise of my own. "You have to pull it off," B.C. told me. "I can't have you crashing."

There were problems in Tennessee from the start. The six-ton steel landing B.C. had towed from California to use in the Polaris event didn't fit through the arena doors in Nashville. To get it inside, we had to cut off the top and weld it back on again—expensive, difficult, last-minute work. And then we still had to ride—on brand-new quads we had never ridden before, in front of the crowd that helped pay our bills, with pressure on everyone, Caleb most of all.

The first night in the arena, with the lights turned down low and the pyrotechnics firing, Caleb was expected to appear on cue, hit a ramp, and do his backflip in front of the entire Polaris sales force, the corporate hotshots, the CEO, everyone. Land it—and the crowd roars. The sponsor feels great about its new quads, the dealers want to sell them, and there are handshakes all around. Crash—and it's a corporate disaster. Call the crisis management team and say good-bye to our contract. Crash—and we never work with Polaris again.

"How are you feeling?" B.C. asked Caleb before the flip.

"I'm fine," Caleb replied.

His answer, while comforting to B.C., didn't mean much. Caleb wouldn't say if he was nervous. But when it came time for the flip, it was clear there was no reason for concern. My brother did not hesitate on his approach, flipping, end over end, and then landing in front of that crowd with mathematical grace and certainty. It was $L = I\omega$—all that stuff. Angular momentum, and moment of inertia, and angular velocity—Caleb had it all figured out. And the crowd was roaring. And the sponsor was giddy. For years, Polaris dealers would tell B.C. they'd never forget that moment in the arena in Tennessee.

The problem, perhaps not unexpectedly, was me. I crashed—not that night, but later that week at the same dealer event, on an outdoor course that Polaris had set up. I came up short on a jump and just crashed—falling off the shiny new Polaris I was riding and bashing my head against the steel landing. I jumped up and mounted the quad again, trying to act like everything was fine. Move along; nothing to see here. At least the four-wheeler wasn't damaged. But on my next approach, I felt dizzy and a bit sick, like the world was suddenly spinning faster on its axis. A concussion, for sure.

Rang my bell a bit on that last landing, I told B.C., trying to explain why I couldn't ride anymore.

"He messed up," Caleb told B.C.

"I just messed up," I agreed.

"But he's good—trust me," Caleb said.

"I swear I'm good," I told B.C. "Sorry I messed up," I added, apologizing. "I swear that doesn't always happen."

I was worried that B.C. would never invite me to ride again. He had made me promise to not crash—and I had crashed. But B.C. didn't seem upset. "It's all right," he kept telling me. "Don't worry about it."

Despite my mistake, and my concussion, Caleb's manager liked what he saw in me. I could be timid, yes. And I wasn't anywhere close to flipping yet, like my brother. But my slow, analytical approach,

B.C. believed, often led to more precise tricks and landings. What I lacked in courage—in *huevos*—I made up with attention to detail and a methodical, if plodding, effort to get things right. Anyway, B.C. told me, everyone crashed. It happened to Christian in England. It could happen to any of us. As we left Tennessee that week, B.C.'s concerns about me had nothing to do with the crash, in fact. He was worried about my personality, my shyness, and how I seemed to shrink from the world, into silence.

"How do I get this kid to talk?" B.C. kept asking himself.

TO PRACTICE
AND BE SAFE

HERE'S HOW you injure yourself: You knuckle the landing, coming up short like I did in Tennessee, and get bucked off the machine, tossed hither and yon, onto the dirt, concrete, or steel. Or you flatland it—going too long and missing the landing altogether. In this case, the quad comes down hard—flatlanding—as if dropped from a third-story window. It bounces on its wheels, or tips, and again, you get tossed, slamming onto the dirt, concrete, or steel. Bogging out is a sure way to crash. You hit the ramp at three-quarter throttle, say, and everything is humming along just fine. And then you bog out. The engine sputters and dies in midair, perhaps because there's water in the fuel line. You should have flushed the line—or bought better gas. But it's too late. You have to throw the machine away from you. You don't want to land with it—because a bogged-out machine, just floating through the air, can land on top of you. If you don't throw the quad far enough away from your body, it's going to land on you, anyway. In this case, it's better to hold on, to stay in the seat as best you can—unless, of course, you're upside down. You never want to land upside down, with four hundred pounds of quad smothering you. Either way, if your machine bogs out, you're probably going to yardsale it, crashing and scattering parts everywhere. And then your four-wheeler will be roached out or clapped out—broken down, a real mess—and people will think you're a goon. You're gooney, they'll say. They'll know you can't ride. You're a goon with no skill and no business being out here. And if you try to flip—which you might, because you're such a goon—you'll panic. We'll hear that dreaded sound—*the panic rev*—as you pull madly on the throttle trying to correct your angular momentum and get your under-rotating machine to come back around. But chances are, it won't. You'll under-rotate, and you'll be lucky if you're conscious after yardsale-ing it all over the place. Oftentimes, it doesn't end well.

Caleb once hit his head so hard, crashing during a practice, that he started having a seizure on the track.

"It's all right, Caleb," my father said, kneeling over his twitching body.

"C'mon, Caleb . . ."

"Listen to my voice . . ."

"Talk to me . . ."

"I ain't going to the hospital," Caleb said, in a fog, after he finally regained consciousness and the seizure stopped. But my father, alarmed by what he had seen—"You scared me," he told my brother—demanded that Caleb get checked out this time. Doctors were worried about a possible brain bleed, and by the next day my brother was screaming with headaches—the worst he'd ever had.

Caleb spent days in an intensive care unit, taking antiseizure medications, and still more days sitting at home in the dark, before ultimately recovering. It was just another concussion, a bad one. We all had them. I once had three in the span of a month—in California, Nevada, and some rodeo arena somewhere. I can't recall exactly where—possibly because of all the concussions. All I remember about the rodeo crash was that I woke up the next morning in my parents' hotel room, with dried blood on the sheets, left over from my wounds—wounds I could clearly see now in the morning light, but could not recall from the night before.

"I guess I wrecked?" I asked my parents.

My father taught us, from a young age, how to handle pain. "Grit your teeth and yell," he said. "We ain't crying." Then, to show us what he meant, he would yell, like a Wookiee in distress. That's how we were supposed to do it—and we usually did. Gritting our teeth and yelling, Caleb and I frequented emergency rooms for dislocated shoulders, cracked wrists, torn-up knees, and broken ankles. I broke my ankle twice—once racing and once jumping. Our grandparents didn't like it, and in time we learned not to speak to them about our injuries. Or, if we had to talk to our grandparents about getting hurt, because we were hospitalized and they were going to find out, we called them directly so they could hear our voices on the phone and know we were okay. We were safe. It was just a concussion, or a fracture, or busted teeth. I knocked mine out in Steel City, Pennsylvania, three months after crashing in Tennessee, with Wes Miller's crew filming.

The jump that day in Steel City was seventy-two feet to the knuckle, which meant an ideal landing would have been around seventy-five feet, nice and smooth, easing down onto the sloped landing. But worried about knuckling it, about coming up short with the *Huevos* crew filming, I overthought the jump, did too many practice runs to gauge the distance, and was heavy on the throttle on my first approach. I cleared the knuckle, all right—and everything else, too, flying about eighty-five feet in the air and flatlanding. On impact, my head slammed into the handlebars, then jerked back as my body bounced off the quad into the dirt. I was already grabbing for my mouth—and Caleb was already there, racing toward me to help—before I even came to a stop on the ground.

"How bad is it?" I asked Caleb, showing him my face.

"It's okay," he said. He was lying.

"Are my teeth bad?"

"Nah," Caleb said. "You're fine."

Again, he was lying. I'd need three surgeries to fix my mouth, replacing the teeth I lost, with dentures and a bridge. But I was tough. It was official. The crash in Pennsylvania made the cut, appearing in *Huevos 10*. There I am, on film, flatlanding it before the crowd in Steel City. There I am in the dirt looking up at Caleb—scared and in pain, but not crying. Finally, there's the close-up, the money shot: my mouth, mangled and bloody, for the cameras.

• • •

THE CONCUSSIONS worried Ashley. "I wish you'd get your head checked out," she told me. They worried my parents, too. B.C. was right: The injuries could indeed wear on your soul, eating away at you and your confidence, your family and your finances. Hospital stays and surgeries were never cheap. But the biggest price was always physical. There were only so many times a rider could break his collarbone, or his wrist, or his leg, before he began to wonder: Why am I doing this? Once that question was buzzing around inside your head, it was hard to bat it away. Riders often retire, walking away from the sport, at age nineteen or twenty, to get a job with an auto body shop or a landscaping crew—manual labor usually, and not exciting work, but safe. One friend, who quit riding while still young, later explained his decision this way: "I was kind of over crashing."

But Caleb wasn't going to quit—maybe not ever—so I couldn't, either. There was no stopping us now—not with B.C. booking us gigs from Colombia to Latvia, Monaco to Mexico. "I'm ready to travel the world," Caleb said. And to go with him—I absolutely needed to go— I was gearing up to learn my own backflip. Just imagine the market, B.C. said, for a pair of quad-flipping brothers from rural Texas. Promoters would really go for that. So to protect us, my father came up with a plan. "To practice and be safe," my father told us, "you need a foam pit."

Neighbors in Krum had never enjoyed the quad riding on our property. Our home was in the country, but it wasn't like we were alone out there. We only had two acres, and the foam pit my father began designing for our backyard was just going to make neighborly relations worse. For starters, the pit was going to be bigger than Scott Murray's contraption in Michigan: thirty-five feet wide by a whopping seventy feet long. The larger it was, my father figured, the safer it would be. And, anyway, this was Texas. Our foam pit had to be big, almost out of principle.

It began with a load of oil field drilling pipe that my grandfather acquired in Wheeler and delivered to Krum. From the pipe, we cut twelve-foot posts, buried them ten feet apart, three feet in the ground, and held them in place with concrete. Next came rebar and hog wire—nine hundred feet of it. We used this to build the walls, purchased silver tarps to line the inside, and acquired dozens of semitruck tires to form the bottom. The truck tires would keep the foam off the ground in wet weather. A crane would be necessary, too. My father designed one, using a steel I-beam, thirty feet long, welded to a second, smaller I-beam to make an elbow, and hooked up to a winch, powered by a car battery. With the crane and winch system, we could hoist quads out of the pit on a hook—no heavy lifting necessary. Now we were just waiting on the shipment of foam—twelve hundred dollars' worth—coming from Georgia. But when it arrived by truck and we tossed it all into the pit, as giddy as children on Christmas morning with the foam piling up at our feet like so much wrapping paper, we realized we had a problem.

"We're going to need more foam," Caleb said, surveying a pit that was still mostly empty.

"A lot more," I nodded.

"You can't even jump a bicycle into this," my father said.

Unable to afford another foam shipment—my parents had already spent thirty thousand dollars on the backyard endeavor, literally throwing money into a pit—we began investigating cheaper

options. My mother, always frugal, went to work, making a compre-
hensive list of local manufacturers that might be able to assist us. "Do
you have scrap foam?" Caleb asked, making the rounds by telephone,
and soon enough we found a place that did: a carpet manufacturer in
an industrial strip outside Dallas. The foam in the warehouse there
was piled up in compressed bales weighing up to 750 pounds. For
about fifty cents a pound, a carpet man informed us, the bales could
be ours. There was just one catch: We had to pay cash, he said, and
he wasn't giving us receipts. "I don't want to know what you're doing
with this," the carpet man said, eyeing Caleb and me. "And I don't
want to be connected with it. I don't want to be liable."

Foam pits, after all, aren't exactly safe. You're practicing—that's
the point of a foam pit—and you're trying new things. So you often
land wrong: nose heavy, sideways, twisted, and upside down. If you
land upright, you can take crunching blows to the crotch. If you land
upside down, you can take it in the head and neck. And since you're
buried under four hundred pounds of machine—sandwiched upside
down between aluminum and foam—you often can't move, or hear,
or breathe very well. Claustrophobia sets in, as your buddies clam-
ber over the foam to help free you. Panic follows, as it takes them too
long. Brake rotors can slice open body parts. Handlebars knock out
teeth. On rare occasions, gas caps pop off, quads start leaking fuel or
oil, and hot exhaust pipes burn up, searing both skin and foam. Fires
aren't unheard of in foam pits—then the neighbors really complain,
with the smoke billowing everywhere and the firefighters barreling
down the street.

There had to be rules to prevent all of this. Once we finished
building our foam pit and finally started jumping into it, my father
insisted on two rules in particular: No one was allowed to jump into
the pit alone—and fire extinguishers had to be kept outside at all
times. Just in case.

PANIC REV

WE BARELY knew him when he showed up at our house in Krum in June 2008—or at least I barely knew him. Caleb was the one who spoke to Darrin Hall on the phone and invited him down to Texas. Sure, he could come, Caleb told Darrin, warm and hospitable. Of course, he'd teach him how to flip. He'd try, anyway. That's why the foam pit was there, Caleb told Darrin. Come on down to Krum.

Caleb was always helping other riders, scouting them out, and then calling B.C. to inform him about some new talent he had discovered. "I have a new rider for you," he would tell our manager on the phone. It often didn't work out. Caleb seemed to assume that everyone had his talents—and it was just a matter of trying. But that wasn't always the case. And, anyway, B.C. didn't like using unproven riders. There were too many risks. Still, B.C. would listen to Caleb and sometimes even agree to use a rider my brother had found. By 2008, Wes Miller, B.C., and the Bomb Squad had one goal: Get ESPN to add an ATV freestyle event to the Summer X Games, the biggest showcase of extreme sports in the world. We needed to be in it. But for that to happen, the sport needed more athletes, more guys who could actually do the stunts. And in Darrin Hall, Caleb believed he had found one—another hot recruit, a young prospect worthy of consideration. Of course, Darrin was welcome to come ride with us in Texas.

Darrin could hardly believe his good fortune. He was twenty-two, tall and lean, and, unlike most of us, he had a career. Darrin worked as a welder in Oklahoma and made good money, traveling the country on construction jobs. He had always been good with his hands—quick and agile. As a child growing up in rural Missouri—a town called Pleasant Hope, nestled into the Ozark Mountains—Darrin excelled at baseball, playing outfield for his local Little League team. But chasing down fly balls didn't hold his attention for long. Darrin was more interested in chasing adrenaline. From a young age, he would climb the dresser in his bedroom and leap to his bed—or seek out other high points and jump from there, too. Even getting injured—breaking his collarbone during one such stunt at the age of three—didn't dissuade Darrin from the business of jumping. As with Caleb, fear had no power over him. Darrin was in control. And when he got his first four-wheeler in high school, that was it: He was gone—off riding somewhere. By 2008, when he first spoke to Caleb, Darrin Hall had been competing in freestyle events for about two years. He had won trophies, like us; earned sponsors, like us; and even crashed badly—like us. In one accident in Arizona, Darrin crushed his trachea, leaving him unable to breathe on his own initially, hooked up to a respirator for days in a drug-induced coma.

"You ready to quit this now?" Darrin's mother, Angie, asked when her son finally came out of it.

"No," Darrin replied, steadfast.

The welding job was great and all. Darrin had a fiancée in Oklahoma and a shot at a normal life—he understood that. But he wanted to ride. He needed to learn to backflip, and he hoped my brother could teach him. "Caleb Moore just called me," he told his mother, in awe, after his phone call with my brother that spring. The Caleb Moore from the *Huevos* movies that filled Darrin's house back in Missouri. The Caleb Moore from the magazine articles that Darrin liked to read. The Caleb Moore who had done backflips across the world for almost two years now—and had his own foam pit in Texas, a big one. *That* Caleb Moore was on the phone with Darrin and soon Darrin was driving south from Oklahoma, towing his quad behind his pickup and sending selfies back home.

He was in Texas. He was in Krum. This was really happening.

. . .

WE ALL liked Darrin right away when he arrived at our house. Caleb showed him around. Then we geared up inside my parents' garage and rode our four-wheelers down the slope to the foam pit in the backyard. Before jumping in—before trying flips or any other serious tricks with Darrin—we warmed up, jumping, from a steel ramp to a dirt landing we had built right next to the foam pit. The landing was about thirteen feet high by forty feet wide, and Darrin, for whatever reason, had trouble hitting it from the start.

On his first jump, he came in nose heavy—a dangerous way to land a flying four-wheeler. Coming in nose down can send a rider right over the handlebars crashing face-first into the ground. Caleb shot me a look, like: *What the hell was that?* But my brother didn't say anything to Darrin, a guy we had only just met. Darrin knew what he was doing. Darrin knew he was nose heavy. He corrected it on the next jump. We all felt better. And then, on maybe Darrin's third jump of the day, we heard it: *a panic rev.*

An ATV in flight is relatively quiet. You don't pull much on the throttle, maybe not at all—unless you know from the start that you're in trouble, that you've under-rotated a flip or a move. Then you might rev the engine in hopes that a little juice will correct your angular momentum and get you back to where you need to be for L to equal $I\omega$. Or maybe it happens just out of panic—a panic rev. With Darrin, we heard it before we saw it—his engine whining, that horrible motorized scream. He was coming in nose heavy again and trying to correct it with the throttle, but there wasn't enough time. He went headfirst over the handlebars, right into the landing, right into the dirt.

I began to scream—a sound I didn't even know I was capable of making. Caleb called for my father and I went running for rags, in part because I had no idea what else to do. There was blood everywhere, Darrin's blood, pouring from his nose and puddling on the ground. He wasn't moving—and this was no concussion. It was much worse. Caleb and my father worked on him, mouth to mouth, chest compressions. A helicopter full of paramedics was summoned. It was on the way. And still, I was screaming—to myself, to no one, and then at my mother. When my father sprinted out of the house, she came outside, too. But I stopped her in the backyard before she reached the dirt landing and saw Darrin. Our mother liked word jumbles and jigsaw puzzles, Bible study and quiet weekends with family. She absolutely couldn't see Darrin—not like this. "It's bad," I told her, shaky with fear. "It's real bad." And then I screamed some more. "Don't come down here!" I told my mother. "Do *not* come down here!"

The helicopter landed a short while later in a neighbor's pasture and flew away with Darrin, whirring off toward Dallas. Some say Darrin Hall died at the hospital. Others say he was dead right there on our ramp. Either way, it didn't matter. Darrin was gone—and I was crying, alone, in our garage.

"Something happened," I told Ashley, calling her later that night.

I couldn't say what it was. Couldn't bear to tell her. I couldn't give it words because to do so would only make it more real. But finally Ashley got it out of me.

"I'm coming over," she said. When she arrived, letting herself into my bedroom upstairs, I cried some more. The walls of my room were painted in two colors, black and fire-engine red. The décor was what I thought of as Kickass Teenager. Racing trophies lined my shelves, racing pictures adorned the walls, and, on one wall, using square mirrors, I had made the outline of my racing number: 21. But that night, with Ashley holding me, I was not the tough, hard-charging racer who had won those trophies. I was a boy and I cried myself to sleep in that room, just up the hill from the landing where Darrin had crashed. We were supposed to be going to Spain in six days for a show. Now we were headed to Missouri for a funeral.

Darrin's mother asked if Caleb and I would be honorary pallbearers. Said it would mean a lot to Darrin to have us there in our riding gear, walking in front of his casket. And of course, we agreed. We went to Missouri to escort a body into a cemetery—a body that didn't look exactly like Darrin anymore. In the open casket, his face looked crooked, from his broken jaw and nose. But his mother was pleased with the work that the funeral home had done and at peace with what had happened in Krum—thanks in part to a letter she had found inside Darrin's pickup truck after they collected his body at the morgue in Texas. "If you're reading this letter, don't worry," Darrin wrote. "I'll be fine. I'm at home."

In the letter, he asked people not to mourn him or the short life he had lived. "I can honestly say I am happy with what I accomplished," Darrin wrote. And he urged his family not to live in regret, hate, or denial. "Live each day with love." He was still with them, he continued, even if they couldn't see him. He was in the cloudless sky and the moonlit night. All they had to do was think of him and look up. "Maybe," he wrote, "you'll see me flying on my quad."

. . .

IT WAS a nice thought, comforting even. Still, for my family, Darrin's death was hard to accept. Caleb blamed himself for what had happened in our backyard. "I should have said something," he told me, replaying the crash afterward. He had seen Darrin come in nose heavy on that first jump. He should have mentioned it to Darrin. He was Caleb Moore—*that* Caleb Moore. Darrin had trusted him—and my brother felt like he had failed a friend.

My mother felt responsible, too, and for a long time couldn't face what had happened at all. She didn't attend Darrin's funeral with the rest of us. Didn't call or even reach out to Darrin's mother. "Don't come down here!" I had told her the day of Darrin's crash—and it was like she was still standing there in the kitchen, paralyzed with guilt and fear and the idea that it could have been one of us, one of her sons dying on the landing in our backyard. "Do not feel bad," Darrin's mother told her when they finally spoke by phone months later. "Don't feel bad," Angie Hall said again. "Darrin's accident was just that—it was an accident."

It helped my mother to hear that, but not me. The fact that it was an accident meant that it could happen to me, to Caleb—to anyone. The risk, for me, was suddenly more real after what had happened to Darrin. I couldn't get certain images and sounds out of my head. Darrin's engine shrieking. The panic rev. Everyone running. *"Don't come down here!"* And the puddle of blood, pooling on the ground. Something had to be done about the blood after the helicopter whisked Darrin away. As my father went inside to wash up in the kitchen, he asked us to take a shovel and cover it with dirt.

•   •   •

I LANDED my first backflip in a show fourteen months later—after scrubbing those sounds and images from my mind as best I could. We had become the people we wanted to be: the backflipping Moore brothers from Texas. But like a carpenter stripping paint off an old house, I couldn't sand away all of the painful memories. They were right there beneath the fresh layers of paint I slathered onto the exterior of my life in order to move forward. And there would be too many reminders, peeling off the layers: more crashes, more friends going down, more paramedics and helicopters coming to our house—not for us, but for others. Darrin's crash wasn't the last time we would see something terrible.

Worst of all, despite all the risks we took, and all the boundaries we pushed, we weren't getting very far. Caleb and I were traveling—playing monster truck jams and rodeos. But in other ways, we were also stuck, going nowhere, risking our lives for five thousand dollars a weekend—and what else?

It was hard to say. ESPN officials finally made a decision: They had no interest in adding freestyle four-wheeler events to the X Games. There weren't enough people who could do what we did—that was the first issue. ESPN already had a freestyle motocross event, with motorcycles—that was the second, and more problematic, issue. What was the point of having flipping quads on television when they already had flipping motorcycles? Who would tune in to watch the quads? No one, ESPN programmers believed. People who flipped motorcycles were heroes—Evel Knievel in red, white, and blue. People who flipped quads were rednecks—Bubba on wheels. It didn't matter that what we were doing was more difficult. That was the perception—and there was nothing we could do to change it. Caleb and I were out of options. If we wanted to be in the X Games, if we wanted to compete on national television, we needed to try something else.

PART II

THE VALLEY

There have been risk-takers since the beginning of time. Young people want to take risks to stretch beyond the boundaries and experience that exhilarating feeling. They've been doing it forever. It's just that, back then, ESPN wasn't there recording it and there weren't product endorsements waiting, if they made it through the chute.

—Allen Sack, sociologist

THIS DARN
CONTRAPTION

AT FIRST, in the beginning, no one called them snowmobiles. North country tinkerers—from Mont-Joli, Quebec, to Moosomin, Saskatchewan—dreamed up far more fantastical names for their newfangled winter machines.

They christened them Snow Flyers and Snow Birds, Snow Sedans and even Snow Planes. In Sayner, Wisconsin, in 1926, Carl Eliason called his first machine a Motor Toboggan—"a motorized sled with a thousand uses," he declared, marketing it to woodsmen, doctors, trappers, and mail carriers, "all men whose daily life takes them through remote snow areas." In Flin Flon, Manitoba, Frank Smerch's engine-powered Huskymobile glided along on skis made "from the best quality solid oak," becoming, he told buyers, "The Motorized Dog Team." And in Almena, Wisconsin—"Small on Size, Big on Friendliness"—John Swansen founded the Eskimobile Company, manufacturers of two vehicles built for snow and mud. With his Eskimobile, Swansen slapped massive tracks, not wheels, to the bottom of a car chassis, selling the new machine for eight hundred dollars. And with his so-called Stilt-Mobile, equipped with large, narrow wheels, Swansen had a vehicle that he believed perfect for navigating through mud or fresh snow. The Stilt-Mobile was a complete machine, brochures boasted, capable of driving in "tall brush, swamps, ditches, and washouts, and over rocks, fallen trees, stumps, etc." The

Stilt-Mobile could pull a tractor—"all day long"—or harrows, discs—
"or what have you." "In other words, it does the work of three average
horses," the brochure concluded. "A STILT-MOBILE has many useful
purposes."

There was no single inventor of the machine, no Henry Ford of the
snow. The idea, to northerners, just made sense: They needed a more
efficient way to travel during winter, something better than horses,
wagons, or the new cars that always got stuck somewhere. And so, the
notion spread—from town to frostbitten town across Canada, New
England, and the American plains, floating, as if on the wind, until,
perhaps inevitably, the idea blew into a small community in the far
reaches of northern Minnesota.

David Johnson, working there in town, hadn't heard of anything
so crazy as a Stilt-Mobile, but he had seen photographs of Eliason's
toboggans. And the orphaned son of Minnesota pioneers intended
to perfect that design—even if his business partner, Edgar Hetteen,
had no interest in building a motorized sled, "this darn contraption,"
Hetteen called it once. Johnson was supposed to be building straw
choppers. The future, Hetteen believed, was straw choppers—and
perhaps, also, grain loaders and weed sprayers, practical products for
practical people, Swedes and Norwegians mostly. That's what they
built at Polaris Industries, their company, in the little town near the
Canadian border. And that's what they needed to keep building, Hetteen declared, to satisfy their small-town investors and to fulfill the
contracts they had been lucky enough to land.

Johnson—a quiet man with blue eyes, parted hair, and a winking
smirk etched on his oval face—couldn't shake the idea from his mind.
He kept picturing it: a snow machine that could take him deer hunting in bad weather, a utility vehicle that farmers could use in winter, a
way to navigate the snow-covered roads of northern Minnesota until
spring. By late 1954, it was all he could think about. So when Hetteen

left town at Christmas, bound for California with his family on vacation, Johnson turned to the other men inside the shop.

"We've got two weeks," he announced.

Two weeks, Johnson said, to build what he was calling the Sno-Traveler.

. . .

THE LITTLE workshop had opened a decade earlier with a clunky name, Hetteen Hoist & Derrick, and a simple slogan. "We Can Build It or Fix It," the sign said outside. Hetteen—lanky, stubborn, and just twenty-four at the time—was brimming with confidence. But business, at least initially, was slow. It was hard to find the cramped shop inside the abandoned dance hall and tucked in behind Hjalmer Sunsten's garage. The shop wasn't in the phone book and it might as well have been off the map. Few, if anyone, ever made their way to the place that Hetteen and Johnson called home: tiny Roseau, Minnesota, about a dozen miles south of the Canadian border, high on the northern prairie.

Hetteen's grandparents—Peter and Betty—came here in 1889 from Sweden for the same reason everyone else did: to build a better life. The Roseau Valley was said to be teeming with animals for hunting: moose, elk, caribou, and deer. The beasts, unafraid, would often gather in large numbers, making the killing easy. And, of course, the Swedes were ready for the weather—the cold, endless winters. A perfect climate for them, or at least so it seemed.

The pioneers hadn't counted on the rain, which fell the rest of the year, one settler noted, with "monotonous recurrence," flooding the prairie, the farmers' fields, and even their homes. Residents complained of "perpetual rainfall," dripping from their saturated rooftops into their saturated houses. Even during dry years, the Roseau lowlands retained water, making travel difficult, if not impossible. Men were known to wade, knee-high, through the slop to get from place to place while women tried to stay dry by converting water troughs into makeshift canoes. Life was reported to be "a factual nightmare of mud and mosquitoes." Wolves—some weighing over one hundred pounds—were also a problem. So settlers turned to poison, buying the product in five-pound cans. But the poison, at times, killed the unintended: people and livestock. And there was almost nothing early settlers could do to drive off the snakes, which slithered into their primitive homes, nesting inside hay mattresses or sugar sacks to escape the rain, floods, snow, or cold. Almost anywhere, it seemed, was better than living in the elements outside.

The Hetteens cut an odd figure in this inhospitable land. Peter was lean and wiry while Betty was round and large—Mother Hetteen, Mör Hetteen, a strong woman who, upon seeing the wide-open land south of Roseau, suggested settlers give it the name of her hometown back in Sweden: Malung. Peter and Betty built a home here out of Gilead trees that had to be hauled from seven miles away, homesteading on 160 acres. The family called it the "homestead shack," nothing much to speak of, but Peter filled it with furniture he built himself. And Mör Hetteen endured the hardships of this new, soggy land, with no complaints. When the family needed food, she bartered with the Native Americans living nearby, trading her homemade bread for moose meat. When the swamp caught fire one summer, threatening their homestead, she prayed to God for mercy—and the winds changed, sparing the Hetteens' little shack. And when the pioneer children needed a school, Mör Hetteen, the mother of Malung, offered to move her family upstairs, so that they could convert the first floor of their home into a schoolhouse. "We will not raise dunces," she declared.

The Hetteens had eleven children—the three they brought with them from Sweden, the seven delivered in the New World, and, finally, the orphan boy they brought home by horse-drawn sleigh in the winter of 1923. David Johnson's mother had died because of complications suffered during childbirth. The woman's midwife, Mör Hetteen, agreed to take little David home with her. He'd keep his last name, but be a Hetteen in almost every other way, growing up with the Hetteens' American-born grandson, Edgar.

• • •

HETTEEN AND Johnson argued about the newly built Sno-Traveler when Edgar returned home that Christmas from California. Johnson was proud of his creation; Hetteen saw no point in it. The machine was slow and flawed, maxing out around 4 mph and routinely bogging down, dying in the snow. Who was going to pay good money for such a thing?

But Johnson's first toboggan sold—to Sliver Pete, the lumber yard operator across the street from their workshop—for about four hundred dollars. Serious money. The second one sold, too—to Harley Jensen, who bought it despite the fact that the throttle got stuck on his test drive, knocking him off into the snow as the snow machine rumbled away.

"I'll take it," Jensen said.

Suddenly, with money coming in, Hetteen was listening. Straw choppers were still the focus. Had to be. But Johnson could build his Sno-Travelers. Polaris built five that first year, a couple dozen the next, and a few hundred the year after that, lining up dealers and placing ads in the *Free Press Prairie Farmer*—everyone read the *Prairie Farmer*—to spread the word about the new machine selling for $999.50 and capable of reaching speeds up to 20 mph with its spring-loaded track and seven-horsepower engine.

"AUTOBOGGAN . . . NEW!" the ads screamed, listing off its features.

"Simplicity of design . . ."

"Rugged construction . . ."

"Responsive Snow Propulsion . . ."

"For the trapper and commercial fisherman," the ad concluded, "the AUTOBOGGAN provides greater versatility than dog team travel and requires no upkeep during the offseason."

Customers, by and large, were pleased with the product, saying it could go anywhere a dog team could—if there was at least a foot of snow. But the promises about the machine's required upkeep and top speeds weren't exactly truthful. Hetteen later admitted the early models wouldn't exceed 20 mph "unless you were going downhill with a tailwind." Throttles iced up and stuck in place, making the vehicles hard to stop, and at times, the machines sank in the snow. As a result, sales were sluggish—even as Hetteen hit the road, traveling by car from Alaska to New York with a trailer full of Sno-Travelers and a briefcase filled with slide shows to push product. To give the appearance that people were buying them, one Wisconsin dealer moved a couple of machines off his lot and into his back storage shed. Even Hetteen grew pessimistic at times, believing he was selling something "that didn't really work to people who didn't really want it." Penning a letter home from New England in 1959, Hetteen reported that his latest sales trip had been mediocre at best. He didn't believe the Sno-Travelers had the power to handle the mountains in New Hampshire or Vermont. Perhaps more troubling, he had been forced to sell the machines to dealers at lower prices in order to move them off his trailer, which was hard to handle, fully loaded, on the icy roads. "I gave them a little break on price," he wrote to the home office back in Roseau, "as this was the only way to convince them to try and sell them in this country."

·   ·   ·

FINALLY, IN March 1960, Hetteen and Johnson began making an argument that persuaded skeptics to consider traveling by sled. It started with a publicity stunt. Hetteen organized a twelve-hundred-mile journey by Sno-Traveler across Alaska. "Once moving, we were alone with our thoughts," one of Hetteen's three companions later wrote in his travel log of the trip. "I wondered about the route, the depth of the snow, the safety of the ice, and the possibility of severe cold." No one knew if the machines could stand up to three weeks of physical abuse under the worst of conditions. But they did, making headlines back in the continental U.S., detailing the journey of what Alaskan children called the "airplanes without wings."

Still, it was speed—more than durability—that changed the fortunes of the little company in Roseau and, really, an entire industry. By the end of 1960, Hetteen was out, quitting Polaris to start a different company. Racing was in—and it was David Johnson, quiet and unassuming, who proved to be the fastest driver of them all, flying across the winter landscape on a red Sno-Traveler. He was without question, rivals said, the "man to beat" at some of the first races ever held at a trapper's festival in a remote Manitoba village called The Pas.

By 1960, the races at the festival were more than just sales demonstrations; men driving their American-built Sno-Travelers or Canadian-built Bombardier Ski-Doos wanted to win. Prizes were at stake, as well as side bets. And soon other snowbound towns—from Lac la Ronge, Saskatchewan, to Boonville, New York—were staging their own races to draw crowds to winter carnivals. By 1963, championships were staged in Beausejour, Manitoba, with a dozen or so contestants racing in three events, including a six-mile cross-country race. (A Winnipeg man won.) By 1965, more than one hundred entries were common at the championships, drawing four thousand spectators to Beausejour's three-day Winter Farewell Festival in late Febru-

ary. The people came for the free Lipton soup and the jig contest, the
pancake breakfast at the town hall, and the mayor's snowshoe race on
Park Avenue. Hayrides were popular—as was the weekend's "Queen
of the North" beauty pageant, featuring the region's most beautiful
women and sparking much talk among the townsfolk. "Pat has big
blue eyes, brown hair and a peaches-and-cream complexion . . . Ter-
ryl Schmidt is blonde . . . Diane is a very comely entry." All the women
wanted to win. "I'll even try driving a dog team if I have to," a fired-up
contestant vowed before one pageant.

But it was the power toboggan races that they came to see most of
all, hoping for excitement, wild crashes, and speed. "This baby can do
38 mph," one driver in Beausejour boasted of his Ski-Doo. Everyone
was making adjustments to go faster. Back in Roseau, Johnson measured the progress of his new Polaris models by giving them to his
children and unleashing them to chase jackrabbits through snowy
fields. Gone were the days of marketing the new machines as utility
vehicles, best suited for mail carriers—this was boring. Smart dealers were now targeting the "hot-rodders" of winter, men and women,
interested in speed and not worried about crashing or anything else.
"Take it easy," one promoter cautioned, "those machines are wild."

Sales of the vehicles—now called snowmobiles—tripled between
1965 and 1968. There were more than thirty thousand of them in
Minnesota alone—and that number was growing by the day, creating
new and unforeseen problems. Homeowners complained that snowmobilers trespassed on their property. Police officers often couldn't
catch the alleged offenders, with the snowmobiles squealing off into
the woods. And state conservation officials worried about the impact
the machines were having on wildlife, especially beaver. In search of
good jumps, where a snowmobiler could really catch some air, many
riders turned to beaver lodges, perfectly banked and covered with
snow. "There was a time you found a beautiful, unbroken expanse of

snowy country and just enjoyed the scenery," one official sighed. "But no more."

Like it or not, the snowmobile had arrived. The Associated Press declared it "the hottest thing to hit the winter recreation market since they invented hockey sticks." And while there were dozens of manufacturers—some fifty-five in North America alone by 1968—few were as established as Polaris, still based in tiny Roseau. The company projected $35 million in annual snowmobile sales and boasted a rapidly expanding factory, just down the road from the town ice skating rink. "Little Detroit," one magazine dubbed the town. If you wanted to make it in American snowmobiling, you needed to find a way to get to Roseau.

ADRENALINE ERA

CALEB SAW the snowmobiles on television—this was how it began. He saw ESPN's Winter X Games and his mind started working backward. We couldn't ride snowmobiles. Had never even tried. But Polaris made the machines. Polaris was one of our quad sponsors. B.C. and Wes Miller had a contract with the Minnesota-based company for vehicles—and executives there just loved Caleb. They loved the way he flipped his quad before the corporate crowd in Tennessee. They loved all the people who came up to B.C. afterward to tell him how great it was. The more Caleb thought about it, talking it over with our father, the more obvious it seemed to him what we had to do. If ESPN wasn't going to create a competition for freestyle ATV riders in the Summer X Games, then we needed a new plan. We needed to call Polaris, Caleb said, request two snowmobiles, and find a way to enter the Winter X Games—riding the snow machines once built by Hetteen and Johnson.

"You guys can do this," my father said.

"We can totally do this," Caleb agreed.

We were sitting in the living room of our parents' house in Krum, watching the Winter X Games on their small television from the couch. And suddenly, it was as if we had peered into the future. The road map was right there, flickering on the screen. We began to watch with almost surgical attention, breaking down what the snowmobilers were doing and translating it to our own skills. Seat grabs—we could do that. Flips, of course—we could do that, too. Outside, in north Texas, it was chilly, but not cold. No chance of snow—not today, this week, or any time soon, probably. The very idea of riding in the snow, of competing in freezing temperatures on a mountain in the night, made me shiver from the cold. We were Texans, not Minnesotans or Canadians. Our bodies weren't built for this. But once the snowmobile idea was out there, once Caleb had latched onto it, he couldn't let it go. By the next day, he was on the phone with B.C. pleading our case for why he absolutely needed to get snowmobiles and get us signed up for the next Winter X Games.

"Really?" B.C. said, skeptical of Caleb's plan.

B.C. had good reason to be dubious of the new—and preposterous—plan. He was going to have to call in favors at Polaris to get us snowmobiles. He wasn't even sure that was possible. Then he was going to need to call the X Games organizers at ESPN and find a way to make an absurd argument—*the quad-riding Moore brothers are now expert freestyle snowmobilers!*—sound at least sort of plausible. Such phone calls were not to be made on a whim. B.C.'s reputation was at stake, among other things. He was a good salesman, yes. But he couldn't go off making requests of important people just because Caleb had this new, half-baked notion about riding—and flipping—*snow*mobiles.

"I don't know, man," B.C. said. "Are you sure you can do it?"

"Yeah," Caleb replied, definitive. "We can."

•   •   •

ESPN HAD a history, at least, of welcoming crazy dreamers to the party at company headquarters in Bristol, Connecticut, and Ron Semiao was proud to consider himself one of them. Semiao didn't come from the entertainment world. He was born in gritty New Bedford, Massachusetts, the son of first-generation Americans from Portugal and Brazil. New Bedford had once been one of the busiest whaling ports in the world, where a single ship might bring in more than seventy thousand gallons of whale oil from just one voyage. Between 1890 and 1920, the population of the city tripled to some 120,000 people as immigrants, many of them Portuguese, moved there to make money in the whaling trade. But by the time Semiao was born in 1956, whaling was long over and New Bedford was a city in decline, with an increasing rate of poverty. The Ivy League would not be in Semiao's future. He attended college at the University of Bridgeport in Connecticut, where he joined the baseball team as a pitcher and majored in accounting—at least in theory. "Let's put it this way," Semiao said once, "if they gave out degrees in partying and baseball, I would have double-majored."

But Semiao's ability to work with numbers got him jobs, at least: first as an accountant in Connecticut, then as an internal auditor at Capitol Records and NBC in California. He was a bean counter when he applied for a job back on the East Coast in 1985. A fledgling cable company with a weird acronym was seeking a program finance analyst—a guy who could track production costs against the budget. Semiao, not quite thirty years old, got the job in Bristol, went to work at ESPN, and soon began to get promoted. He went on location, working in production, at the College World Series or the Holiday Bowl. When ESPN—now more established—set out to launch a second network in 1993, Semiao got his big break, cracking into the programming department that would help build a new venture called ESPN2.

The network was designed to capture younger viewers, ages eighteen to thirty-four, by giving them an around-the-clock menu of sports they couldn't find elsewhere: rodeo, arena football, NHL hockey, and *SportsNight*, an irreverent, three-hour news show. Television critics hated it—pretty much all of it—from the start. At the network's launch in late 1993, *New York Times* critic Richard San-

domir ripped ESPN2—"The Deuce," as it was known—for opening
with a gaffe: sixteen minutes of silence, dead air. "Is silence hip?" Sandomir wrote. "Neither ESPN nor my cable company take the blame."
He disliked the anchors' wardrobes: Suzy Kolber in sneakers, Keith
Olbermann in "zany shirts," and too many others in leather jackets. "Leather!" Sandomir screamed. "The Official Fabric of ESPN2!"
And above all, he trashed the content itself: fawning puff pieces,
video shown in quick cuts with flashy type, and way too many terrible sports, like wrestling. "ESPN2 has a new deal to televise the National Professional Soccer League, an indoor league you never heard
of," Sandomir joked in one column that fall. "But at least it won't be a
Calgary Stampede rerun." Even Olbermann—one of ESPN's marquee
names and biggest stars—couldn't resist making fun of his own company's new network. In the debut of ESPN2, the bespectacled anchor,
prone to smirking, looked into the cameras and said, "Welcome to the
end of our careers."

There was serious debate in the industry at the time about whether
America's appetite for sports programming had reached a saturation
point. As it was, ESPN was already covering sixty-five sports twenty-
four hours a day. Some cable providers wondered whether people
wanted more. Even if they did, there was no guarantee ESPN could sell
enough commercials to make the Deuce profitable. "The eighteen-to-
thirty-four demographic is attractive," one advertising executive said
just before the launch. "But how much does it cannibalize ESPN? Just
because you put on another sports network doesn't mean Budweiser
and other major advertisers increase their sports budgets."

Steve Bornstein, ESPN's president, saw it differently. "Viewers
keep asking us for more sports," he told skeptics, "and more in-depth
services." Bornstein intended to give it to them—"This is what the affiliates want," he declared—and Ron Semiao wanted to help. In late
1993, he had hatched an idea of his own while visiting a Barnes &

Noble bookstore in suburban West Hartford. Standing before a magazine rack in the store, Semiao was stunned by just how many publications catered to the sports fans that ESPN2 was hoping to capture. There was no *Sports Illustrated* of extreme sports—no single magazine that covered that world—but there was a raft of magazines covering each individual subculture. Publications for skateboarders and snowboarders, snowmobilers and surfers. He went home with a large stack of them—maybe one hundred dollars' worth—and soon made a few realizations.

These sports adhered to no borders; the following for the biggest stars was global. The people featured in the magazines weren't longhaired burnouts or backyard hobbyists, Semiao learned, but true professionals—world-class athletes. And their fans respected them. In their minds, Tony Hawk, the skateboarding icon, and Michael Jordan, the best basketball player to ever live, had equal stature. And Madison Avenue advertisers clearly respected them, too. Semiao began analyzing television commercials for proof of his hypothesis. Images of surfing, biking, and other extreme sports were everywhere as advertisers tried to associate their product with something different, something cool.

That fall, Semiao was just an infantry soldier in Steve Bornstein's army at ESPN—a television grunt who still didn't rate enough to get his own office. He was sharing space in Bristol. But after his visit to the Barnes & Noble, Semiao floated an idea to an old friend in the production department: What if ESPN created an Olympics of extreme sports and televised it? The friend found the idea interesting and encouraged Semiao to take it to his bosses in programming. They liked it, too. How was this any worse than Olbermann wearing sneakers, leather jackets, and a mustache at the anchor desk? And soon Semiao was sitting in Bornstein's office on Third Avenue in New York, making his pitch for the Extreme Games: eight days of televised insanity. Bornstein bought the idea in early 1994. ESPN began planning. The first Extreme Games launched in Newport, Rhode Island, about a year later with nine sports, including in-line skating, skysurfing, and something called street luge. And, again, critics pounced.

They called the Extreme Games boring. "The events I watched—freestyle bungee jumping, downhill slalom on mountain bikes, and the 'Eco-challenge'—were interesting for about three minutes," one critic wrote. They mocked the "MTV-style ads" that promoted the event and joked that no one would tune in to watch. "We'd be happy to get a 1.0 rating," Bornstein admitted beforehand, which in television-speak was almost nothing—a fact that sneering reporters took great pleasure in pointing out. "To cite a common industry explanation," one critic wrote, "a 1.0 rating can result from household pets who happen to hit television remote controls." Whether they were pets or actual humans almost didn't matter, critics said. In the critics' estimations, viewers were only going to tune in "to witness some poor sap crashing to the pavement from the bungee platform." For that reason alone, many critics said, the Extreme Games with their death-defying "trash sports" were a terrible idea. "Its stunts might kill," declared *USA Today*. "Maybe on live TV." This wasn't just extreme. It was psycho—"a weeklong psycho Olympics," one critic wrote—with massive consequences for us all. "I don't know if the Extreme Games presage the fall of Western Civilization," Sandomir wrote, again in the *New York Times*. But his implication was maybe—maybe it did.

Still, ESPN defended the idea, putting Semiao—not its president—front and center in its marketing blitz. There was the man from New Bedford, with his ink-black hair and smoky voice, telling reporters the Extreme Games were going to catch on. "A lot of people questioned us when we wanted to televise the NFL draft," he said, "but it's become a franchise for us now." There he was promoting the participants of the sports—as ludicrous as the events might sound. "Are they thrill-seekers?" he said. "Yeah. They're also athletes. They consider what they do athletics." And there was Semiao connecting the dots to ESPN's own unlikely story. Critics had doubted ESPN from its inception in 1979, questioning the need for a twenty-four-hour cable sports network. "But now," Semiao said, with just the right amount of bluster, "we have two of them."

Most important, ESPN itself declared the first Extreme Games a success. Sponsorships and advertising slots sold out. The programming drew about 65 million viewers to each prime-time telecast—a far bigger audience than critics, and even Bornstein, had expected. No one had died, crashing to the pavement, as many had feared. The worst thing that had happened was that a kite skier got blown off course, coming down miles away from Newport. "When he finally made land," Semiao later told reporters, "he flagged down a cab, put his kite ski in the trunk, and took the cab back to the venue."

The first Extreme Games had barely ended when ESPN announced plans for a second one the following summer. Soon, it was just the X Games, no "Extreme" necessary. And by 1997, there were two of them every year—one in the summer, one in the winter, and growing, as Semiao tinkered behind the scenes, adding new entries, deleting others. Autogyro—a contest in which men build their own flying machines—never made the cut. Street luge and bungee jumping were soon phased out. And Semiao had to do something about the disaster that was super-modified shovel racing—an event in the first Winter X Games in 1997 that injured one rider and confirmed critics' opinions of the games as a whole. Even Semiao himself had to admit it: Shovel racing required no athletic ability whatsoever, which was the exact opposite of what ESPN wanted. The sports in the X Games needed to be nontraditional and exciting. But they also couldn't be silly, Semiao had decided. What he and ESPN wanted by 1997 were real sports, albeit existing on the fringe.

Joe Duncan—a stocky, ruddy-faced Minnesotan—thought he had just the idea for ESPN, flying in to meet Semiao and other corporate executives in the spring of that year. What Duncan was proposing was a race—fast-paced and wild, with hills and tight turns, under extreme conditions. Snocross, it was called. The riders would race snowmobiles, not unlike what they had done back in The Pas and Beausejour, in the days of Hetteen and Johnson. Duncan felt strongly about it; the Albertville, Minnesota, native was a former snowmobile racer himself, turned race organizer. He knew what it felt like to go screaming across frozen ponds in negative-thirty-degree tempera- tures, rumbling along with a herd of machines. Semiao felt Duncan's passion—here was a regular guy, a sportsman, who lived what he was selling—and ESPN bought his snocross idea in the room. Semiao and Duncan inked a multiyear deal for the new sport that day, before re- tiring to celebrate over drinks—a lot of them. The event debuted the following winter in 1998, with Duncan designing the course, running the competition, and recruiting riders. Nine years later, in 2007, ESPN added freestyle—the flipping of the snowmobiles—again with Dun- can's help. And the crowds followed, flocking to Aspen, the annual site of the winter games. "Not only are we an action sport," Duncan boasted to reporters in the first year of freestyle, "but we're an action sport that brings in motorsports enthusiasts."

The X Games, by then, had a lot of enthusiasts—starting with sponsors. Gillette, Sony, and other major corporations advertised, hoping to reach teenagers and tweens—both of whom were watch- ing. In the first four years of the new millennium, television ratings for the X Games soared—up 88 percent for the winter, 150 percent for the summer. Some 37 million people were tuning in for some part of the winter games—whether they were coming to see Shaun White on his snowboard or Duncan's band of merry men careering around on snowmobiles. And Caleb and I were right there with them. We were watching on TV from Krum, wishing we were there competing, and identifying with the athletes. "We come from the adrenaline era," said one of them, Todd Richards, a snowboarder, at the first Winter X Games. "When I grew up on the East Coast, you were either someone who played sports, or you were one of the nerds who didn't."

Richards believed he didn't fit into either category. Neither a jock nor a nerd. And Caleb and I felt the same way. There were a lot of us like that—young men and women who didn't fit inside the perfect little boxes the world had laid out for us. But now, thanks to Semiao and ESPN, we all had a place to go—a place where we were not only welcome, but understood. Not in spite of our long hair or our tattoos or our proclivity for taking risks, but because of all that.

Guys like us belonged in the X Games.

SEVEN HUNDRED POUNDS

B.C. UNDERSTOOD what we wanted—even if our stunts worried him at times, leaving him pacing in the shadows or shrieking in front of fans. He handled everything for us: the promoters, the negotiations for payment, even the airline travel. B.C.—managing both Caleb and me—booked the tickets. We didn't have to do anything, except show up and flip and not crash. But once we got to the show, wherever it was, B.C. could lose his cool at times, concerned that something would go wrong. He didn't like us trying new tricks at shows. "Do that at your house," he told us. He didn't want us competing against each other, as we inevitably would, to see who could do which trick bigger—and how. "You're making me nervous," he worried. He had a mantra that he repeated so much that it played on a loop inside my head. "It's better to be safe than sorry," he said. But safety was a relative term.

Once in Manizales, Colombia, Caleb and I were forced to jump our quads in an unusually small arena, with almost no space for landing. It was early August 2008, just six weeks after Darrin had died from the crash in our backyard in Krum. Everyone was still rattled, the memories still fresh of the helicopter landing in the pasture and my mother standing by the window. And now we were in Colombia, jumping our quads inside this crowded, too-small deathtrap of an arena. A wooden platform had to be erected at one end, extending the landing area upward, almost like a ramp to nowhere, arching up into the seats themselves, just so we had enough room to come down. No one liked it. The quarters were too close. And in our finale, in which Caleb and I jumped parallel to each other, we briefly collided in midair, making contact thirty feet above the makeshift landing down below. "OHHHHH, MY GOD!" B.C. shouted, too loud, standing off to the side. "OH, MY GOD!" "I thought we were going to the hospital," he told us later, in an attempt to explain all his screaming. No one wanted to go to the hospital—in Colombia.

By then, B.C. had been with us for years. We were almost like family—with him playing the role of the nervous uncle and us playing the role of the rascal kids. We didn't always agree—or understand what made him so anxious. While he was bouncing with nerves after our jump in Colombia, Caleb and I danced in the spotlight, helmets off, sliding down the ramps, headfirst, just for fun, like children playing on a snow hill. "Quit stressing," Caleb told B.C. But we trusted our manager completely. We knew B.C. would do everything he could to help us, whenever he could. So, when Caleb called him with his X Games idea and told him that we needed snowmobiles, we knew B.C. would get to work. He started by phoning Polaris and explaining the situation with his usual frankness.

The way B.C. saw it, it was simple: On the sponsorship contract we had with Polaris that year, the company still owed us four quads. In a *Let's Make a Deal* moment, B.C. offered to swap the quads that we were still owed in exchange for the unknown, our dream—whatever was behind Door No. 3.

"I'll trade those four quads for two snowmobiles," B.C. told the Polaris rep on the phone. But not just any snowmobile. B.C. wanted two Polaris 600 IQs, light-body, high-performance, limited-release race sleds.

"For who?" the rep asked.

"The Moore brothers," B.C. replied.

My father holding Caleb as a baby. *(Courtesy of Michele Moore)*

My mother with Caleb in Wheeler, 1987. *(Courtesy of Michele Moore)*

Caleb and me on the trampoline where we first learned to flip, ages ten and eight. On the back of the snapshot, my mother wrote, "Best buds forever."
(Courtesy of Michele Moore)

Caleb on his first ATV in the dusty hills of Texas. *(Courtesy of Michele Moore)*

Me on my quad, preparing to race. *(Courtesy of Michele Moore)*

Me taking the checkered flag on my quad. By late 2004, we had decided to go national. *(Courtesy of Michele Moore)*

Caleb and his racing trophies. *(Courtesy of Michele Moore)*

Caleb making his legendary canyon jump in Caineville, Utah, in 2006.
(Courtesy of Michele Moore)

Caleb making his first flip in Montreal's Le Stade Olympique,
November 2006. *(Courtesy of Michele Moore)*

My family in Montreal after Caleb survived his flip at Le Stade
Olympique. *(Courtesy of Michele Moore)*

Caleb practicing at Wes Miller's compound in California in 2009.
(Enrico Pavia)

Caleb and I were soon flipping our quads together all over the world.
(Courtesy of B. C. Vaught)

Caleb acknowledging the crowd in Russia. *(Courtesy of B. C. Vaught)*

By 2010, our first X Games, we had at least one major sponsor.

Caleb and me getting interviewed at our second X Games, 2011.

(Todd Williams)

Caleb and me executing the first tandem two-man flip at the X Games in 2011.

(Courtesy of MorningPhotography.com)

Me flipping my sled, practicing for X Games 2012. *(Todd Williams)*

Caleb and me sitting on our sleds together the day before X Games 2012. *(Todd Williams)*

My father standing with me and my brother after I won my first gold medal at the X Games in 2012. *(Todd Williams)*

Caleb and me with our manager, B. C. Vaught, in 2012. *(Todd Williams)*

Caleb and me laughing in Guadalajara, Mexico, in May 2012.
(Courtesy of B. C. Vaught)

Caleb and me, together, as brothers in Guadalajara in May 2012.
(Courtesy of B. C. Vaught)

Caleb, my brother, peering up at the sky, Guadalajara, 2012.
(Courtesy of B. C. Vaught)

Caleb gets interviewed while on tour in Pont-de-Vaux, France, in 2012, just months before his crash. *(Pete Cobbe Photography)*

Caleb and me checking in with each other before our runs at the X Games in 2013. *(Wayne Davis Photography)*

Caleb in Aspen, just moments before his crash in 2013. *(Wayne Davis Photography)*

The Texas flag flying above our trailer at the X Games in Aspen. *(Wayne Davis Photography)*

Me riding at the X Games in 2013, just after my brother's crash,
but before I knew the severity of it. I too would crash moments later.
(Wayne Davis Photography)

"But they live in Texas. How are they going to ride them in Texas, man?"

B.C. told the rep not to worry about it, that there was the foam pit in Krum, and other exciting ideas in the works. The Moores, B.C. said, had big plans for the snowmobiles. "How soon can you send them?" he asked.

• • •

THE SNOWMOBILE factory in Roseau employs more people in a single twenty-four-hour, three-shift day than live in the town itself, making the 710,000-square-foot facility a city within a city. The employees come from five counties and two countries, from deep into Canada to the north and all the way to Red River Valley to the west, working seven days a week at times and building as many as 225 sleds in a shift. Each sled begins with a single piece called a tunnel—an aluminum sheet, folded several times by massive press brakes to form the chassis. Assembly-line workers, wearing eye protection and wielding rivet guns, come in next, reinforcing the freshly folded aluminum with plates and brackets. The workers then pass the metal slab to three yellow robots for still more riveting, stamping, and, finally, glue—an aerospace-grade adhesive to make the tunnels stronger while also reducing their overall weight. The chassis, silver and shiny, now looks like something—the beginning of something. And line workers move back in to start adding the guts of the machine: the chain case and the bulkhead cooler, the A-arms on the front suspension and engine in the back. Four screws bolt the engine into place. Tunnel grips—where we place our boots when riding—go on next, soon followed by K braces and rear track shocks, before the workers hand off the partially constructed machine to the moving line.

The snowmobile is in motion now—inching along, never stopping—suspended from a metal elbow in midair while the assembly-line workers walk along next to it, adding still more detail.

Here come the snowmobile tracks (made with metal-reinforced rubber) and the fuel tank (the seat gets mounted right on top of it). Here come the spindles (where the skis attach) and the decals (placed on by hand). "Excuse me," the operators say with perfect Minnesotan manners, working around the moving line, which goes straight, then bends left, then hooks back around to the right—into the test shack, where operators start up the engine and check the taillights, before the machines get shrink-wrapped, placed in crates, and stacked four high, ready for shipment.

Our two sleds arrived in Krum by crate in late December 2009, barely a month before the Winter X Games in Aspen. B.C.—and Polaris—had held up their end of the bargain. Caleb and I had the machines we had requested: two 600 IQs, brand new and perfect for the tricks we hoped to perform. The new generation racing sleds cost a lot of money—Polaris wouldn't say how much, but probably more than ten thousand dollars. And the price wasn't the only reason the IQs were hard to get. Polaris built only 268 of them in 2009, knowing the race-ready machines weren't for everyone. "You like to ride the big bumps? Bigger the better?" snowmobile expert and industry reviewer Jerry Bassett wrote of the retail version of the new sled when it first hit the market. "You like to fly? Higher the better? If this is you, meet your ride."

The IQ was lighter than most other snowmobiles. Its 121-inch Ripsaw track offered riders great handling in the snow. And its two-stroke carbureted engine was built to rev fast. Top speeds were estimated to be 80 mph. But speed, in freestyle, wasn't as important as agility—so the IQ had that, too. It was designed with a higher seat, a lower center of gravity, and steering posts moved up closer to the nose, positioning riders to attack moguls and bumps—or ramps, in our case. It was, in short, a durable, rugged, and even rambunctious machine, Bassett wrote in his review, a machine that was "ready to rock." "Polaris got this sled right," the review concluded.

But that's not what Caleb and I first noticed when the IQs arrived in Krum on the back of a flatbed truck. We had never ridden snowmobiles before—not even on vacation. So the specs for the IQ's engine, horsepower, weight, and track size meant almost nothing to us. All we noticed was the hulking size of the new snow machines in our driveway—just how much bigger the Polaris sleds were than the quads we had been riding all these years.

"This should be interesting," I said.

"We've got work to do," Caleb agreed.

"These things are massive," I said.

Caleb just nodded. "Huge."

We modified the factory models to fit our tastes and needs. First, we installed longer handlebars—to give us more leverage when pulling for flips. Next, we modified the engines to make the machines even faster. We needed to account for the speed we'd lose when running at elevation in Colorado. And we had to make adjustments to make sure the engines didn't overheat. Snowmobiles use the snow itself—kicked up by the track—to keep the engine from running too hot. Since we had no snow in Texas, radiators had to be installed and connected. So did small wheels, on the skis up front. Skis don't run so well on the Texas dirt, where we'd be practicing. Caleb and I, still not finished, then paid a local shop to make aluminum seat risers to fit. The result was an even higher seat, which would reduce the distance we'd need to move our bodies in the air when jumping on and off. Finally we turned to the cushioned seat itself, hacking away at it with a most unlikely tool: an electric carving knife, like the kind you use at Thanksgiving, to slice the turkey. Caleb carefully cut a snug, cylinder-shaped hole in each seat, melted down a stretch of PVC pipe in the oven, inserted the pipes into the holes in the seats, and then stitched the cushions back up again. Now we'd have something solid to grab on to when floating off the seat, high above the snow. We were ready to go, except for one thing. We didn't have the slightest idea how to ride—much less flip—a snowmobile.

. . .

EVERYONE SAID it was impossible, that he was going to kill himself, or at least seriously injure himself. In the beginning, people told Jim Rippey all sorts of things to stop him from trying to flip a snowmobile. Still, the professional snowboarder from Northern California wanted to try it. And he didn't appreciate everyone telling him it was a stupid, no-good, dangerous idea. If they wanted to tell him once, just to express their concern, that was fine. "I'll listen to you," Rippey said. But if they continued to press the issue, bringing it up again and again, all it did was raise doubts in his mind—lingering doubts. And that wasn't productive when he was trying to become the first person to successfully flip a snowmobile. Because even Rippey understood the math. He figured his Ski-Doo snowmobile—fifteen years ago—weighed close to seven hundred pounds with a full tank of gas. "Imagine seven hundred pounds," he said. "If that comes down on top of you, it's game over. That's basically like a small car."

James Ira Rippey was born in 1970 in a small gold rush town in the Sierra Nevada Mountains. His home, Quincy, California, got on average more than fifty inches of snow every winter, so, like most kids in town, Rippey grew up skiing on the weekends. But he didn't begin to take winter sports seriously until after high school when he got a job as a chair-lift operator in Truckee. Within three years, he was a professional snowboarder—one of the first and one of the best, too. Burton, the famous snowboard manufacturer, soon signed Rippey to a sponsorship deal and even named a board after him. "The man, the myth, the legend," the *Tahoe Daily News* once dubbed him, in part because Rippey was willing to try anything: cliff diving, jumping out of airplanes, or even letting helicopters abandon him on high, craggy mountaintops, with nothing but his snowboard to get him home again. Rippey would find a way down, usually flipping on the way for fun—and for the cameras that inevitably followed him. Rippey was always flipping, and soon he had it in his mind that he wanted to flip a snowmobile.

The snowboarding star was no expert at driving a sled; he only used them to get into the backcountry, where he could find the best powder for boarding. He was acutely aware of the inherent dangers involved—for even the most experienced snowmobiler. In the winter of 2001, saying you wanted to flip a snowmobile was a little like saying you wanted to play defense for the New York Rangers because you were an Olympic figure skater. Was it possible? Maybe. You *could* skate. But most likely, you were going to get bloodied in your black satin and gold lamé. You were going to get creamed.

"I don't think you should do it," a member of Rippey's film crew told him.

"Why?" Rippey asked.

"I don't think it will work."

Rippey was unafraid. He had found God, just months earlier, sitting on one of those remote mountaintops and scanning the snow-capped horizon in Alaska. Overwhelmed by the natural beauty laid out before him, Rippey heard himself praying, speaking to God. And not long after that he was baptized, born-again at age thirty. He understood why everyone else was so worried about his snowmobile plans. But he was comfortable with the idea, comfortable with the risk, quoting Philippians 4:6–7 to the naysayers around him. "Be anxious for nothing," the verse says. Instead, make your request known to God, trust in him "with prayer and supplication," and you will experience a peace "that surpasses all understanding."

That's where Rippey was when he made the trip to Utah in the late winter of 2001. He was at peace, as he and his crew scouted out a jump location in the mountains near Salt Lake City and then sculpted a ramp out of earth and snow. "Here, you work on this," he instructed his crew. "You start packing this in. I'll shave from the top." He wasn't working with any exact specs in mind; no one really knew what kind of ramp was best for flipping a snowmobile. And he was nowhere near a hospital, if something went wrong. It was maybe a forty-five-minute snowmobile ride just to get back to a lodge.

But Rippey felt good about his ramp. It was built into a wind lip—a natural transition on the mountain, with about a twenty-five-foot drop-off. He liked the physics of the snowmobile, too, with that rubber track rotating in the back. The track was an internal torque, which could change his moment of inertia, which in turn could alter his angular momentum and bring the seven-hundred-pound sled all the way around. Rippey believed in God—and, also, Sir Isaac Newton. He was no physics professor, but there was beauty in the simplicity of $L = I\omega$. And when the sun broke through the clouds on his second day in Utah, he and his crew went up to the mountain to make history.

On his first flip attempt, Rippey came up short, planting the skis of his snowmobile into the snow, going right over the handlebars, and landing headfirst—hard.

"You all right?" a friend hollered.

"Yeah," Rippey replied, bouncing up.

"Oh, man. That was awesome."

"Let's get this thing out of here. I gotta do it again."

Rippey—wearing a yellow Burton jacket and a helmet adorned with his last name—had failed miserably in the first jump. In the air, he knew he was close. He could feel the centrifugal force of the track working in favor of the flip. He just needed a bit more throttle and a bit less ramp. The ramp was too steep. But he was right there—everyone on the mountain that day agreed.

"Yeah, Rippey. You almost had it, dude."

"We're going to have to tighten up your bars a bit, Jim." They had gotten banged up in the crash. "Or do you like them loose?"

"Don't worry about it, man," Rippey said.

He was in a hurry to go again before he lost daylight—and the second effort was better. He didn't come up short this time, but the ramp was still too steep. The whole flip was off kilter from the start, almost sideways, and Rippey bailed out before landing. The next three tries were only marginally better. He came all the way around on the snowmobile, only to crash, unable to stay on the rotating sled as it landed, track down, but hard, in the snow. Rippey was tired now and aching, having bruised his thighs and tweaked his wrists, and his friends were concerned.

"You all right, Jim?" they asked.

"How are you feeling?"

"You want to go again?"

"One more time," Rippey said.

He thought he had it figured out. He was going too fast on the approach, he had decided. As a result, he was catching way too much air, and that made it impossible for him to stay on when the sled finally made landfall. He needed to slow everything down, he thought, pinning the throttle on only the last part of the ramp—the last five to eight feet, maybe; that was it—and then hold it wide open in the air, to let the machine do the work. The snowmobile would bring him back around if he let it. The snowmobile would flip if he truly committed to it—and he was right. Rippey's last jump that day was perfect. He flipped, landed, and rode away—not dead, like the naysayers had predicted, but just fine—pointing to the heavens while his friends cheered.

COCKAMAMIE

WE DIDN'T know Rippey. Couldn't call him. By the time Caleb and I got our snowmobiles in late 2009, Jim Rippey had effectively retired from the world of extreme sports. He was almost forty years old and working as a preacher in Nevada. Even if Rippey had still been on the scene at the time, he wouldn't have known us, a couple of no-name, quad-riding kids from rural Texas. None of the world's best snowmobilers knew us—*why would they?*—and we didn't know them, either. Staring at the newly delivered and seemingly massive snowmobiles in our parents' driveway in Krum, Caleb and I were alone—almost alone, anyway.

A year earlier, on a tour doing shows in Colombia, we had met a snowmobiler named Sam Rogers. Sam was about our age—lean, tall, and wallpapered with detailed tattoos of skulls, goblins, snowmobiles covered with skulls, more goblins, and logos of companies related to snowmobiling. We liked him right away—and he liked us. He was from Cooke City, Montana, population almost nobody, somewhere near the Wyoming border. "Super tiny," Sam said, but perfect for what he loved: snowmobiling. Sam got his first Polaris sled before he was even in first grade. He had competed, flipped, and even medaled in the Winter X Games. We bonded immediately in Colombia, where we had way too much free time on our hands—to drink, sleep in, party, stay up late, and discuss the finer points of snowmobile flipping, somewhere in South America, on the road.

Caleb wanted to know everything. "Does it feel heavy in the

air?" he asked Sam. "Does it feel like the machine is riding you? How's the rotation? Does it pull the same?" Caleb inquired about the mechanics—the twin-cylinder, two-stroke engine versus the one-cylinder, four-stroke we were used to operating on our quad. "How did that change things?" Caleb wanted to know—and Sam had the answers. They talked for hours about snowmobiling—casually at first and later more seriously. By the time our sleds arrived, Caleb was on the phone with Sam all the time, asking about everything from the shocks to the transmission.

"How do you shift gears on these things?" Caleb asked.

Oh, boy, Sam thought. It was worse than he feared. Snowmobiles, he informed Caleb, ran on an automatic transmission.

"You *don't* shift gears," Sam said.

It was just a few weeks before the X Games in Aspen—and we didn't even know the basics of our new machines. We were lost, with almost no chance of competing that year. ESPN officials had told B.C. as much. Joe Duncan—the man who had sold ESPN and Ron Semiao on the snowmobile competition in the first place—knew Caleb and liked him. Duncan had seen Caleb flip a quad before. We all crossed paths on the extreme sports circuit. And he also knew that Caleb, if not I, was a true professional, with drive and real talent. But Duncan, the gatekeeper and event organizer, dismissed our plan out of hand. There was simply no chance we'd be ready in time, he informed B.C. It would take several months or even a year to make the transition from quads to sleds. And to expect it to happen faster than that was lunacy—a "cockamamie idea," Duncan called it.

"No way," he told B.C.

Duncan couldn't tolerate inexperienced snowmobilers crashing—and potentially seriously injuring themselves—during his event. He couldn't put himself, or the X Games, at risk like that, he said, no matter how much he respected Caleb or how great B.C. assured him we would be by January. "I've got enough stuff going on," Duncan told B.C. "No way," he said again.

But Caleb refused to accept that answer. All we needed, he figured, was Sam Rogers and his help—if Sam could only get to Texas. *Could he get to Texas?* Would he mind coming down? In exchange for his expertise, we offered him our foam pit. While we learned, Sam could practice, getting ready for the X Games himself. We invited him to Krum—and Sam agreed to make the trip. But only if we promised not to touch the snowmobiles in the meantime. Even Sam—our friend—didn't trust us alone with the new machines.

"Just wait for me to get there, man."

• • •

SAM MADE the twenty-three-hour drive from Montana just before Christmas, without stopping and hardly eating. At night, he lived on energy drinks. During the day, he ran on coffee—with milk and lots of sugar. When he got tired of driving his pickup truck and towing the loaded-down, fifty-two-foot gooseneck trailer rattling along behind him, Sam rolled down the windows, feeling the cold on his tattooed body. As he saw it, there was no time to waste. He arrived with two snowmobiles, one ramp, about 130 feet of turf to help replicate the feeling of snow on the ground, and lots of instructions. "We're going to start," Sam told us, "with the ramp up close."

From about forty-five feet away, Sam showed us how it was done, hitting the metal ramp he had brought from Montana and landing to the dirt where Darrin had once crashed—a straight jump, with no flips or tricks. "Do the same thing I'm doing," Sam told us. Not too fast and not too slow. "Hit it just like that," he said. And we followed along next to him, speed-checking his machine as he hit the ramp. The key, Sam said, was timing and the throttle. "Don't get too crazy on the throttle."

Caleb nodded—he had this—queuing up to go first. He made the approach on the turf and hit the throttle on the ramp, as Sam had instructed. But he was heavy on the gas. Like Rippey in his first attempt nearly a decade earlier, Caleb was going too fast. He was too steep, and nose high, as a result. As his snowmobile left the lip of the ramp, my brother's sled was straight up and down to the ground, like a motorized pencil arcing through the sky. There was no way this was going to end well. Caleb knew it and he bailed, throwing the snowmobile—his brand-new, after-market-modified, race-ready, ten-thousand-dollar snowmobile—away from his body. He landed on his hands and knees in the dirt while the sled skittered away, cartwheeling toward the trees, shedding parts, yardsale-ing it all over the place.

"I can't believe that just happened," Caleb said.

"You okay?" Sam asked.

Caleb was fine. "But the sled," he replied. "The sled is screwed."

My brother was furious, glaring at the sled as it tumbled away, coming to a rest on its side. He wasn't used to crashing anymore. Coming in too steep? Nose high? With too much throttle? That didn't happen to him—or me—on quads anymore. Our flips, these days, were almost always seamless. And for a long time, after crashing the new snowmobile, Caleb just sat there in the dirt, stewing in angry silence. Maybe this wasn't going to be as easy as we thought. Maybe Duncan had been right. What if this did take months? Worse still, the snowmobile was a mess. The tunnel—the sled's aluminum chassis— was bent. The skis were mangled and the handlebars twisted. The machine had been delivered from Roseau polished and perfect, and we had already broken it—with just one jump.

We lost time replacing parts, but there was no question about whether Caleb would try again that day. He was itching to go again. But before he did so, Sam suggested three changes. First, we were moving to the foam pit; no more fooling around on dirt, where someone could really get injured. Second, Sam wanted to push back the

ramp to the distance we'd be hitting in Aspen: seventy feet. Sometimes, it was just easier to go longer, especially since we had experience at that distance on our quads. And finally, Sam said, we needed
to lay off the throttle. There was no need to come in so fast.

Caleb understood. He hit the ramp again, and, this time, landed
safely in the foam—a straight seventy-foot jump, with no tricks and
no problems. With just his second try, Caleb had it, he thought. He
could feel it now. It was true what they said about snowmobiles, Caleb
told us. You could feel the spinning track working in your favor. So on
his next try—without so much as a word to anyone—Caleb hit the
throttle on the ramp and pulled for a backflip in the air. He pulled
so hard, worried about under-rotating, that he yanked his left hand
right off the handlebar. But Caleb was able to get his grip again, finding the handlebar upside down in the air, and he stuck the landing,
coming all the way around and touching down safely in the foam. A
perfect flip, on his third jump.

"No way," Sam said.

"It's on now," I said, smiling.

"Wow," Sam kept saying. "No way."

· · ·

WITHIN MINUTES, Caleb was doing heelclickers—tricks no one
had ever done on a sled—bringing his feet up and over the handlebars and briefly touching them together before landing. Then it was
my turn. "You're going to be fine," Caleb told me, sensing my worry.

My brother, at that point, was a much better rider than I was—
more confident, yes, but also more experienced and more talented. I
had only been flipping quads for three months; Caleb had been flipping for three years. And now, despite my relative inexperience, I was
being asked to flip something totally different. Or, at least, I was asking myself to do it, forcing myself, really. As much as I feared failing

and crashing, as much as I pondered all the ways it could go wrong, I feared something else even more: being left behind by my brother. I grew panicked—physically panicked—just thinking Caleb might be good enough to compete in the X Games while I watched from the hill in Aspen with my parents, the little brother, the spectator, the twenty-year-old waif of a kid who wasn't good enough to ride with the big boys. I couldn't live with that reality, so I lived with the risk instead.

I listened to Sam and Caleb, climbed aboard the sled, and jumped it into the foam—a straight jump, with no flips and no tricks. Wobbly at first, filled with doubt, I got better—and quickly. "I think I got it," I told them after several attempts. By the end of the first day, I was flipping, too. Sam was impressed. B.C. was excited. Maybe we had a chance, after all. And right after Christmas, we headed north, back to Michigan, where several snowmobilers, including Sam, would be doing their final preparations for the games. We needed to leave the safety of the foam and the warm weather in Texas, to prove our skills in real snow. But with temperatures hovering around zero for most of the week, we didn't last long in the elements, taking breaks far more often than Sam and the other northern riders, who had warmer gear, thicker clothes, and tougher skin.

"Dude, I can't feel my toes," I told my brother on the first day.

"I can't feel my hands."

"Is it going to be this cold in Aspen?"

"Don't know."

"You want to go warm up in the trailer?"

"Yeah," Caleb said.

We'd retreat inside, huddling up around propane-powered heaters, our chapped faces and frigid fingers awash in their orange glow. But we couldn't stay in the warmth for long. Our jumps were still sloppy. We'd come in nose high one time, too straight the next. We needed to be dialed in, almost perfect, because B.C. was back on the

phone with Duncan, making one final—and desperate—sales pitch
to get us in the X Games.

"These boys can really put on a show," B.C. told Duncan, working his salesman shtick up into a lather. "They'll bring a whole new
element to the X Games. And it will be one hell of a story." Two brothers from rural Texas? Kids who grew up without mountains or snow?
Now flipping snow machines on the biggest stage for extreme sports?
That was good television, B.C. told Duncan. A great story. "And a
story," B.C. said, "is as good as any rider out there."

Silence on the line.

"You know that," B.C. told Duncan.

Still more silence.

"C'mon, Joe," B.C. begged.

Duncan softened, letting his guard down, in part because he had
a problem of his own. There had been some last-minute cancellations
at the X Games. Riders had gotten injured in the weeks before and
fallen out. They weren't coming. Duncan needed more bodies on the
mountain. And if he had to add unproven talent, he at least wanted
to add a professional, like Caleb, and not some idiot who might do
something stupid on national television. He liked what he was hearing from B.C. and started to think that maybe we could fill the void.
Maybe we had what it took to compete.

Get me video, he told B.C. in an email. He wanted to see the tricks
we were doing—and could potentially attempt at the X Games. "Ones
that you have in your bag right now." And get the boys to Aspen, Duncan added. If we could prove that we could do it on the mountain, he
said, we were in.

FOLLOW ME

THE OTHER riders were all there on the mountain, looking like pros—real riders. Jeff Mullin hailed from Kipawa, Quebec; Jimmy "Blaze" Fejes from Anchorage, Alaska. Riders came from Idaho and Montana—and even northern Europe. Daniel Bodin—who had finished fourth, just off the medal stand, in the previous three years of freestyle snowmobile at the X Games—was Scandinavian. His hometown was Malung, Sweden, the birthplace of another snowmobiling icon: Mör Hetteen, the sturdy Minnesota pioneer and God-fearing grandmother of Edgar, one of the machine's inventors back in tiny Roseau.

Yet the north country roots of the other riders—our competition—weren't our only concern as we arrived in Aspen. The other riders had bona fides, actual accomplishments on real snowmobiles. Justin Hoyer, from Wisconsin, was the previous year's silver medalist, gunning now for gold. Joe Parsons, from Washington, had collected four snowmobiling medals—in the past two years—including two silver and one gold. Heath Frisby was a freestyle original and something of a snowmobiling god. The son of an Idaho potato farmer, Frisby had been doing tricks on his sled for nearly a decade, long before Jim Rippey had ever even attempted a flip. Though just twenty-five, Frisby had been around forever, it seemed, competing in the X Games' freestyle snowmobiling events since their inaugural year, 2007. He had never finished worse than fourth—mediocrity didn't suit Heath—and he had picked up three medals along the way. How were we going to

compete with that? With Heath Frisby? Or, better yet: How were we
going to compete with Levi LaVallee?

Everyone in Aspen loved Levi. He was from Longville, Minnesota, population 156, about two hundred miles south of Roseau. His
mother worked at the post office and his father owned the sanitation
company in town. From a young age, Levi did two things: bag groceries at the local store and ride snowmobiles. He was particularly
good at the latter. Before he even graduated from high school, he had
turned semipro, racing sleds in snocross events. The Polaris factory
team signed him soon thereafter. Winter X Games started extending
invites in 2004, and Levi made an impact right away, winning gold
in the hillcross event in his first year. By 2010, he was a five-time X
Games medalist, with big-time sponsors lined up behind him. But
Levi was perhaps best known for the medal he didn't win—on national television the year before.

In 2009, with Caleb and me watching the X Games back in Texas,
Levi announced that he planned to throw down a double backflip
in the best trick competition. It was the sporting equivalent of Kobe
Bryant saying he planned to beat Wilt Chamberlain's single-game
scoring record of 100 points in an NBA game, not by scoring 101, but
by scoring 200. It simply wasn't possible. No one had ever attempted a
double backflip on a snowmobile in competition, much less executed
one. As the Associated Press reporter in Aspen pointed out, there was
almost a "coin flip's" chance of injury. "And if that did happen," the
AP reported, "it probably would be serious." Head trauma, paralysis,
even death—it all seemed possible. The same laws of physics applied,
of course. It was still $L = I\omega$. But with Levi's plans, everything seemed
to be multiplied by a factor of two: the torque, the moment of inertia,
and especially the fear. "I hope I don't wind up underneath this big
thing," Levi admitted at the time.

For months, he tried and failed, double-flipping into his own foam pit. He and his team tweaked his ramp, raising it; the usual ramps weren't giving him the lift he needed to go around twice. And the more Levi tried it, the more comfortable he became committing—fully committing—to the trick. He stuck a few double backflips into the foam, started trying it on snow, and then brought the trick with him to Aspen. "I think he's going for it," ESPN's play-by-play man said from the broadcast booth under the lights. And he was right. Levi went tearing off on his snowmobile, barreling toward his thirteen-foot ramp, tilted at a sixty-three-degree angle, while the crowd roared and the broadcasters fell silent.

There was nervous energy on the mountain. Everyone who was there could feel it—then liftoff. Levi's sled took flight, and like a comet streaking across the night sky, it had a tail. White snow was spinning off the rotating track of his Polaris snowmobile, as it went around once, as it went around twice, and then came back down to earth. Levi was right side up, but he had flown too far, maybe seventy-five feet through the air, nearly missing the landing altogether. Basically flatlanding it from roughly four stories up in the air, maybe higher, Levi came down hard, nearly smashed his face into his handlebars, and bounced off, tumbling into the snow. He had fallen. By rule, there could be no medal. But he had done it. Levi had proven that a double backflip was possible—and he was alive. "Fortunately," he said afterward, feeling genuinely lucky, "God was on my side and I walked away from this one."

Freestyle snowmobiling dominated the sports headlines that night. Levi's agent tabulated at least twenty minutes of coverage dedicated to the preposterous flip. "Way more than the next closest athlete," Levi pointed out to reporters later. With one trick, he had become something of a star, snowmobiling's version of Shaun White, the famous snowboarder and de facto poster boy of the X Games. "That guy," Levi said, "always has the buzz around him." Now—at least momentarily—it was around snowmobiles and Levi. By the time Caleb and I arrived in Aspen, fans had lined up for Levi's autograph—"That is the coolest thing," he said, marveling at his newfound fame—and ESPN followed him everywhere. The cameras loved Levi LaVallee.

. . .

OUR PROBLEM—we needed sponsors. While Levi was giving interviews, basking in the spotlight, B.C. worked the phone trying to find a way to bankroll the costs of sending us across the country to Aspen for several days. This wasn't the monster truck circuit any longer; this was ESPN with millions of viewers and a global reach. Most riders who compete here have their sleds blanketed in decals paid for by sponsors looking for airtime. Levi didn't seem to have one square inch of real estate unclaimed—from the gear he wore, to his helmet, to the seat of his sled, decorated with two words: "Levi LaVallee." And then there was us. Our sleds from Polaris were still pretty much naked, except for the Polaris logos themselves.

"I'm working on it," B.C. assured us.

Joe Duncan's invite to come to Aspen was like a golden ticket to a chocolate factory. By merely mentioning that the Moore brothers were headed to the X Games, B.C. found corporate sponsors lining up to pay us to do what we loved—one at least, anyway: Rockstar Energy Drinks. As we rolled into Aspen, the company's yellow star was plastered on just about everything we had with us: our snowmobiles and our gear, the helmets we wore while riding and the caps we wore when we weren't. And ideally, of course, we'd have a Rockstar drink in our hands, if the camera happened to pan to us. At home, the canned beverages would soon begin arriving by the case or even the pallet. Pure Zeros to start the day, fruit punch or lemonade at meals—our refrigerators, all of them, were full.

The Rockstar sponsorship had other perks, too. It made us look the part of X Games competitors; the company sponsored other snowmobile riders, including Justin Hoyer, the reigning silver medalist. Still, we didn't fit in—and we didn't feel welcome. On the mountain in Aspen from the moment we arrived, there were whispers about the two brothers from Texas—of all places—who rode ATVs and now were trying to do *this*? We'd been riding snowmobiles for less than a month. And now we were standing next to men—tough, winter-tested, north-country men—who had been riding them for more than a decade, most of their lives. We didn't belong, no matter who sponsored us or what we wore. How could we? At the rider's meeting that Joe Duncan called at the foot of the mountain to start the week, I tried to stand as close to Caleb and Sam Rogers as I could. Every other rider was a stranger—and not always friendly. No one offered any help or any suggestions. As Duncan finished talking—"All right," he said, "let's go have fun"—and we hit the course for our practice runs, the other riders stood back, eyeing us as if we had fallen from the sky. They wanted to see what we had, and I could feel their gaze upon me, cold and calculating.

"Dude, it's no big deal," Caleb said.

"We're not here to make friends," B.C. agreed.

We were in Aspen to ride and to prove to Duncan that we belonged in this group of twelve. I needed to focus on that, Caleb said, and not worry about anything else. But thinking about the riding only made me more nervous. We weren't competing for plastic trophies anymore, like we had on the quad racing circuit back in Texas. Serious money—life-changing money, to us, anyway—was at stake in Aspen. Gold medalists took home thirty thousand dollars. Plus, everyone had clauses in their sponsorship contracts for medal bonuses. By medaling, riders could easily double their payouts and, in turn, attract still more sponsors wanting to be connected with a winner.

"Can you imagine if we got gold," Caleb said in the days before the X Games, "and had that much money handed to us?"

"What if we both medaled?" I replied, dreaming big—really big—since I still felt shaky on a snowmobile.

We could do the backflip and the double grab and the cliffhanger. I had the backflip heelclicker and Caleb already had the super flip—a KOD, or kiss of death flip—where you let your body dangle dangerously off the sled while spinning upside down. Duncan wouldn't have invited us to Aspen if he thought we couldn't handle it. "It's all the same jumps," Caleb told me.

But as usual, I was thinking too much, tunneling down into a hole of doubt and worry. What if I under-jumped it and knuckled the landing? What if I over-jumped—OJ, the riders called it—and flatlanded, blowing out my teeth—again? What if I landed upside down? *Darrin.* What if I forgot everything? *Blood in the snow.* How fast do I go? How do I hit that again? What if I made even just the smallest mistake, and there I went, and there I was, chased down and crushed in the snow by a 450-pound snowmobile?

"Don't let all this get to you," Caleb told me. "I'll go hit the jumps. You just follow me out there."

I speed-checked my brother, running along next to him as he hit the five ramps on the course, including a twelve-foot ramp that was about thirty feet long, intended to throw the riders one hundred feet to the knuckle—the hundred-footer. Then I started hitting the ramps myself, straight air at first—no tricks—then gradually building up to stunts and backflips. Duncan was watching and liked what he saw. We looked at ease, he thought, and in control—more comfortable on a sled than even some veteran riders who had competed in the past. What might take others an entire season to learn—four or five months, at least—we had learned in less than five weeks. To Duncan, it looked as if we had been riding for years.

We were in.

ROOKIES

"IT IS dangerous! It is fast! It is loud! It is snowmobile freestyle elimination!"

The ESPN broadcast began with announcer Sal Masekela standing in the snow in a crisp red X Games parka and detailing all the ways we could injure ourselves today on national television. "Last night in practice—*we're talking practice*," Masekela said, "things were crazy."

"They definitely were, Sal," play-by-play man Cameron Steele replied.

Daniel Bodin had lost his grip on the handlebars thirty feet in the air and plummeted, arms flailing, to the snow, like an injured bird crashing to the ground. "We're talking about a risk factor many people can't really fathom," Steele told viewers. Isaac Sherbine bailed out—midflip—after his sled under-rotated. "The riders are pushing the limits," Steele said. Paul Thacker crashed, too, planting his skis into the landing after his snowmobile ran out of gas—again midflip. "Brutal," the color man Chris Burandt noted.

Burandt was no armchair critic. He was Chris "Big Air" Burandt: winner of the first gold medal the X Games ever awarded for freestyle snowmobiling, three years earlier. That day, he had attempted a backflip off the hundred-foot ramp, even though he'd never done a flip that big in competition before—a huge risk that he didn't really want to take, but did, and it paid off. With his winnings, and name recognition, Burandt opened a backcountry snowmobile tour company in Colorado. He was in his early thirties now and retired from freestyle, no longer interested in flipping and risking serious injury. "Uhhh, that would be a big negative," Burandt told people that day. He had a company to run now, clients to serve, and real responsibilities. "If I get hurt," he said, "I don't make money." But it was also about fear. Freestyle's first gold medalist developed a fear of flipping after a crash in practice just months after his 2007 victory. He botched a flip, hit his head, and briefly went blind. "I couldn't see," he said. "I couldn't see for a few seconds." And that was it: Burandt was out. "You can't do this sport if you're not all in."

Yet here in Aspen, he was still Big Air. He understood what the riders were doing and how, what they were risking and why. He had been where we sat, straddling the gas tank of a snowmobile and attempting the impossible in the face of the unknown. Above all, Burandt knew just how tough—how fearless—you had to be, just to try. And in his mind, one man stood out from the field: LaVallee.

"Levi," Burandt told viewers. "Toughest guy in the business." There he was crashing in practice. "That was nothing for him," Burandt said. And there he was, in a flashback to the year before, throwing down the double backflip—a failure by the judges' standards, but not by anyone else's. The only question now was this: What sort of history would LaVallee make this year?

• • •

THE TWELVE-MAN competition started in the afternoon under blue skies with three heats of four. Everyone got two seventy-five-second runs. The riders with the top eight scores would advance to the next round that night under the lights. The best four from that group would then move on to the medal round, where each would get two final chances to impress the judges with their best tricks.

In the first round, several riders flamed out. Thacker fouled up his Superman jump, forcing him to skip the next ramp—a big mistake in the eyes of the judges. Jimmy "Blaze" Fejes crashed twice, under-rotating and ejecting in midair—both times. "He knows that's not a trick, right?" Steele said. Sherbine crashed, too, bailing out midflip, unable to commit. Even for skilled, experienced riders, it wasn't always easy to have faith that the sled would come back around. Sherbine scampered away, narrowly avoiding being tackled by his runaway sled. "Not fun," Burandt noted. And I had problems of my own.

The judges, and the guys in the booth, loved my big flips.

"Whoa!" Steele shouted.

"Look at that!" Burandt nodded. He loved my pendulum backflip and my heelclicker flip, too. "You know, Cam," Burandt admitted. "I don't think I've actually done an actual heelclicker before."

"Really?"

"Yeah. And he's doing one upside down."

But my heart was racing, pounding beneath my new black-and-white-polka-dotted Rockstar gear. I don't even remember much of my first two runs, blind with nerves. And the judges penalized me: for being tentative, for dead sailors—straight-jumping ramps without doing any tricks at all, after my mind froze up—and, in general, as Burandt described it, for "not poking it out." I was the youngest competitor out there—and, a lot of the time, I looked like it.

"Maybe he should stick to doing backflip variations?" Burandt said.

"Just stay inverted?" Steele asked.

"Yeah."

Caleb, on the other hand, impressed everyone from his first jump—a big holy man off the hundred-footer, in which he let go and momentarily soared, unattached and flying above the seat of his sled. His flips were huge—fully committed and fully extended. And when Caleb hit the hundred-footer again at the end of his first run—

catching the sky he went so high—Burandt didn't shout, but fell silent instead. Big Air was in awe.

"Get out of here," he said, almost in a whisper.

"You're impressed," Steele said.

"Yeah. That was really big. For all you guys at home, that was 110 feet. And—oh, yeah—flipping. And doing—you know—a Superman. While upside down. No big deal."

The only problem Burandt and Steele had with Caleb's first run was the judging. The judges had underscored Caleb, giving him just a 76.

"Wow," Burandt said.

"That big Superman flip? The variations?" Steele said. "I'm a little disappointed, to be honest with you."

Caleb was, too, and set out to make an even bigger statement with his second run. This time, all revved up, he made a few mistakes. He didn't get full extension on his Superman, costing him points. And in another jump, he yanked so hard for the flip that he pulled his hand off—just as he had done once back in Krum. Many wondered if he was playing it safe to make sure he made it to the next round or just being inconsistent. But on the hundred-foot ramp, in his second run, Caleb showed his promise yet again.

"Ohhhh!" Steele shouted.

"Wow!" Burandt said.

"Was that a flying squirrel?"

In the trick, Caleb let go of the sled entirely, flying above it in mid-air and then reaching back—fully extending back—for something.

"Did he go back and grab his ankles?" Steele asked. "I've never seen that done before."

Caleb was underscored—again. The total for his second run was almost six points lower than his first, 70.33. But our scores were high enough for us to move on to the next round. Just barely. Caleb had finished seventh. I placed eighth.

• • •

THE PRIME-TIME telecast that night opened with ESPN's cameras trained on Levi—of course. The talk was about his toughness— he was fighting through a heel injury—and also about history. Levi was attempting to become the first X Games athlete to medal in four events in a single games. But the talk now was also about us. Levi had some stiff competition, Steele pointed out from the telecast booth. "And some *new* competition," Steele added, as the camera panned to Caleb sitting atop his sled in his gold-and-maroon-checkered Rockstar gear. "Check these two guys out. The Moore brothers."

Caleb didn't acknowledge the camera. He was thinking about his run.

He wasn't going to do the same set of tricks he had pulled earlier that day. "He actually has a trick in his arsenal that we haven't seen yet," sideline reporter Tes Sewell informed the viewing audience. "And he's going to pull it, if he thinks he needs the points."

There was, in fact, no mystery about it.

"Dude," he told me, just before he sped off, "I'm going for it."

"Are you serious?"

"Yeah," he said.

I knew what that meant. Caleb was doing the volt. "He has the volt," Sewell reported, "in his bag of tricks." The body varial Caleb was planning came from the world of freestyle motocross, invented about two years earlier by a rider named Kyle Loza. Loza, who, as a rookie at the time, used the volt to win gold, busting it out in the Moto X best trick competition. In the move, as Loza designed it, the rider lets go of the handlebars in midair and does a complete 360-degree rotation in the seat, turning left, backward, then all the way back around before landing. Timing here is key. Every movement matters. In the trick, the rider has to lift his leg over the seat four times: the right leg to the left, both legs across the back, and then the left leg back swinging around again to get the rider back into a normal riding position. All while flying in the air and holding on to nothing. Loza, from Southern California, admitted to praying before attempting it the first time. "I was super nervous," he said that night. And Caleb had reason to be nervous, too. For starters, the volt was going to be harder to pull off on a sled. The chassis was much wider than that of a motorcycle. No one had ever done it before on a snowmobile—and Caleb had never practiced it, not even into the foam pit. Attempting it now, on national TV at the X Games, broke all of B.C.'s rules. *"It's better to be safe than sorry."* Even I thought Caleb was a little crazy to try it—right now, right here.

"Are you sure?" I asked him.

Caleb just nodded.

In his first run of the prime-time telecast, he started off slowly—with a holy man, followed by a heelclicker, followed by a cliffhanger, with a no-handed landing. No flips—and Burandt noticed from the booth. "I'm a little surprised Caleb's taking it easy on this first run," he said. Maybe the pressure was getting to him. Maybe we had hit our ceiling. You could only expect so much out of a couple of kids from rural Texas. "Not only is this his first X Games," Burandt noted, "it's his first competition—period—on a sled." Maybe next year we'd do better—*if* we got invited back. People on the mountain were already writing us off. We were a cute story, nothing more. And that's when Caleb went for it. With thirteen seconds left in his run, he hit a ramp, let go of the sled, and spun his body in the air.

"Oh, the volt!" Steele shouted.

"Oh, my gosh," Burandt said.

"He does it—and he stays on the sled!"

Coming down, Caleb found the handlebars, but missed the seat entirely. Only his left foot kept him from falling off, planting into the running board. That probably cost him points with the judges—as did a minor crash two jumps later. Caleb—too excited to think—over-rotated his last flip of the run and tumbled off, harmlessly, into the snow. His score: 80.66. Good—better than earlier that day—but still not great, considering the ground he was breaking.

Caleb was determined to do better. Realizing that the judges weren't going to give him anything for free, he set out on his second run with a simple goal: Be perfect. For seventy-five seconds, he almost was. No falls. No bobbles. And when he went to pull the volt a second time, there was no shouting in the broadcast booth. Steele and Burandt were quiet as they watched, almost speechless. His volt, this time, was clean.

"What in the world?" Burandt said.

"Wow," Steele added. "He just did that like it wasn't even anything."

"He just pulled one of the cleanest runs I've seen at X."

This time, the judges awarded Caleb a score of 85.33—which, again, was great, but not as good as we were expecting. Earlier that day, Hoyer had scored an 87, doing pretty much the same old tricks, the same old way. Still, in the moment, Caleb felt good, destined, it seemed, to qualify for the medal round.

"Colten," he said, calling me. "Colten."

We bumped fists. I was up next. "You got this," he told me.

But I didn't. My first run in the round of eight was weak, with rough landings, mental mistakes, and straight-air jumps, more dead sailors. And my second run was worse, with me crashing and going to the ground.

"Oh, he's coming off!" Steele shouted.

"Came off," Burandt said.

"Both feet off," Steele continued. "Decks it ... ugh ... brutal."

I wasn't alone. Frisby crashed, coming up short on a flip, sticking his skis into the snow, and going over the handlebars—dangerously.

"Get away from the sled!" Burandt shouted. "Oh, no." Frisby was fine, but he was out. The great Levi LaVallee crashed, too, bailing out of a flip. The handlebars on his Polaris sled were mangled, loose. For equipment reasons, Levi wouldn't be making any history tonight. The story was Caleb. "He is a rookie," Steele said, "and he is going for gold—your number-one qualifier."

In the round of eight, Caleb had outscored the entire field. And the fans now were rooting for the man from the place with neither mountains nor snow. My parents had established a cheering section next to the course, waving Texas flags in the night with friends, family, and my girlfriend, Ashley. Everyone felt like something special was about to happen for Caleb, even those attempting to be impartial. Off camera, during a commercial break just before the finals, Burandt had to admit it: "I've got butterflies for the boy," he said.

·   ·   ·

CALEB WASN'T nervous; he was angry. Despite the fact that he had the leading score heading into the finals, he—and B.C., my father, all of us—believed the judges were underscoring him.

"*What?*" Caleb said, off camera, as the scores posted all day.

"Don't say anything," B.C. scolded him. For the cameras, for the crowds, and even for the fellow riders around us, it needed to be smiles—all smiles, everybody. B.C. didn't want Caleb—or anyone else—complaining, making a stink at our first X Games.

"Keep it cool," B.C. said.

But it was hard for my parents, standing there, witnessing it all.

"Of course, they're going to screw you," my father told us. Because we were new, the outsiders on ATVs who couldn't handle the cold and sat there huddled around a propane heater. "They've actually been sitting in the pit area with a heater," one reporter noted, with a mocking tone. "They're not used to the snow." Because we were brash. My father walked around in a cowboy hat and flew the Texas flag—high and proud—on a pole by our trailer at the course. "Gotta let them know where we're from," he said. And because the other riders couldn't lose to us—the thin-blooded rookies from the flatlands. "They don't want someone coming in," our father said, "and whupping their butts in the first year."

We didn't know if the underscoring was intentional; B.C. figured it was subconscious for the judges. The judges knew the other riders—often personally—while they didn't know us at all. Regardless, as the finals began, Caleb was thinking about it. He believed—rightly or wrongly—that he needed to be more than perfect to win against the three other competitors still riding. Parsons was the defending gold medalist. Bodin was a perennial finalist. And Hoyer had landed the best score of the day—that 87. All three of them went out on their first runs and scored 83 or better. On their second runs, all three improved their scores. Caleb truly needed to be flawless now, but it didn't happen.

In his first run, he had problems. "All kinds of problems," Steele told viewers. His cliffhanger was called "squirrelly." His cordova flip was deemed "shaky." He still did the volt, making the fantastic now mundane, but twice he nearly missed ramps, with his sled hanging off too far to one side.

"Oh, my gosh," Steele said.

"He's going to have to bail," Burandt added.

"This is his first time in the big show, Chris. Do you think maybe the wheels are coming off?"

Burandt wasn't sure. About the ramp misfires, he only knew one thing. "That could have been catastrophic," he said.

Caleb corrected these mistakes on his second and final run, hitting the hundred-foot ramp as hard as he could. The crowd watched, mouths agape, as he floated across the night sky for what seemed like forever. But it wasn't enough. Caleb settled for the bronze—an achievement that for everyone else didn't feel like settling at all.

ESPN wanted interviews. "Thank you so much," Caleb told the crowd. Fellow riders were impressed; Levi LaVallee said as much. "You had a heck of a run," he told Caleb afterward. The underscoring would continue later that week, we believed. Neither of us did well in the best trick competition, finishing off the medal stand. But we belonged. Levi knew he'd see us again the next year—and that alone felt like a victory. We hadn't won, but we hadn't failed either. As Caleb climbed onto the podium that night, he had a bronze medal around his neck, a Rockstar energy drink in his hand, and a smile across his face.

He was happy.

GOING BIG

OUR LIVES took on a certain rhythm after our first year in Aspen. From January to April, we hit the road with the Nuclear Cowboyz tour, jumping our quads in arenas from Atlanta to Kansas City, Columbus to Tacoma. In the summer, we'd go international; France and Russia became annual destinations. And then, in the fall, when the shows ended and the work dried up, we would return, once again, to the snowmobiles, practicing flips into the foam pit in the backyard in preparation once again for Aspen. We rode the sleds only a few weeks a year—and even less than that on actual snow. Because of the visibility of the X Games, the millions of people who tuned in to watch, and the success Caleb had enjoyed there in our first year, we became known for the thing we did the least: flipping snowmobiles.

In California, B.C. picked up more sponsors. Western Power Sports—makers of Fly Racing motorsports gear—signed on with us that spring, giving us yet another big-time supporter. Between our quad-flipping shows and our sponsors, Caleb and I were now making more money than we ever could have conceived when we first set out to jump our ATVs on that little, nowhere ranch near Plano, Texas. But B.C. wasn't finished. He wanted us to have deals like the other serious contenders in Aspen. So, with our sponsors, he secured contingencies—bonuses that we would be paid, over and above the X Games prize money, if we happened to win a medal. As our contracts were now written, Caleb and I stood to earn a total of more than $70,000 for winning gold at the X Games, $25,000 for silver, and about $15,000 for bronze. With a single day's work in Aspen, we could take home more than our parents earned in an entire year—an exciting thought, but one that came with a suitcase full of pressure. What if we lost? What if we crashed? What if we went all the way out to Aspen and didn't win anything? There was no money for doing that. Or what if we did so poorly—what if *I* did so poorly—that sponsors backed out, making the X Games almost impossible? I worried about that. To fail in Aspen was to not get paid.

Still, it wasn't all about the money. That summer, on the Fourth of July, we staged a show—for almost no fee—back home, on the Texas panhandle, in Wheeler County. Just about everyone we knew would be there—our grandparents, aunts, uncles, and cousins—plus hundreds of others coming out for the show. We were supposed to flip our quads at the rodeo. But when it started raining and we couldn't flip for safety reasons, Caleb and I came up with an alternative plan.

"You think Uncle Todd would let us borrow his Razor?" Caleb asked.

A Razor—officially known as a Polaris RZR—is a larger, off-road, all-terrain vehicle with seatbelts and roll bars. Basically, a larger, more expensive ATV. And Uncle Todd's was brand new, shiny in his shop in Wheeler. Asking to use it at the rodeo was a big request; Caleb understood that. But Todd agreed to let Caleb have it for the day, so the show could go on. "We need to do something for the people," Caleb explained. His suggestion was free Razor rides to anyone in the crowd. Caleb would give rides to anyone at the rodeo—one jump over the ramp. For at least one afternoon, the people in Wheeler could fly, like us.

"C'mon," he said, smiling at each fan. "Climb on in."

That day, Caleb must have jumped the Razor two hundred times, giving rides like a carnival showman. Young and old, male and female, friends and total strangers, they all sat down next to my brother, got fitted with helmets, buckled up, and then looked to Caleb—anxious with anticipation.

"Don't worry," he told them. "Here we go."

Again and again, he jumped. And again and again, people thanked him.

"I appreciate you doing this for my son."

"Thanks for the ride."

"Can I go one more time?"

It became a Fourth of July tradition in Wheeler. Like the turtle races or the fireworks themselves, we would be there on the pan-handle at the rodeo or on the baseball field by the town swimming pool—and maybe, if you were lucky, you could get a ride. One year, we even talked my grandfather, the aging cowboy, into climbing into the Razor with Caleb. They hit the ramp a few times, flying in the air before the crowd. And when it was over, the emcee of the festiv-ities stuck a microphone in our grandfather's face to ask him what he thought about it. At the pinnacle of each jump, Granddad told the crowd, when all he could see were the tops of the cottonwood trees, and he wondered if the ground was still there, down below, he was only thinking one thing.

"Oh, shit," he said.

Later, our grandfather would blame his risk-taking hubris on beer. "I drank too much damn beer," he said, chuckling. But he didn't regret jumping with Caleb. "I had faith," he said, "in my driver."

• • •

HEADING IN to our second X Games in 2011, we were determined to do better than we had the year before. We made plans to once again go to Michigan for a couple of weeks of training on snow. This time we asked B.C. to come to Texas and help us drive north. We wanted to make sure we were well rested when we got to Michigan and ready to go. "We've got to get to work," Caleb said.

We felt more comfortable on the sleds, more at home on the snow. And we had a routine now. In Michigan, B.C. woke us up early. We ate breakfast, fought through the cold, and practiced for as long as we could. In Colorado, we practiced some more, getting accustomed to riding at altitude, and then we moved into a rental house in Aspen.

As comfortable as we felt back at the X Games, neither Caleb nor I felt complacent. ESPN was beginning to push the snowmobile freestyle and best trick competitions, running ads to drum up interest. "Backflip. Snowmobile," one ad that winter read. "They don't belong in the same sentence. That's why we put a period in between them." And for months we had worried about being underscored—yet again. Just because we felt more at home in Aspen didn't necessarily mean we were welcome.

At home, in Krum, to guard against being snubbed by the judges, we began working on a new trick, in secret. We wanted to have something big in store—our own version of Levi's death-defying, news-making double backflip—to make headlines, if not win, and prove once and for all that we belonged. Once we had started thinking about it—once we began mulling over this unorthodox flip—we almost had to do it.

"That's a good idea," Caleb said.

"We'll practice it," I agreed.

Once we began practicing it—first in the foam pit in Krum and later on snow in Michigan—we realized something: "It's actually easier than I thought," Caleb said. There was no need to practice it more than a few times.

"We're dialed," Caleb said. "We've got this."

"Hell, yeah we do," I said.

At the freestyle competition, with the Texas flags waving on the mountain, we had no need to unveil our top-secret plan. I came in fifth—off the medal stand, but my best finish to date. And Caleb, once again, took home bronze—not the gold he was seeking, but still, third place for the second year in a row. He could be happy with that.

The problems started in the best trick competition. Caleb went big, doing a corolla—another trick that had never been performed on a sled. In the move, the rider lets go of the handlebars, slides down to the seat, and then lets go, spinning his body above the flying snow-mobile like a floating screwdriver, before grabbing back on again and landing. The move is all about timing, body control—and risk. If you do it wrong, you can spin yourself right off into oblivion while the sled flies away from you. But if you do it right, Caleb figured, it's a gold medal. "Easy," he said.

The judges in Aspen disagreed. They gave his first corolla jump a score of 88.33—good enough for second place, but more than two points behind Daniel Bodin, the rider from Malung, Sweden. Bodin had somehow managed to lay claim to the lead by doing a flip that everyone had seen before. Frustrated, but not giving up, Caleb de-cided to increase the risk with his second attempt: He'd do the co-rolla again, spinning his body above his sled in the night—but land, this time, without using his hands.

"A no-handed lander!" Steele shouted from the telecast booth.

"Didn't even check the bars, Cam," Burandt added.

"Wow."

"That's bringing it to a whole 'nother level," Steele said. "It's in-sane," an injured LaVallee said, chiming in. "It's one thing just to do this trick. But then to do a no-handed lander like that—"

"Wow, that's gnarly," Burandt said.

But again, the judges disagreed. Caleb's score only went up two points. He was still sitting in second place, three-tenths of a point be-hind Bodin. There would be no gold medal for him, and he threw his hands in the air in disgust. I did, too. On television, for the first time, Caleb complained, calling out the judges for their low scores. "What can I do?" he asked me.

In between jumps, huddling with B.C. and my parents, we decided it was time—time to employ the trick we had practiced in secret. Secret because if we told ESPN, we thought they wouldn't allow us to do it. Secret because, as our father put it, "it's an in-your-face move," basically taunting the judges. Secret because, by the rules, what we were about to attempt wasn't allowed. When it was my turn to ride, I was going to let Caleb go with me. I was even going to let him drive. We were going to do a tandem backflip, two of us flipping on one sled together, sacrificing my run—and my shot at a medal—to make a statement: You don't trifle with the Moore brothers.

"They're going to no-score you, Colten," our father told me.

I know that, I said.

"They're not going to give you a medal, Colten."

I know that, too.

And, of course, there was the possibility that this move—this "in-your-face move"—could come right back in our own faces. "If you don't land it," our father said, "it's going to be kind of ugly."

B.C. agreed—at first, anyway. In his mind, he was playing out all the ways this could go wrong. Crash and get injured—both of us, on one jump. That was bad for business. Crash and embarrass ESPN, and maybe never get invited back to the X Games again. That was bad for business, too. But everyone—B.C. included—believed we could do it. We at least needed to try. "If we crash," I said, "we crash together."

Out on the course, when it was my turn to go a second time, I stopped my snowmobile, waved my hands in the air, and pretended I was having mechanical problems. Caleb raced out on his sled and I climbed on board, sitting behind him and slipping my hands across his chest through small holes we had cut into his gear. I had no intention of just sitting on the back. I was going to do an Indian air, a super flip, throwing my legs away from the snowmobile, attached not to the sled in midair, but only to my brother. "Hold on," I told him as he raced toward the ramp. "I'm going big."

I had total trust in him. I had more faith in Caleb than I had in myself. And as we hit the ramp, there was no question in my mind what was going to happen: We were going to flip. The crowd was going to cheer. We were going to come back around and stick the landing, which we did.

"Do they both get medals?" Burandt asked.

Not a chance, X Games officials decided.

"You're disqualified," Duncan told B.C.

"Who cares, man?" B.C. replied. We had won the gold without winning the gold—and once again Caleb was coming home with hardware: a bronze in freestyle, a silver in best trick. ESPN wanted interviews. *SportsCenter* wanted the highlight. And sponsors—like Craig Shoemaker, the CEO of Western Power Sports—wanted a word with us.

"Get Colten and Caleb over here," Shoemaker said later that night. He told us how much he had enjoyed the tandem backflip and then handed us a check for several thousand dollars—just a little something extra, for our trouble. "You are the kind of boys," he said, "that we want representing our brand."

CRUEL

THE PARTY that night in Aspen raged into the wee hours of the morning, fueled by Crown Royal and Cokes and the feeling that our lives had changed—were changing—and that Caleb and I had crossed over into new territory and would never be the same again.

Back in Texas, we used the money we were making to pay back our parents for all the sacrifices they had made when we were young. And then Caleb and I bought a home of our own. He was twenty-three, I was twenty-one, and we found a place that was perfect for us in Corinth, in the distant suburbs north of Dallas. The house had everything we could possibly need: a two-car garage and five bedrooms upstairs; a loft for playing video games on giant beanbags; a swimming pool in the backyard with a fountain attached; and a doorbell programmed to ring with a tiger's growl or a trumpet's fanfare. *Da, da, da, DUT, da, DUH! Charge!*

The best part was that the sellers were interested in unloading their furniture, too. Two hundred dollars for their flat-screen television. Three hundred dollars for the poker table. Bedroom furniture for two grand, the billiard table in the front room for fifteen hundred dollars. We bought it all and the sellers threw in their bar for free, making our new house in Corinth a home, almost overnight, stocked with food, drinks, and shot glasses we had collected from around the world. Ashley and I moved into the master bedroom in one corner of the house; Caleb moved in on the other side of the atrium. He turned a third bedroom into a massive walk-in closet for his helmets, gear, and clothes. To impress a girl we all hated, he dropped twelve hundred dollars on a single pair of black-leather, red-soled, French-made loafers and scooped up expensive watches. Both of us spent money on new toys: guitars, lasers, skateboards, knives, mini-scooters, trucks, speedboats, and motorcycles. Caleb wanted to make sure his machines were especially fast. What was the point, he said, if they couldn't go fast? In the garage, in time, he parked everything: his stripped-down, modified, race-ready street bike; his supercharged eight-hundred-horsepower Ford Lightning pickup truck; and finally a deep blue, limited edition Mustang GT, designed by race car driver Carroll Shelby, with a glowing speedometer that maxed out at 160 mph.

I started to grow my hair out, wearing it long. When I rode my snowmobile or four-wheeler now, you could easily spot me on the course, my hair sticking out from beneath my helmet and flying along behind me, fluttering in the wind—a real rock star. Still, I wasn't allowed to drive my brother's Mustang—not really. It was going to be a collectible, Caleb said. An investment, he called it. And, anyway, I had already proven that I was not to be trusted with his toys, crashing his Ford Lightning on the Interstate 35 service road near Krum. I lost control of the truck, trying to go too fast, and ended up slamming into a curb, while my brother looked on from the passenger seat—almost amused by my inability to drive.

"Nooooo!" I shouted as the impact of the crash sheared a wheel off the truck's rear axle and we came to a rest with a thud.

"Really?" Caleb said, just looking at me.

Only he could test the limits, pushing the needle of his machines on the city streets of Dallas, the back roads near Krum, and the flatlands of Wheeler, most of all. On visits to the panhandle, our cousins would take us out to what the local kids called the Quarter—a quarter-mile stretch of flat, straight two-lane highway, going west, away from the cemetery and the little farmhouse where Caleb had once scampered up the TV antenna, hand over little hand.

There, facing the sunset, our cousin Jaten honked his horn three times in steady succession. On the third honk, off they went, racing side by side in the two lanes, windows down and engines roaring, until Caleb decided he'd had enough—he was finished fooling around—and pulled away from Jaten's truck, like it was standing still, winning easily.

"I wondered when you were going to start," he cracked, circling back to our cousin, with a smile on his face.

"I had it floored, man," Jaten replied. "That was all she had."

The parties we threw were even more elaborate. On the road, we stayed up late, turned hotels into jungle gyms climbing from balcony to balcony, and once, in Colombia, we tossed ceramic room service dishes off the roof like Frisbees.

"All right," B.C. said in the morning, banging on the door and waking us up. "Which one of you all did it?"

"Did what?" I asked.

"You know. Which one of you threw the plates off the roof?"

We were caught and we paid for it, covering the damages with money out of our own pockets. Everyone agreed that the South American plate incident was a stupid mistake, fueled by alcohol, boredom, and testosterone. On the road, under B.C.'s watch, we learned to behave—or else. But at our new house in Corinth, there were no rules. We could stay up as late as we wanted and often did, living off of chicken wings and tequila shots, like the college students we never were.

There were parties—at least one got out of hand, drawing the ire of neighbors and the attention of the local police. They didn't appreciate the noise, or the two-story beer bong we had set up, or the fact that there were naked girls in the pool and the bounce house that we had rented. By the end of the night, it wasn't even fun. Someone—we didn't know him—was passed out on a table in our foyer. Someone else had apparently fired a gun outside in the yard. Neighbors found the bullet casings. The garage smelled like an ashtray. The green felt surface on the pool table had been stained black by goodness knows what. And Caleb, Ashley, and I were forced to admit it: We didn't know most of the people in our own house, people who were trashing our white carpets and stubbing out cigarettes on the wall. One guy Caleb met even claimed the party was his.

"Really?" Caleb said. "That's interesting, because this is my house."

"Get the *HELL* out!" I started shouting.

The next day, I slept in, well into the afternoon as usual. But Caleb almost always got up early and went to work. He ran our books, paid our bills, handled B.C.'s phone calls and requests, knew our schedule, and generally organized our lives—both of them—while I slept in most days. "Wake up!" he'd shout down the hall every morning while I rolled over, ignoring him.

At least once, we fought. I was upset about a girl he was dating, and money he'd spent on her out of our shared bank account, and maybe a little bit about everything—that he was Caleb and I was me, that he was a winner and I was an also-ran, that he was comfortable in front of cameras and I was nervous, that I was almost twenty-two years old and was still best known for being the great Caleb Moore's little brother, a sidekick. At some level, whether I was willing to admit it or not, I was frustrated about all of that. And right there after dinner one night in our kitchen in Corinth, we fought, throwing punches and wrestling on the tile floor while Ashley and friends looked on, stunned and shouting.

"Do I need to stop this?" one friend asked.

"No," Ashley said. "They need this."

•   •   •

THAT WINTER, at the X Games, lots of riders came in banged up, nursing injuries that limited their abilities or knocked them out altogether. Levi LaVallee had a broken leg. He had shattered his tibia in early January, just days before the X Games, while practicing his famous double backflip into his foam pit into Minnesota. Slammed his leg into the dashboard of his sled, he reported, and that was it. He couldn't compete in Aspen. Two days later, practicing in the same foam pit, Bodin, the reigning gold medalist, crashed as well, fracturing vertebrae in his neck. There was no spinal cord damage—that was the good news. Bodin would ride and walk again, but not this year. He was going to be wearing a halo neck brace for a while—and, obviously, he was also out. "I love our sport," Levi told the press at the time, "but it can be cruel sometimes." Bodin's injury—suffered while attempting a front flip—was especially frightening, even for veterans like us. "Jeez Louise," Levi said, "that's scary stuff."

But it was hardly the only stuff. Jimmy Blaze was coming into the competition off a broken femur that he had suffered less than three months earlier. Blaze wasn't sure about riding—"I don't know if it's the right thing to do," he said—but he was doing it, anyway. And Caleb was riding through his own injuries. Right about the time LaVallee and Bodin hurt themselves in Minnesota, Caleb crashed in a Nuclear Cowboyz show in Baltimore or Kansas City or some such place. The towns all ran together after a while. His right hip was injured. He couldn't push off with his foot. Flips—and his usual tricks—were nearly impossible to perform in the days leading up to the X Games. He was only riding because he was Caleb. "I ain't quitting," he said. But once we got to Aspen, it was clear: If a Moore brother was going to compete this year, it was going to have to be me. Caleb just wasn't himself.

He crashed again and again—in practice and in competition—bruising his already battered body and bloodying the bridge of his nose. By the best trick competition, people on the mountain could see it: Caleb, for once, was playing it safe, unwilling to push himself, knowing that, physically, he didn't have it. And, at least initially, I didn't have it, either. In the freestyle qualifying round, I crashed badly, unable to reach my seat after letting go during a trick. As the sled floated away from me, I fell to the snow from thirty-five feet up in the air and just missed coming down on my head, tucking at the last possible moment to land with a thud on my back—bruised but safe.

Still, even after my fall, I wasn't rattled. For weeks, I had been training harder than ever before—at first in our foam pit, then up north on snow. While Caleb struggled with his physical ailments, I was determined not to give the judges any excuse to underscore me. "I'm not going to leave any doubt this year," I said. I practiced KOD flips, in which you stretch your body completely away from the sled while upside down. I even practiced crashing. Just one week before losing my sled in midair at the X Games, I had crashed the very same way in a training run. "Instinct is, you don't want to land on your face," I told the press. "So I just tucked, bounced out of that one. You could almost say I practiced for it."

I managed to recover from my early mistakes, making the finals—sore, but relatively unscathed. Because of the depleted field—no La-Vallee, no Bodin, and a physically limited Caleb—I finally won. I took home silver in best trick and gold in freestyle—my first-ever medals in Aspen. Somehow I had become the first in our family to take the top spot on the podium. And for once, the reporters came to talk to me, not Caleb.

"Honestly, I don't even know what I'm feeling," I told them. "I can't even breathe. . . . Best moment of my life right here. . . . Did that really happen?"

It had—and hasty plans were made for a celebration that night at our rental house. The place was massive—a six-bedroom, A-frame behemoth with plenty of room for family and friends and an ironic address that my family appreciated: North Little Texas Lane. And inside, the party raged till dawn. There was dancing, laughing, and tequila shots for all. Caleb passed the bottle around the living room, toasting me.

He could have been jealous. He was only taking home bronze— yet again. Both of us knew the truth: Had he been healthy, the scores in Aspen might have been different. But Caleb didn't feel the need to point that out—to me, to reporters, or anyone else. "Let's go get that medal for you," he said after I won, smiling and slapping me on the back.

Still, I knew it was possible for him to feel two things: happiness for me, his little brother, and also a burning desire to prove that he still was the best. "It's going to be different next year," Caleb said that night during the party at the house, joking about the future, but not really. "I can't let you win again."

. . .

I UNDERSTOOD what he meant. I believed that he would beat me—and LaVallee and Frisby and every other rider—the following year. Heading into the X Games in January 2013, I might have been the reigning freestyle gold medalist, the champion, but most people thought Caleb would win. It was his time.

Then the snowstorm closed in on the mountain. And Caleb under-rotated his flip—until L did not equal $I\omega$. The angular momentum was all wrong.

And he and the snowmobile began to roll down the landing, tumbling end over end, until the sled popped up and speared him in the chest—"Just pummeled him," Burandt said—450 pounds of Minnesota-made machine hurtling into his sternum. And everything stopped. Everything changed.

"Caleb?" I said, leaning over my brother's body in the snow.

"Caleb?"

"C'mon, Caleb. Wake up."

AS THE SNOW FALLS

THE CONCUSSION—it had to be a concussion—was the primary concern. For a full thirty seconds, Caleb lay there unconscious on national television, on his back in the snow, with his arms spread wide and the palms of his hands turned up toward the sky. Briefly, after the snowmobile slammed into his chest and tumbled away, it appeared that Caleb might try to get up. But it was just an illusion, just gravity, only the momentum of the fall, pushing him down the landing, or maybe it was just his body twitching—an unconscious twitch. Either way, he was down. He wasn't moving. Caleb wasn't getting up.

Three X Games officials, dressed in parkas and running through the snow, arrived at his side first, kneeling down, hands on his body. I was next, followed by still more officials, medical experts, B.C., and then my father, who had watched Caleb's crash while standing next to my mother with all the other fans on the hill, and came running, leaping a barricade to be at Caleb's side.

"Go," my mother implored my father up on the hill, knowing he wanted to be down in the snow with Caleb.

"Let me talk to him," my father said when he finally arrived.

"Get up," my mother whispered.

From up on the hill, she kept talking to Caleb, clutching hope in one hand and her Texas flag in the other. But still, there was nothing. No movement in the snow. Soon, my mother couldn't see Caleb at all. He was lost in a sea of bodies. Everyone was hovering over him.

"Get up," she said again. "C'mon, Caleb. Get up."

· · ·

MY FIRST thought was about his back. In the days before the X Games that year, Caleb had been hobbled by lower back pain. It was a chronic problem for him, dating to a fall he had suffered at a show in Amarillo years before. But in Colorado, the pain had become acute for Caleb, forcing him to sit out for long stretches while we practiced at a retreat called Electric Mountain.

There were no roads in, only trails. The retreat, nestled in the snowy hills two hours west of Aspen, was reachable only by snowshoe, cross-country skis, or snowmobile. Visitors needed to park at a remote trailhead about a dozen miles away and make the journey in, going up a path through an evergreen forest and deep into the Colorado wilderness. There was nothing else out there, making it a perfect place to train. Caleb and I had been coming to Electric Mountain for years, always right before the X Games. This year hadn't been any different. Together, with our father, we had holed up there, sleeping in one of the cabins, eating warm meals at the lodge, and stepping outside every morning, onto the snow, to ride.

Caleb wanted to work on his biggest tricks—the corolla and the volt, the varials where he let go of his sled altogether, flying above the snowmobile or next to it, before landing. "I need to have those dialed," he said. But at least a few times, he crashed, failing to get back on the snowmobile in time, and these crashes took a toll on his body—his back, in particular.

He tried everything to make it better: resting, lying on the floor, taking ibuprofen, and even leaving Electric Mountain for a day. He and my father rode out on their snowmobiles—in search of a town, a chiropractor, and some relief. I was worried about how he'd fare at the X Games, injured again, just like the year before.

"I don't want you going in hurt again," I told him.

Obviously, Caleb didn't want that, either.

"Can you help me with my back?" he asked me one night in the cabin.

"Of course," I said.

Down on the floor, I did what he told me to do, pushing and prodding, trying, as Caleb said, to "pop" his spine or discs—something—back into place. He didn't know what it was, but he knew it when he felt it.

"Like this?" I asked. "Am I in the right spot? Want me to push harder? Any better?"

Everyone at the lodge seemed to have suggestions for him about what he needed to do and whom he needed to see. Most people believed he needed a professional to examine him—and right away. But Caleb disagreed.

"Naw," he said, "I've got my brother."

It felt good at the time, knowing that Caleb trusted me, that I was his brother and I could help him. On the course, though, after his crash, with the television cameras rolling and Caleb lying there on his back, there was nothing I could do. The medical staff was going to take care of him, B.C. assured me, as Caleb finally regained consciousness, sat up, and walked off the course with my father. He was shaky, taking my father's arm to steady himself. But he was also smiling. "I feel like I just had the longest dream ever," Caleb said.

He ducked into the medical tent with my father, and everyone made a snap, if subconscious, decision: Caleb was going to be just fine. He was walking off. Once again, we believed, he had managed to accomplish the impossible. He had survived a blow to the chest from a flipping, tumbling machine. But out of sight—away from me, the other riders, and the relieved commentating team in the telecast booth, Tes Sewell and Chris Burandt—Caleb promptly wilted, falling to the ground, eyes closed.

"He's passing out," my father told the medical experts around him.

And he wasn't coming out of it. Maybe it was a seizure—another seizure. He'd had them before.

"Caleb?"

His body had gone limp and he wasn't responding.

"Talk to me."

The medical staff on the ground made the call: They strapped Caleb on a backboard, put him in a waiting ambulance, and sent him to the hospital with my mother, riding along in the passenger seat up front.

It was 8:23 p.m. as they pulled away. About fifteen minutes since the accident. And for my mother, anyway, things felt suddenly urgent. Caleb seemed in and out of consciousness, making noises, but not making sense. He briefly became combative, not cooperating. Paramedics knocked him out with a fast-acting sedative, put him on oxygen, inserted intravenous tubes into his body—and gave him a number. Caleb's weighted trauma score was a 6.9—an early assessment of his status based on his blood pressure and respiratory rate. By this initial, if cursory, measure, Caleb was likely to survive; 6.9 was a good score. Still, everyone was moving fast. The ambulance raced to the hospital, rumbling down the streets of Aspen, as the snow continued to fall. "As the snow falls," Sewell told viewers, "on Buttermilk Mountain."

•   •   •

I COULDN'T shake the thought of what I'd seen: my brother, down and out, in the snow. Even after Caleb got up and walked off, holding my father's arm, I felt uneasy about everything: the night, this snow, my run, my brother. Was he okay? "He's going to be fine," B.C. assured me. Either way, the program had to go on. We were live on cable TV—and I was riding soon. As Caleb ducked inside the tent with my father to get checked out, I ran back to my snowmobile, stripped off my black winter coat covered with sponsorship logos, and prepared for my turn on the course.

"The younger of the two Moore brothers," Sewell said, introducing me from the telecast booth. "Colten Moore . . . the gold medalist from last year . . . one of the most entertaining people in Aspen."

"I cannot wait to see this run," Burandt said.

"Here we go."

At the starting line, the sport's organizer, course designer, and producer, Joe Duncan, looked at me as the snow swirled around him.

"Ready?" he asked, getting his cues for the live telecast through a headset.

"Ready." I nodded.

Then, as usual, Duncan counted it down.

"One minute," he said.

"Thirty seconds."

Three, two, one . . .

I tore off across the snow, pumping my fist for the crowd. But behind my goggles and inside my helmet, I wasn't ready at all. I was lost and distracted—and it showed. My first jump, throwing my feet off the back of the sled, was conservative, and poorly executed. "A little high on the landing," Burandt noted. My second jump, a cliffhanger, nearly ended in disaster when I knocked the handlebars off line with my knees. At the last moment, I was able to turn them straight again, to avoid crashing on landing. But with no time to recover before I hit the next ramp, I was doomed to fail. I over-rotated my third jump, a flip, so badly that Burandt was groaning before I even crashed—which I did, falling off the back of the sled and slamming my head, back, and tailbone into the ground.

Here came the medical staff again—running. Here came B.C. and my father again—running. And here came Ashley, too—running and also crying.

"I can't move my right leg," I told them.

Couldn't walk, couldn't even stand. I was pretty sure I'd broken my hip or leg in the fall. It felt almost like my leg had come unglued from my body—and I knew where I was headed. I was going to the hospital, just like Caleb. In the ambulance, to distract myself from the terrible pain in my hip, I thought of how much Caleb would tease me when he learned that I hadn't walked away from my crash—while he did—even though his accident appeared, in comparison, much worse than mine. I could hear him cracking jokes at my expense about my toughness, or lack thereof, mocking me with the nurses. And I thought about how I would laugh it all off when I joined him at the hospital. *"Couldn't leave a brother hanging . . . couldn't leave you here all alone."* But mostly, in the ambulance, I was worried, increasingly panicked and filled with an almost inexplicable dread: about me, my brother, everything.

"Where are my parents?" I asked.

They're meeting you at the hospital, paramedics informed me.

"Am I going to be okay?"

Yes.

"Is everything okay?"

• • •

THE AMBULANCE carrying my brother arrived at Aspen Valley Hospital just six minutes after it left the freestyle course on the mountain. Caleb was now about twenty-one minutes removed from his crash. The emergency room staff, pulling the night shift and prepared for the large crowds in town for the X Games, snapped into action.

They unloaded him out of the ambulance and checked his vital signs. His breathing was reported as good, nonlabored. But doctors noted a weak pulse and couldn't obtain a blood pressure reading. They rushed him inside and sent him away for a battery of tests—CT scans of his head, spine, and chest. By 8:46 p.m.—thirty-two minutes after the crash—Caleb was lying on a narrow examination table inside a CT scanner while my mother waited outside, soon getting word that another rider was bound for the hospital. *That can't be Colten,* she thought. Minutes later, paramedics rolled me inside, with my father, B.C., Ashley, and others in tow.

There was no need for our fans to stay on the mountain now; the Moore brothers were done for the night, probably the week. In the waiting room, our friends sat huddled, deflated, and quiet, their Texas flags folded across their laps. Forget about medals and prize money and sponsorship contingencies playing out on national television. We had worked all year to get back to the X Games, and in just two jumps we were out. I was angry—ornery with pain.

"Where's Caleb?" I asked.

My mother tried to explain.

"Is he all right?" I asked.

My mother said she didn't know.

I went away for my own battery of scans and returned to my parents in a wheelchair a short while later, asking still more questions about my brother. We were in different rooms; I didn't like that. No one was telling me anything; I didn't like that, either. I wanted to know what was going on, and when I could see Caleb, and why he wasn't conscious.

"Why is he asleep?" I asked.

. . .

A RADIOLOGIST, reviewing Caleb's films, was the first to identify the problem. Caleb's head scans revealed no sign of trauma. There was no bleeding or brain hemorrhage to explain his collapse in the medical tent. And the images of his spine revealed no fractured vertebrae. Like his head scans, everything in Caleb's back was normal. The problem, the radiologist reported, was in his chest. On the CT scan of Caleb's torso, the doctor noted pulmonary contusions, a broken rib, a lacerated liver with some possible bleeding, and a worrisome finding in his upper left chest, right where the nose of the snowmobile had barreled into him like a motorized arrow. "The heart size is normal," the radiologist noted, but in the pericardium—the sac around the heart—there was blood, an effusion. "A large pericardial effusion," the radiologist called it, "measuring up to two centimeters in thickness." Caleb appeared to be bleeding internally, into the sac around his heart. The buildup of blood was making it hard for the organ to do its most important job: pump. On the scans, the radiologist could apparently see that, too. "There appears to be right ventricular compression," he reported, calling in this finding to the emergency room at 10:17 p.m.—more than two hours after Caleb's crash and ninety minutes since the doctors had sent him away for his scans.

An ultrasound was performed to confirm the bleeding. Doctors finally had a definitive medical explanation for why Caleb had collapsed, why his pulse had been weak upon arrival, why they initially couldn't get a blood pressure reading, and why—even now—his blood pressure fluctuated from minute to minute, ranging far away from the normal reading of 120 over 80. As doctors received the radiologist's news of the bleeding around his heart, Caleb's blood pressure was low while his pulse was racing—tachycardic, too fast.

111 over 76.

90 over 56.

65 over 42.

Around 10:50 p.m., roughly a half hour after the radiologist had made the call, doctors met with my parents at Caleb's bedside and informed them in detail of both the plan—and the problem.

Doctors needed to perform either pericardiocentesis or a pericardial window—or possibly both. In pericardiocentesis, a doctor—typically a cardiothoracic surgeon or a cardiologist—would guide a long needle into Caleb's chest, piercing the sac around his heart and withdrawing the blood putting pressure on the right ventricle. But this was probably just a temporary fix. Ultimately, a cardiothoracic surgeon would need to cut Caleb open, slicing through his sternum with a reciprocating saw, opening a sort of window on his heart, identifying the bleed and stopping it. Yet doctors in Aspen decided not to perform the procedures there—so long as Caleb's vital signs remained stable.

Aspen Valley Hospital had a trauma surgeon and an orthopedic surgeon on call that night, along with a full complement of well-trained physicians and nurses in the emergency room. But it was a small facility, with only twenty-five beds—a center capable of handling many traumas, but not all, given its lack of specialized care. Aspen—home of the X Games—didn't have the experts necessary to perform the surgery that Caleb, one of the X Games' biggest stars, needed. There was no cardiothoracic surgeon in town, no heart surgeon. And emergency room doctors didn't call in the staff physician, who could have potentially helped: Aspen Valley Hospital's lone cardiologist. A cardiologist could have at least decided whether or not to drain the blood pooling up around Caleb's heart.

Instead, plans were made to send my brother 130 miles away to St. Mary's Hospital and Medical Center in Grand Junction. That hospital had the surgeon Caleb needed. And under normal conditions, it was a quick flight by helicopter. But outside, the snow was still falling, grounding all helicopters for now. And at 11:10 p.m.—three hours after the crash—there we were, still waiting with Caleb, the patient, age twenty-five.

"Pt's brother Colten in to see," the nurse noted in her chart.

"Pt sedated and intubated."

Patient's heart is racing. "Remains tachycardic @ 150s." Doctor is aware. But for the moment, we are stuck—stuck in Aspen. "Planning transport to St. Mary's . . . Awaiting weather conditions."

∙   ∙   ∙

DOCTORS WERE whispering. Off to the side—hushed among themselves—I heard the medical staffers talking to each other about Caleb, the snow, and the plan to get him to Grand Junction. They finally decided on an airplane, leaving not out of Aspen, but from a town called Rifle, sixty-seven miles away. Before Caleb could get to the doctors in Grand Junction, before he could even get on a plane, he needed to get back inside another ambulance—this time, for a long ride—to an airstrip in the middle of the mountains, in the middle of the night.

"I'm going with him," I told my parents.

"They're not going to let you do that," my father said.

In my crash on the mountain, I had seriously injured my pelvis. Tests revealed what doctors call an open-book fracture—the bones in my pelvis had opened like a book, due to the impact of my fall. And it was potentially life threatening, given the possibility of ruptured veins and blood loss. I still couldn't stand, walk, or even move very much. The hospital, wisely, wanted to keep me under observation overnight. I wasn't going anywhere—and I certainly wasn't riding on any plane with my brother, no matter how much I protested. My parents weren't even flying with Caleb to the second hospital.

They were driving to Grand Junction in my father's pickup truck and leaving right away. "Colten," my father said, "we'll get you over there tomorrow."

I didn't say anything. I just sat there in pain, holding Caleb's hand, until the doctors came and took him away and we said half-hearted good-byes, talking about how we'd see him later and everything was going to be all right. It wasn't as if Caleb was listening. He had been resedated after briefly stirring in his bed. He was chemically paralyzed for his flight and breathing on a ventilator, all tubes and wires, when they finally loaded him into the ambulance at 12:36 a.m.

For the next eighty minutes, the ambulance pushed west over icy roads in the dark, with Caleb in the back, his vital signs unchanged. His blood pressure continued to spike and fall—and his heart continued to race. From 1:18 a.m. to 1:56 a.m., his pulse never dipped below 154 beats per minute—well above the normal rate of 60 to 100. He was sweating now and pale, with pupils the size of pinpoints. But when the ambulance arrived in Rifle around 2:00 a.m., the snow had stopped. The hospital's plane—a twin-engine turbo-prop—was waiting on the tarmac. Paramedics deemed Caleb to be "stable, still stable," as they placed him on a stretcher and loaded him on board.

It was 2:10 a.m. when the turbo-prop pointed its nose west, whistled down the airstrip in Rifle, and took off, wheels up and lights blinking, soaring into the night—almost exactly six hours since Caleb's crash on the mountain. Way too long, it seemed to us, given what happened next: Somewhere near the airport in Grand Junction—either just after the plane touched down, or perhaps in the air just before—my brother's heart stopped beating.

TWENTY MINUTES

MY PARENTS didn't talk much on the drive west. They were exhausted. The day, for them, had begun that morning with talk of medals—about which brother was going to win gold and which brother was going to win silver and how we would celebrate at the house that night on North Little Texas Lane. Everyone was excited: B.C., the sponsors, and, of course, my parents, handing out Texas flags for friends to wave on the mountain. But now, driving to Grand Junction through the dark and the snow, all that excitement felt like days, even weeks, ago. It was all my father could do just to keep his weary eyes focused on the twisting, unfamiliar roads. He leaned into the steering wheel and squinted into the snow coming at him, white in the headlights of the truck.

In the passenger seat—in her head, to herself—my mother prayed for us, for her sons. She felt guilty about leaving me behind in Aspen and worried about Caleb. "God," she said, "please help them be okay." Ashley, at least, was with me, back at the hospital. She slept that night on the couch in my room. I was going to be discharged the next day. Despite everything the doctors had said in Aspen about Caleb's problems, my parents, even now at two in the morning, were optimistic—cautious, of course, but upbeat about the heart surgery that Caleb needed. He was going where he needed to go: Grand Junction. After hours of waiting, he was finally going to get the care he required. And he was going to recover; my parents were sure of that. In the truck, on the drive, my father kept coming back to the same idea: Caleb walked away from the crash. *Walked away*, he kept telling my mother. He was talking and laughing. He was Caleb. He was fine. Of course, he was going to recover.

At the hospital in Grand Junction, my parents learned differently—right after they walked through the doors. In a small room, at the end of a long hall, at the end of a long night—sometime in the darkest hours before dawn—a doctor sat down before them and told them about Caleb's cardiac arrest in transport and what had happened next.

The flight crew began chest compressions, flooded his body with epinephrine—three rounds of it, to get his heart going again—and performed the procedure that doctors hadn't tried in Aspen: the pericardiocentesis. With nothing to lose—Caleb's heart had stopped beating—they inserted the long needle through his chest, into the blood-filled sac around his heart, and pulled out about twenty-five milliliters of blood. Not much. But together with the chest compressions and the medication, it was enough to resuscitate Caleb. His heart started beating again, the doctor said, after about twenty minutes.

The doctor continued talking about what was happening now: the heart surgery they were doing on Caleb in the operating room, and the hospital stay to follow in intensive care, and how it might be at least a day before they knew what effect the cardiac arrest might have had on Caleb's brain. A brain injury—caused by a lack of oxygen—was now the new concern. But my parents were no longer listening. They were nodding, they were there in the room with the doctor in the middle of the night, but they were gone, blown away by the number.

Twenty minutes.

Twenty minutes with no pulse.

To my parents, it was inconceivable.

• • •

THE STORIES on ESPN that night, and in the newspapers the next morning, included nothing about Caleb's heart problems, his troubled transport to Grand Junction, or anything about what had happened after the plane landed. No one back in Aspen—not even Chelsea Lawson, the spokeswoman we had hired to handle press inquiries—knew the full extent of Caleb's problems. As Chelsea told a *Denver Post* reporter on deadline that night, Caleb was okay, going to be just fine. "Got knocked out," she said, on the record, for the reporter's article, "but is awake and answering questions."

The stories that night, and in the morning, focused primarily on the medal winners: Hoyer taking bronze, Parsons taking silver, and LaVallee, after a two-year hiatus because of injuries, storming back into Aspen to take gold—too good, of course. "I feel terrible about the accidents that happened," LaVallee told reporters after his win in the snow. Bodin had crashed, too—and, also, badly—narrowly escaping serious injury as his runaway sled rammed into him. Unaware of the fallout from those accidents and not worried about Caleb—*he walked away*—Levi was just thrilled with the medal around his neck. "It's like, 'Pinch me!'" he said. "Is this for real?"

I awoke that morning, a Friday, to the same news as everyone else—nothing more. My parents didn't call to give me all the details about what had happened en route to Grand Junction. All I knew was that doctors had performed heart surgery on Caleb and that it had gone well. Surgeons stopped the internal bleeding in his chest wall and around his ribs. They also opened up the sac around his heart. They noted a cardiac contusion on his right ventricle, a small hematoma of his pulmonary artery, and, as they reported, "quite a bit of blood." But this, they just suctioned out. There was no artery, or heart tissue, that had perforated, requiring significant repair. Whatever had caused the buildup of blood around Caleb's heart had apparently stopped. As the surgeon noted in his report, "there was no active ongoing bleeding at this point." His prognosis was considered "guarded." As far as I knew, Caleb had survived the worst of his ordeal. I only learned the full extent of Caleb's problems after I got discharged from the hospital and together with Ashley, against the advice of my doctors, who were still worried about my pelvis injury, made the drive to Grand Junction that Saturday.

My mother, at first, only wanted to see me. Ashley waited outside. I needed to know, she said, that things were worse than I'd been told, that Caleb had survived the crash and his heart was on the mend, but that his brain was the problem now. Neither she nor my father mentioned the fact that Caleb's heart had stopped beating for twenty minutes. They couldn't bear to tell me—or anyone else—everything they knew. But they wanted me to know that Caleb, my brother, or at least the brother I knew, might not be coming back.

"I'm sorry," my mother told me.

I just looked at her, silent and dumbfounded—totally confused.

* * *

MY MOTHER still had hope. She believed in miracles and she was asking for one now. Or maybe we didn't even need a miracle. Maybe the doctors had it all wrong about Caleb. Maybe his heart hadn't stopped for as long as they believed. Or maybe somehow Caleb was strong enough to overcome it. He was strong, after all. What did these doctors know about him? They didn't know what he could do. Had they seen him get up and walk away after being speared by a snowmobile? Did they know how tough he was? When my mother's mind got to thinking, which it did with the long hours inside the hospital, she could talk herself into almost any positive outcome.

"We're hoping and praying," she told a friend.

"Doctors say we need to give it time," she told another.

"We should know something soon."

My father, on the other hand, slipped away into quiet resignation. Telling no one—not me or my mother—he began making calls to friends and family back in Texas, informing them that they needed to get to Grand Junction right away if they wanted to see Caleb one last time before he died.

"I'm sorry to have to tell you that," he said on the phone, wandering the halls of the hospital, far away from us. Admittedly, he didn't know what was going to happen in the days ahead, either. "Right now," he told his father back in Wheeler, "it's just a waiting game. Just gotta wait and see what happens." As soon as he heard the doctor's description—*twenty minutes without a pulse*—my father shut down, lost hope, and started planning for a dark and, to him, inevitable future. "From what I'm seeing and hearing," he told folks on the phone in a voice that was both solemn and distant, "he's not going to make it."

Early indications suggested my father was right. Caleb didn't wake up Saturday afternoon, even after doctors took him off the sedatives. By Saturday night, not long after I arrived at the hospital, neurologists had performed both an EEG and an MRI to check for activity in Caleb's brain. The results of both tests were abnormal—"severely abnormal," one neurologist reported. There was a lack of electrical impulses and not enough blood flow in his brain. Caleb's cerebral cortex—the core of human thought, reasoning, emotions, speech, memory, and movement—appeared dead, with no blood flow at all. For the first time, there was talk of irreversible damage—a finding that doctors made clear to us in a series of cold, written medical assessments.

"He is comatose."

"He does not follow any commands."

"He does not arouse to deep pain."

"We're here, baby," my mother whispered at Caleb's bedside,

stroking his face, perfectly at peace, looking just like Caleb. "We're not going to leave you. We're going to be here when you wake up. Take as long as you need."

I agreed with my mother, refusing to eat, sleep, shower, or even use the bathroom. I wasn't leaving Caleb's bedside and I wasn't letting go of his hand—even when my own condition worsened.

"Colten," my father said, "you need to get checked out by a doctor."

I refused to go.

"You're in bad shape, son."

I didn't care.

"I'll sit right here and hold Caleb's hand until you get back."

Okay, I finally agreed. I'd leave Caleb to see a doctor—under one condition.

"We can't give up on him," I told my parents.

By Monday, four days after the crash, doctors had officially diagnosed Caleb's problem as anoxic encephalopathy: brain damage caused by a lack of oxygen. By Tuesday, yet another neurologist in Grand Junction agreed, examining Caleb and his brain scans with fresh eyes, but coming to the same conclusion. "At this point in time," the neurologist said, "I feel his overall prognosis is very poor." My parents—with my Uncle Todd and Aunt Tammy's help—had Caleb's medical records shipped overnight to still another brain expert in California, hoping he might be able to give us better news. But he couldn't, either. "It doesn't look good," he told my mother on the phone that Wednesday. "I don't think there's anything I can do for you."

• • •

OUTSIDE, REPORTERS were circling, notepads in hand, chasing down scraps of information—anything—about Caleb. Chelsea, our publicist, made it clear to everyone that we weren't to speak to the press. Don't talk, she said. No pictures. Don't give them your name, don't give them anything. At the house in Aspen, my mother's best friend, Kelly Gonzalez, ran interference, not answering the door when reporters knocked, not talking when they called, and drawing the blinds to make it appear as if no one was home. "No comment," Kelly said again and again as reporters called. She was polite but stern, hanging up.

Still, despite our best efforts to contain the information, to control Caleb's story and protect him from the outside world, news was leaking out, making headlines across the country—and the world. From *USA Today*: "Snowmobiler Caleb Moore has brain complication." From the *Denver Post*: "Caleb Moore in desperate condition." *The Huffington Post* declared, "Family of Snowmobiler Not Hopeful," and the *Daily Mail* in London announced, "Champion snowmobiler 'not expected to survive.'" The press had squeezed it out of my grandfather, tracking him down in Wheeler, of all places, to break the story of what we were facing at the hospital. "Caleb is not doing good at all," Granddad told a reporter. "It's almost certain he's not going to make it."

Even my mother was admitting it now.

"It's not looking good," she told Kelly, crying in the hospital in Grand Junction. Down in the cafeteria, taking a break from standing vigil at Caleb's bedside with me and my father, my mother vented to her friend, rolling everything over in her mind. She regretted not hugging Caleb right before he rode that night. "I didn't get to tell him I loved him," she said. She fretted about the future. "I may never get to tell him again," she said. And she discussed, at length, the terrible, no-good choices we, as a family, were now facing about whether to keep Caleb on life support or to take him off and let him die. "How," she asked, "do I make that choice for my son?"

Years earlier, around our kitchen table back in Krum, our parents had talked to us about what we wanted in case something like this ever happened. Both Caleb and I agreed we didn't want to live our lives hooked up to ventilators, wires, or machines, like Caleb was now. "I know what I believe," Caleb said at the time. "And I know where I'm going," he added.

My mother liked to tell that story. And she told it again now to her friend.

"Well, Michele," Kelly said, "there's your answer."

My mother began to cry.

"You're not making this decision for Caleb," Kelly said. "Caleb already made it."

The patient in the hospital bed was my brother. But he was no longer there, doctors agreed. The Caleb we knew was gone—and it was time for us to let go. Still, knowing that didn't make it any easier on my mother, my father, or me.

"What am I going to do?" I shouted at my parents, crying, when they finally told me their decision.

My parents just looked at me, blinking back tears of their own.

"What am I going to do?"

• • •

STARTING THAT Wednesday, friends and family began saying their good-byes. They came by invitation to the hospital room—alone, in pairs, or in groups, huddling around Caleb's bed. Some whispered, some cried, many laughed. "I'll see you again," they said. They told stories: about the time he jumped over that canyon on his quad in Utah, or the time he gave everyone a ride on the Fourth of July in Wheeler, or the time we flipped, together, at the X Games. A few toasted him with shots of tequila. Many thanked him for being a part of their lives. "I was glad to have you in the family," Uncle Todd said. Others thanked Caleb for his guidance—for showing them how to live right. "I taught you a lot," B.C. told Caleb in the hospital room. "But I think you taught me more."

Caleb had taught him, B.C. said, about being tough and never being complacent. About respecting people and trusting people, about the value of working hard and the importance of doing more—faster—with the time we have now. "I'll never forget you," B.C. said at Caleb's bedside. And then our manager made him one other promise. "I'll do my best," he said, "to take care of your brother."

Time was now a factor—especially for my father. If we were doing this, if we were taking Caleb off life support, my father wanted to do it on Thursday, six days after the crash. The date—January 31—had significance. Thirty-one was Caleb's racing number. "That's Caleb's day," my father told the doctors, making it clear to them that it absolutely had to be Thursday, the thirty-first. But we also wanted to donate his organs. Caleb was so young and—except for his brain now—so healthy. If he had to die, he would have wanted someone else to live. Yet the organ donation required planning—more doctors, and schedules, and still more flight teams. And waiting.

My father began to worry about whether it would happen on the thirty-first, piling stress on top of stress. In a crisis where seemingly nothing had gone our way, my father wanted this. He needed this: the symbolism of a number that meant something to our family, 31.

At 9:30 a.m. on Thursday, my father got his wish: Doctors declared Caleb dead. Legally, anyway, it was over. But the final farewell—our last good-byes—would have to wait another twelve hours, until the organ transplant team finally got into place late Thursday night. They were prepped and ready in the operating room in Grand Junction, when doctors finally informed us.

It was time.

"I love you," my father told Caleb, whispering and crying in his ear.

"I'm so proud of you," my mother said, draping her arms around his neck.

And then it was my turn. I was sobbing. I was scared. For once in my life, I knew what to say. "I'm going to keep riding for you," I told him, holding a hand that was lifeless, but still warm. "I'm going to carry on your name."

We walked Caleb down the hall to the operating room, where surgeons were waiting in scrubs and gloves to open him up and take his organs. We left him at the doors, unable to go any farther. I let go of my brother's hand for the last time, they rolled him away, and what was left of my family, the Moores still standing, walked out of the hospital, stepping into the cold winter night. We had a long drive ahead of us.

We were going back to Wheeler, for a funeral.

PART III

THE MOUNTAINTOP

One of the things I found most memorable was Walden, *by Henry David Thoreau. My favorite quote is when he says, "I wanted to live deep and suck out all the marrow of life." . . . I agree with him. We only get one shot in this life, so go for it.*

—Caleb Moore, my brother, in a high school English essay

STREETS OF GOLD

THE PREACHER and his wife were watching on television the night Caleb crashed. She was sitting on the loveseat in the den on the back-side of their doublewide trailer in Oklahoma, nestled under her favorite quilt. He was sitting next to her, and together—as darkness fell on the great American plains—they were excited. Uncle Stanley and Aunt Connie had waited all day to see us competing in the X Games. They rushed through dinner to make sure they'd be ready when the ESPN telecast began, watching on their small television in the corner of the room and settling in for the night. As Aunt Connie told me later, with sadness and regret, "I was ready to be entertained."

Connie was my grandfather's sister, the daughter of panhandle pioneers, who had married Stanley a half century earlier. He was a cattle rancher and a hay farmer in Wheeler—just like the men before him—until Uncle Stanley heard the call of the Lord and left the cows behind for the Bible and ministering jobs in Oklahoma. He had seen my father grow up, presiding over my parents' marriage in Wheeler some thirty years earlier on the lawn at my grandfather's house that hot summer day. It was he who told my father, "You may kiss your bride." It was he who had turned my parents around to face the congregation, in their white handmade dress and white rented tuxedo, declaring, "I now introduce you to Mr. and Mrs. Wade Moore." And it was he, the Reverend Stanley Baker, of Cache, Oklahoma, with his wife beside him beneath that quilt in the den in the doublewide, who jumped up out of his seat, speaking to the television—and God—as Caleb crashed.

"Oh, no."

"Oh, Lord."

"Let him be okay."

Uncle Stanley and Aunt Connie—like all of our friends and family—had seen us crash many times before, if not in person, then at least on television. But right away, they thought, this crash looked different: the way Caleb went over the handlebars headfirst into the snow; the way the snowmobile—my goodness, look at the size of it—came down with all that force, nose pointed right into his chest; and the way he was just lying there, not moving, arms spread wide for so long. As ESPN showed the replays of Caleb's crash, in slow motion, from multiple angles, again and again, Uncle Stanley and Aunt Connie and everyone else watching at home soon came to the same conclusion.

"How can he *not* be hurt?" Aunt Connie asked.

Together, with the replays still running, our aunt and uncle began to pray: for healing, for my parents, for Caleb to get up—why wasn't he getting up?—and for the medical staff that was helping him, kneeling in the snow at Caleb's side. They prayed for the Lord to comfort us. "They need your comfort," they said. And they prayed for me, too. "Lord," they said, "help Colten." I was still to ride, still to crash. Uncle Stanley and Aunt Connie saw that, too, before they finally switched off the television and went to bed, uneasy and apprehensive.

By morning, they learned of the complications as phones rang across Texas and Oklahoma, with relatives calling relatives and friends calling friends with the terrible, and increasingly devastating, news. Aunt Connie heard from Aunt Shirley. Aunt Shirley heard from my grandfather. My grandfather had heard from my father and soon, it seemed, everyone knew something awful was happening in Colorado—with messages pouring in from around the world.

"Dear Mrs. Moore," one began, "I know you are probably being bombarded with messages."

"Our family is praying for Caleb," said another.

"Despite being an atheist, I prayed for him," said still one more.

Calls for prayer went out over the radio in Texas while friends penned notes from as far away as Finland and England. Some of those who wrote had known Caleb for years, others not at all. But each person seemed to feel the same way: The world was a better place with Caleb living in it. When the news finally broke that he had died, and we were returning to Wheeler with his body for the funeral, they wrote to say they were coming.

"Because of this tragic accident."

"Because he had so many friends."

"We will never forget Caleb."

"I will never forget the laughs."

More than a thousand people in all. They were coming, coming to Wheeler. They would see us soon—in the dirt and the dust on the panhandle of Texas. "If nothing else," wrote one woman, an old high school classmate of my mother's, "I feel that you guys have taught us all to love deeper and hug harder this week—and to live life grand."

. . .

WE HELD the funeral a week after Caleb died. It was inside a large warehouse of a church on the outskirts of Wheeler. The main hall didn't come close to accommodating the crowd, so the church created an auxiliary hall on site, where a few hundred more people could watch the service on large television screens. The casket—brushed metal and covered with red and white flowers—sat up front, holding my brother's body. And Uncle Stanley, serving as the preacher, spoke first. With his hands on the pulpit and a rose in the lapel of his suit coat, he looked out over the crowd and discussed the shortness of life. "We need to be prepared," he said. He talked about how none of us was assured tomorrow. "In fact," he said, "we're not any of us assured the next few hours." From the start, he addressed the question of risk—about how Caleb and I knew we were taking chances every time we climbed aboard our quads or snowmobiles, but did it anyway, living with our eyes wide open. "They knew it was dangerous," Uncle Stanley said. "They knew just one second off, or just one moment of not being committed and concentrating on what's happening, and it could be terrible. That's exactly what happened last week with Caleb."

In the front pews of the church, just a few feet from Uncle Stanley and my brother's casket, I sat listening—physically present, but not really there. At the hospital in Grand Junction, I felt like I had a job to do: Sit next to Caleb, hold his hand, and be there for him, fighting with him, especially as grim-faced doctors increasingly told us it was hopeless. But now that his fight was over, and my brother was gone, and we were sitting here inside the church in Wheeler, I was lost, swimming through darkness.

"Colten, you need to eat," well-meaning relatives told me in the days leading up to the funeral.

"Colten, get some rest."

Everyone was concerned about my fractured pelvis, all bent out of shape; doctors said it would take weeks for the injured bones to heal. "Don't get up," they told me around my Uncle Todd's house, where I was staying in Wheeler. "Take it easy. . . . Let me help you out." But I wanted to feel the pain. I wanted to hurt. I wasn't listening to anyone: not Ashley, not my parents, and not the parade of loved ones walking now to the pulpit next to Uncle Stanley to eulogize my brother before the crowd inside the church. Their words—carefully chosen—reached me as if they had traveled down a tunnel from far away.

Austin Wilson—a fellow rider and longtime friend—noted Caleb's charisma and confidence. "He was always our leader," Austin said. "Our fearless leader." B.C. told mourners about how Caleb used to tease him for getting bogged down in worries. *"Awwww, shut up, B.C.,"* our manager from California said, putting on his best Texas accent from the pulpit. Caleb had no time for such things, B.C. explained, recalling the time he and I jumped off a towering train trestle over the Colorado River, with Caleb beating me to the top. "He didn't jump off that bridge to be the first one to do it," B.C. said, recalling the day and choking back tears. "He did it first to make sure his brother was going to be safe in jumping off that bridge."

Angie Hall made the drive from Missouri for the funeral—and she spoke, too. "My son Darrin was the young man who lost his life on his quad at the Moore compound four and a half years ago," she said, dressed in black, reading from notes, and introducing herself to the crowd from the pulpit, a small woman on a big stage. "But that's not why I'm up here."

She was there, she said, because Caleb had always helped her after Darrin died, sending her messages on the anniversary of her son's death, checking in, and always calling her anytime he was riding near her home in the Ozarks. When a parent loses a child, Darrin's mother told the crowd, friends often don't know what to do, especially after the funeral ends and everyday life resumes. Fearing that they'll do or say the wrong thing, she said, or just being uncomfortable amid all the sadness, many friends grow distant and disappear over time. "But not Caleb," she said. "He always kept in touch with me—and that speaks volumes about him." My parents and I were in for a long road paved with bricks of grief, Darrin's mother explained. "It's a long, never-ending road," she explained, "and straight uphill." But she wanted me to know that Caleb was going to be right there with me. "Colten," she said, singling me out in the crowd and addressing me directly, "now you will have two guardian angels. One on each shoulder."

My mother, in her eulogy, also spoke about angels, and heaven, nervous and tapping the microphone. "Is it on?" she asked. "Are y'all hearing me?" She told the crowd she was a terrible public speaker and wouldn't get through her talk if she didn't read it off the paper in her hand. "Forgive me," she said, "if I don't look at you." But my mother undersold herself. Standing before the crowd, she was strong, the best speaker of us all, hesitating at times, but not crying, as she talked about the life Caleb had lived and the legacy he was leaving behind. "I know some really tough days are ahead for me and my family. And we're going to miss Caleb—a lot," she said. But, my mother added, with a pause, she knew some other things, too.

That Caleb had lived an extraordinary life. That the number of his days wasn't as important as the quality of them. That he was gone, that his body was dead, and that a part of my mother had died with him in Colorado. But she believed he was at peace, she told the crowd. She believed he was healed of all his injuries, riding down streets of gold, she said, and we would all see him again—someday. "I'm sure," my mother said, "he will have some pretty incredible tricks to show us by then."

• • •

THEY WANTED me to speak. At the beginning of the week, everyone made it clear that I needed to speak at the funeral, too. And while I wanted that—I wanted to honor my brother in Wheeler—I also dreaded standing up there before the crowd, a dread that only grew after my mother finished her eulogy and sat back down. She had been so poised, so perfect. And here I was already trembling before Uncle Stanley even called on me. "Colten," he said, beckoning me to the pulpit, "come and share with us."

I didn't want to go, for a million reasons. Not just because I didn't like to speak in front of others, but because standing there and looking down at my brother's casket would give his death still greater finality, a finality I almost couldn't bear. A talk like this one—this kind of challenge—was the sort of thing I always did with Caleb, with his help. He would have told me that I had to go. He would have pushed me to do it or made some joke about it, easing the anxiety of a difficult moment. Now, I had to do it by myself, stepping to the altar alone, wearing dark slacks, my long hair parted, and my brother's black-and-red riding jersey with his number—31—on the back.

"Sorry," I told the crowd.

Silence. Sniffles.

"I'm not very good at this."

Awkward laughter. Silence. More sniffles.

I stared down at my handwritten notes scrawled on a piece of white printer paper and began to talk.

"Caleb was the greatest brother that anyone could ever ask for . . ."

"One of the nicest people you'd ever meet . . ."

"He was always there . . ."

I told the crowd inside the church that Caleb had taught me everything: how to flip on the trampoline as a little boy, how to jump my bicycle at the old Cow Palace in Clyde, and, later, how to flip my quad into the foam pit in Krum. "We weren't your normal brothers," I said. "We were inseparable." Working together, riding together, traveling the world together. "Without Caleb, I don't know what I would have done growing up," I said. "I probably would have grown up just being a wuss."

The church in Wheeler erupted in laughter, breaking the tension of the moment. Yet it was no joke, I told the crowd, smiling. It was true. "I probably wouldn't have ever tried anything dangerous," I said, going on. "But with Caleb there to help me, I could do anything because I trusted him more than anyone in the world. I trusted him with my life."

"I love you, Caleb," I said at the end. And then, turning to Uncle Stanley at my side, I let out a deep breath, a weighty sigh.

"That was hard," I confessed.

Uncle Stanley wrapped me in his big cowboy arms and the crowd cheered, getting up on its feet, a standing ovation inside the church. The applause was for me—I knew that—but I believed it was for Caleb, too. I wasn't just wearing his riding jersey and number up there. Around my neck, I was wearing a gift that ESPN officials had flown to Texas, presenting it to my family just before the funeral. It was an X Games gold medal for Caleb. "It's the medal that he earned," I said, holding it up for the crowd to see. Or the medal that he should have earned. Or would have earned—someday—had it not been for what had happened in Aspen. "He just wasn't able to receive it," I said.

·   ·   ·

WE SAID our good-byes inside the church and carried Caleb's casket outside under the big Texas sky. A black hearse was waiting, loaded with flowers, to drive his body the short distance up the road to the cemetery. It was so close you could see it from the parking lot of the church—gravestones hemmed in by the electrical substation and the alfalfa fields stretching west toward Amarillo. The funeral procession, even with a crowd this large, wouldn't take any time at all by car. But my father made it clear early in the week that he had no intention of doing things the usual way. He wasn't going to send his son—his firstborn son, who loved machines and lived a life of speed and risk while driving them—to his final resting place inside a sad, clunky vehicle being driven by a funeral home director who didn't know the first thing about flying.

"I don't want his last ride to be in a hearse," my father told us. Caleb was going to the cemetery inside a car he loved.

"Colten," my father said, "get the Lightning."

The Ford Lightning pickup truck—the vehicle I had once crashed, the one he prized more than any other, opening the hood so everyone could see the engine, and then roaring off down this very road, challenging my cousins to drag races on the Quarter—was waiting outside in the parking lot to take his body to the cemetery. Pallbearers loaded his casket into the truck bed. My father drove. I sat next to him. My mother rode with our grandparents in the car behind us, her eyes fixed on the casket, and, together, with hundreds of other cars, we inched toward the cemetery—too slow for Caleb's liking, perhaps, but with a style he would have appreciated.

And then we left him. We left him there, lowering his body into the soil that my ancestors had farmed, not a mile from the old house where Caleb had once climbed up the television antenna to the rooftop as a toddler. We left him there under a tombstone, engraved with "No. 31," in the windswept dust with all the other bygone cowboys: Shorty and Bubbles, Buster and Curlie; men named Domer Lee and Buck; women named Jerry Sue and Delma Ray. We left him not far from the Hillhouse boy, who died too young, his toy trucks sinking into the red sand, and the child named Texas—"our baby," says the cracked stone—who died six months to the day he was born. We left Caleb out there, his body, with the Hales and the Millers, the Espinos and the Dollars, the Virgils and the Wingos, and everyone else who once called Wheeler home. We left my brother there on the Texas prairie, with the hot wind blowing hard from the west.

STAKEHOLDERS

ASHLEY AND I went home after the funeral, returning to the house we had shared with Caleb in suburban Corinth. She went back to work—Ashley held down a regular desk job at an insurance company—and I sat around in an empty house surrounded by my brother's vehicles, the guitars I never learned to play, and the swimming pool I didn't bother to clean, with way too much time to think. In the morning, if I was awake when Ashley left for work, she would tell me to have a good day, to get out and do something. But who was I kidding? I was never awake when she left for work, sleeping into the afternoon and subsisting on Rockstar beverages and fast-food purchases. It's not like I was riding. Because of my injured pelvis, I couldn't get back on my quad and hit the road on the tour B.C. had booked for me. I was going to be out for weeks, probably. So with nothing to do, I played video games—*Call of Duty*—and bought scratch-off lottery tickets by the fistful at the gas station up the road, and hung pictures of Caleb on every possible wall of the house, and just sat there on the couch when reporters showed up, as they inevitably did, ringing our doorbell and flooding the quiet house with its gimmicky ring tones. *Da, da, da, DUT, da, DUH! Charge!*

I never answered the door. I wasn't granting interviews. And neither were my parents. We weren't ready to talk about Caleb and what had happened; we couldn't even talk about it with each other. A hard silence had fallen upon us like a heavy snow as we grappled with the return of ordinary, everyday life. Back to work, back to routines, with everyone else the same, except us. But that wasn't the only reason we ignored the reporters chasing us down for comment. The story now was far bigger than just us: one family, moving forward. Caleb's death, in fact, was only the beginning of it, the first domino in a fast-moving public relations crisis for ESPN, the X Games, and the massive global corporation that owned both: the Walt Disney Company.

In journalism, three makes a trend. Find three events, tie them together—and you've got yourself a story. It was easy for reporters to connect the dots here, making the case that the X Games in particular—and extreme sports in general—had become too dangerous for our collective health. Just one year earlier, twenty-nine-year-old Sarah Burke died after crashing while practicing on a halfpipe in Utah. Burke wasn't just a four-time X Games gold medalist; she was a freestyle skiing pioneer who had successfully lobbied the International Olympic Committee to add her sport—freestyle skiing—to the Winter Olympics in Sochi, Russia, in 2014. The Canadian star—blond, beautiful, and well liked—would have been a favorite for the gold medal there. Instead, just like Caleb, Burke had died after internal bleeding, a cardiac arrest, and—according to a statement her family released at the time—"irreversible brain damage due to a lack of oxygen."

Before Burke, it was Paul Thacker who had made headlines. Thacker, a freestyle snowmobiler, suffered a serious spinal cord injury—again, in practice—doing basic tricks, nothing fancy, just weeks before the 2011 X Games. The injury didn't keep him from riding again—in adaptive snocross, for disabled athletes—or walking once more, with the help of a robotic exoskeleton. "Since my injury," he told ESPN just before Caleb's crash, "I have done everything except slow down." But the fractured vertabra in his back did leave him paralyzed from the waist down. And the mishaps at this year's X Games gave the press plenty more fodder for criticism. In slopestyle, a skier suffered a lumbar fracture. In the snowmobile best trick, yet another rider crashed. Worse still, his snowmobile tore off into the crowd—a "runaway sled," the *New York Times* called it, "that rocketed toward spectators, injuring a boy."

Such things happened in our world; it wasn't any secret. But Caleb's death—the first fatality during competition in X Games history—brought scrutiny to ESPN's event like never before. "Its stunts might kill," *USA Today* had declared of Ron Semiao's first Extreme Games back in 1995. "Maybe on live TV." And now that it had happened—now that this dark prophecy had effectively come to pass—the press was there to cover it. Headline, CNN: "X Games too extreme?" Headline, the *Denver Post*: "Are there no limits?" The *Washington Post* ran an editorial questioning "the dangers of extreme competition." The *Sporting News* published a column predicting there would be more tragedies. "Thousands have tweeted #prayforCaleb," the columnist wrote. "Keep those hashtags handy because flipping snowmobiles is a growth industry." At least one publication demanded immediate changes. Two weeks after Caleb's death, *The Atlantic* magazine called for ESPN to "permanently ban" the snowmobile freestyle and best trick competitions in Aspen. "ESPN has a choice," *The Atlantic* declared, "and it should choose to sacrifice a small part of a profitable competition for the overall health and safety of the extreme sports industry and its wannabe participants."

The news reports were to be expected. Caleb's death made headlines across the world. It was the response from others that surprised us at times. In internet chat rooms, on Twitter, or in the comment sections beneath the digital versions of news stories, critics weighed in, attacking me and my family. Many were just plain mean, talking about Caleb as if he was no one's brother, no one's son.

"What a dumb way to die," one person wrote.

"Extremely stupid," said another.

"My god . . . you're asking for death."

The sarcasm at times was thick and angry. *"Gee, you can actually get killed on a snowmobile? Who would have guessed?"* But internet yahoos weren't the only ones discussing Caleb's death and what it meant for all of us. Even people within the sport were asking questions now. As the paralyzed Paul Thacker put it after Caleb's crash, "When is enough enough?"

    •   •   •

THACKER—WHO had given something to the sport and, in fact, lost something—had a point. Where *was* the ceiling for guys like us? How far could we go or take it? "We're modern-day explorers," Jimmy Blaze explained at the time. "There are no new places in the world to see and discover, so you have to try to create new things. That's who everybody is." Or was. That's who we used to be, before Caleb's crash. None of us knew where we were heading now.

Within hours of Caleb's death, ESPN announced that it was conducting a "thorough review" of the sport and would adopt "any appropriate changes to future X Games." The network was now in the odd—and unenviable—position of having to cover itself, trotting out its own executives to be interviewed on its own shows about what happened, and why, and what they were going to do about it. The afternoon of Caleb's death, ESPN's investigative show *Outside the Lines* dedicated a half hour to the topic of X Games safety, interviewing several experts on the topic. "How safe does the competition appear to be?" the show's host asked his guests, shortly after announcing the news—"the sad news," he said—that Caleb had died.

Denver Post reporter Jason Blevins, who had interviewed us multiple times in Aspen, maintained on the show that our sport was safe—as safe as possible, anyway. "That said, these guys are assuming more risk," Blevins noted. "When you're spinning upside down, underneath a snowmobile and letting go of it and flopping around, turning around backwards and landing," Blevins explained, "you are assuming more risk."

Dan Lebowitz, director of Northeastern University's Center for the Study of Sport in Society, said the question now was how to mitigate that risk. "The bar keeps getting raised and the envelope keeps getting pushed," he said. "And in some ways it's a Pandora's box." How do you convince someone not to attempt a double backflip now that it's already been attempted? Or a front flip? Or some harder version of Caleb's volt? "It's tough to go backward," Lebowitz conceded. But at the same time many wondered how ESPN could go forward.

In Colorado after Caleb's death, Joe Duncan, who had originally sold ESPN's Semiao on snowmobiles in that meeting in Bristol sixteen years earlier, found it hard to believe that we would return the following year. "Why *would* snowmobiles be back?" he wondered. "It's not just this little event anymore," Duncan said. "It's ESPN. It's Disney." The lawyers were on it, presumably. And the stakeholders, too—corporate-speak for everyone who mattered. In his comments on *Outside the Lines* on the day of Caleb's death, an ESPN senior vice president of programming, Scott Guglielmino, said the "stakeholders" needed to have a conversation about pretty much everything related to this event. "We're going to take a hard look at snowmobile," he said. "We do not want to see snowmobiles landing on athletes."

MENTAL LISTS

B.C. DIDN'T call. For a few weeks after Caleb's death, he and I didn't speak—not about riding, not about the past, and not about the future, nothing. While ESPN executives began discussing their options internally, we weren't discussing anything at all. B.C. wanted to give me time to grieve alone. But the truth is, he needed time, too.

Before Caleb's death, our manager had already been angling for ways to get us out of the business of flipping heavy machines—or at least reduce our reliance on that business as a major source of our income. As he saw it, our freestyle careers had a short shelf life, just like the career of any other professional athlete, and it was never too early to plan for a future after riding. "At some point," B.C. told us, "we've got to get into some other type of business. . . . *It's better to be safe than sorry.*"

His idea, months before Caleb's death, had been tacos—buying into a Mexican restaurant chain and opening a franchise near our house in Texas. Caleb ultimately dismissed the idea. The investment was too pricey for starters—and us? We didn't know the first thing about making tacos or running a restaurant. Still, talk of the future was out there. It was on B.C.'s mind, anyway. "You're not going to be able to do this forever," he had been telling us. And as he returned home to California after the funeral, he was thinking once again about escape hatches. B.C. was no longer a hard-rocking drummer in his twenties or a young, inexperienced snowmobile manager in his thirties, like he was when Caleb first met him in Minnesota. He was closing in on forty-three and, with Caleb's death, B.C. now had hard evidence that he'd had good reason to be worried about us all these years, and maybe he hadn't been worried enough. His plan now was silence. And waiting. And thinking. He was increasingly unwilling to be part of something where people, his loved ones, could die. "I'm not going to call Colten," he told others, making a conscious decision about it.

. . .

THE SILENCE, between B.C. and me, felt normal, actually. Just about the only normal thing in a life that had been turned upside down. Caleb had always done the talking with B.C.—and then told me where to be and what to do. Caleb had also paid our bills, filed our taxes, fixed our machines. He knew we had a show in Las Vegas next week or in Mexico the week after that. And he remembered important things—like to bring his passport with him—while I forgot, leaving my documents at home. Without him now, the bills piled up, the swimming pool in the backyard crawled with black mold, the lawn outside grew into a jungle of Texas crabgrass, tall and waving in the breeze, and even the simplest shopping errands at a local Walmart or Target felt impossible to consider, much less accomplish.

"You need underwear?" Ashley asked me.

"Maybe."

"Maybe isn't really a helpful answer," she said.

"Maybe, yeah?"

"I'm trying to make a mental list here, Colten."

Mental list . . .

My list included the following: Sleep late and take pain medication for ailing pelvis. Call a friend. Was Sonic open yet? No? Sit around. Play video games, *Call of Duty*, shooting mythical enemies with a fake gun on a massive television in our upstairs loft. Eat. Come back to the house. More *Call of Duty*. If I were playing the video game—joystick in hand and guns firing—I couldn't think. I was occupied. My mind couldn't wander off into dark places, chasing memories and getting into trouble. I had a mission and a job to do, even if the mission and the job were make-believe. Play until Ashley gets home. Then have dinner. Broiled steak, pasta, or takeout. Then maybe start drinking? A couple of beers, sometimes more. Nights were the hardest. Sleep was impossible. I began guzzling Nyquil to make it more likely that I'd doze off, but even that didn't seem to help after a while. Ashley would awake in our bed to find me sobbing, my body hot and heaving between the sheets, inconsolable, as I pondered everything, asking questions with no answers.

What if the hospital in Aspen had had a cardiothoracic surgeon on staff? What if doctors had paged the cardiologist? What if it hadn't snowed that night, and helicopters had been flying, and time hadn't been lost in Aspen, just waiting? Might that have changed things? It was hard for me not to think about that. One surgeon in Grand Junction put it this way in a written report, summarizing the problems we had faced in a single, haunting line: "For reasons that are not totally clear," he said, "there was a long delay."

Nobody talked about these things on *Outside the Lines*, or in the magazine articles they wrote calling for the ban of our sport, or in the mean-spirited comments they made on the internet. Because nobody knew of these details. They were ours to consider and ours alone. And yet, at the bottom of it all, underneath all of the what-ifs and could-have-beens, I knew that even if everything had gone perfectly that night, Caleb still might not have lived. He had been flipping a large machine in the air—and he had crashed, badly. This choice had been ours. We were responsible for what had happened. No one forced us to flip, no one told us to go. We did it because we loved it, and now my brother was dead. And that was hard to accept, too—maybe the hardest part of all.

Late at night, back in Texas, I was burdened by these thoughts. Unwilling to discuss my feelings with Ashley—cowboys don't cry and cowboys don't talk—I often just got out of bed and went back to the video games in the loft.

"I'm going to go play," I told her.

"Really, Colten?" she asked, disapproving.

I just shrugged and walked out of our bedroom, padding across the carpet in the dark and plopping back down again on the giant beanbags in front of the television, where a war was raging and other players, with their made-up, anonymous names, whoever they were, were waiting for me to join. SOLDIER_53_ was there and Canadian-Girl, babymoney1, and TheExpert. They didn't know me and I didn't know them. We were strangers playing video games—together, but alone in the middle of the night, asking nothing of each other, and not wanting to, either, while the voice inside the game spoke to us, telling us what to do.

"Search and destroy."

"Defend the objective."

"Get moving."

"He's gone."

Sometimes, afraid of the silence, I played until dawn.

"Finish the mission. You're all that remains."

·   ·   ·

ASHLEY WAS getting worried about me.

"I'm fine," I told her.

She didn't think so. And it wasn't just because of the all-night *Call of Duty* binges in the dark. We had started arguing. She didn't think it was necessary for me to plaster the walls of the house with photos of

Caleb, turning our foyer into a museum to the Brothers Moore and the corner of our living room into something of a shrine. I don't mean to sound cold, she told me, "but we can't make our whole lives about this."

She was concerned that Caleb's death was consuming me from the inside out—and she was also worried about my consumption, in general. The beer didn't trouble her as much as the shots of whiskey that friends bought for me—or I bought for myself—whenever we went out at night. Maybe, Ashley suggested, I could at least stop taking shots? But I didn't listen—and, again, we argued.

She told me I had problems.

"No, I don't," I snapped.

She told me I needed to get my act together.

"I've got it together," I insisted.

Both she and my parents thought I needed to talk to a therapist about my pain—or, at the very least, I needed to talk to them about it. That wasn't happening. I didn't want to give anyone anything. But finally one night in the kitchen, I broke down, crying while Ashley cried, too.

"I know you're sad," she told me. "But you can't treat me like this just because you're sad."

She wanted me to know that we were in this together. "I'm sad, too," she sobbed.

"I'm sorry," I told her, apologizing. I didn't want to act this way—Ashley didn't deserve it—and I didn't want to feel this way, either. But I didn't know how to make it stop.

"I'm just so *angry*," I confessed.

Sometimes, for reasons I couldn't explain, I even courted the anger, seeking it out, staring it down, and wrestling it to the floor. I'd swing back and forth like a silver ball on a pendulum, wanting to feel nothing in one moment, then everything the next. I'd let the pain fill me up inside until it spilled over, watching the video of Caleb's crash on the internet or just standing there in the workshop at my parents' house in Krum, surveying the remains of my brother's life. There are the quads he rode and the trophies he won. There's the snowmobile from Aspen, still bent and mangled from the crash, the chassis and handlebars in need of repair. And there's me standing alone in the middle of it all, shouting, wailing—screaming at the world.

•   •   •

MY PARENTS weren't doing much better. In the mornings before Caleb's death—not every day, but as often as they could—the two of them prayed together, holding hands in the living room, before heading off to work and going their separate ways. After the crash, that stopped. My father didn't feel so much like holding hands anymore and my mother didn't want to press him. She still read the Bible every morning at the kitchen table, but she stopped going to Bible study on Tuesday nights with the women in Ponder, the next town over. Couldn't explain why. Just didn't feel like it, my mother said. For one thing, it was exhausting to have people tell you the same thing over and over, even if they meant well. *"Oh, you're just so strong."*

My mother didn't feel strong at all—that was the problem. She was second-guessing everything. She had prayed for a miracle in Grand Junction. "Why didn't we get one?" she asked. Was it something she had done—or hadn't done? At night, when darkness set in on the Texas prairie, my mother worried that she bore some responsibility for what had happened, that somehow she was to blame for Caleb's bad luck, and both of my parents worried about me—a lot.

My father focused on practical matters. All of our bills were in Caleb's name. We needed to get those switched over into my name, my father said. Caleb had always paid the mortgage. I needed to start doing that now, too, my father instructed me. In the sadness we were all feeling, there was also a lesson, subtle and unstated, but true: It was time for me to grow up, to be my own man, and start making decisions for myself.

Did I want to keep Caleb's Ford Lightning?

Yes, I said. Absolutely.

What about the Mustang?

Again, yes. No debate about it, I told my father. There was no way I was selling the objects that meant the most to Caleb, even if the vehicles were just going to sit, unused, in our garage, like monuments on wheels.

Okay, then, my father said. I needed to start paying those bills, too. Which were expensive. And switch the car insurance into my name. Which also cost money out of pocket. Rockstar had paid for Caleb's funeral, covering every detail: from the flowers, to the casket, to the airplane flight that ferried his body from Colorado to Oklahoma and then, overland by hearse, to Wheeler. My parents hadn't paid a dime for any of that. But we were on our own now, wading through paperwork in the house, organizing documents into stacks, and making phone calls, chasing down the hidden details of a life, the life my brother lived.

There was at least one receipt that didn't make any sense to us. Caleb had recently spent a large sum of money at a high-end jewelry store in a mall north of Dallas—a big purchase that, for the most part, was out of character for him. But we didn't have anything to show for it—no actual piece of jewelry to correspond with the paper trail. My father called the store and asked if perhaps they had something under the name Caleb Moore. Maybe something on layaway? They did, we were told. Caleb had bought a watch in recent weeks, they informed us, and it was there, we could see it, if we wanted to drive down.

We had no intention of keeping the watch. The mystery timepiece, a David Yurman design, had cost Caleb about eight thousand dollars—a lot of money, way too much, given the questions about the future of the X Games and freestyle snowmobiling in general and all my sponsorship deals connected with both. Before we made the trip to the jewelry store, my father informed a manager there that we hoped they would allow us to return the watch and get out of Caleb's layaway deal, in light of what had happened, the unfortunate circumstances.

"Is that possible?" my father asked.

Of course, the manager told us. They knew Caleb, knew what had happened to him, and had been expecting our call. They were willing to work with us.

"Sorry for your loss," a saleswoman said when we arrived, before disappearing to retrieve the watch from the back of the store. My father and I waited together until she returned, carrying a large, fancy box, setting it on the counter, and then opening it for us to see.

"Oh, no," my father gasped.

The watch had been purchased in conjunction with Caleb's Mustang. Like the car, this piece was an exclusive design. The watchmaker had only manufactured 150 of them, and Caleb had clearly requested which one he wanted. On the back of the new watch—black and shiny, in vulcanized steel—the timepiece was engraved with its limited-edition number.

"*31.*"

We looked at each other, just shaking our heads.

"It's still a lot of money," my father told me. But he knew what I wanted to do. "It's your call," he said.

We took the watch home. I was keeping it.

SOME PEOPLE
HAVE IT

FOR A long time—weeks—promoters didn't call B.C. about me. No one wanted to press him—much less me—about my plans for the future and whether I intended to ride again. It was the biggest question on everyone's minds and also the one nobody wanted to ask, for fear of offending me, sounding callous in the face of my loss, or coming off as petty—a petty, self-interested promoter just looking for a rider to fill a slot in a show. My friends and family didn't even want to ask the question, tiptoeing around the topic as if broaching it might threaten to shatter whatever trust existed between us. The feeling was, when I was ready to tell them something, I would speak my mind. Until then, it was better to stay quiet, whispering about the possibilities and asking friends behind my back. Nick Hickey, a close friend and former rider, got the questions all the time.

"Is he going to keep riding?"

"I'm not sure," Nick replied.

"Do you know?"

"It's up to him," Nick said.

Riders, Nick included, had certainly walked away over less. Nick was a happy bear of a man, with a large Celtic cross tattooed on one arm and an eternally scruffy beard. He was chatty, loud, and unable to keep a secret—my opposite in almost every way. We had met him nearly a decade earlier racing quads in Texas. He joined us on the road for our first season of nationals, traveling across America in the back of my father's old trailer with us. And we had remained close friends, bonding in part over the many riding injuries Nick had suffered—often right in our own backyard. The worst was his broken foot and leg in 2010 that required four surgeries, put him in a wheelchair for nine months, and ultimately forced him out of the sport at age twenty-one and into a string of regular jobs, such as his latest: installing heating and air-conditioning units.

"Some people have it," Nick said once, "and some people don't." Even those who did have it—this ability to flip and tolerance for risk—could lose it, just like that. With just the slightest hesitation, you could lose your edge. And if you did, then you quit, and people understood, no judging. You could ride through a lot of things, including pain, but not doubt, not the questions. "Why am I doing this?" Nick asked himself after his rash of injuries and just before he gave up riding for good. "Is it necessary for me to do this?"

That's all people wanted to know from me now: Was I doing this? Was I coming back this season, or what? What was I thinking? It was important to know because, among other things, I was under contract. I was supposed to flip my quad on tour for months with the Nuclear Cowboyz, the traveling freestyle motocross show. The eleven-stop tour had started before the X Games. I had missed gigs just to be in Aspen. And now, with everything that had happened there, I had missed several more: Pittsburgh and San Antonio, Detroit and Tampa. Finally, a Nuclear Cowboyz tour manager called B.C., politely asking for the answer that everyone wanted: Could he count on me to ride in, say, New Orleans or Atlanta? Was I coming back?

You're calling the wrong guy, B.C. told the manager on the phone. "I'm not pressuring him to do anything," B.C. said. As far as he was concerned, my riding days were over. "Colten can find another career," he explained. "And I'm going to help him with that." But B.C.

gave the tour manager my phone number. If he wanted to know what I was thinking, B.C. said, he could call me himself. Suddenly my phone was ringing in Texas and I was asking myself a question of my own: Why were the Nuclear Cowboyz calling me instead of B.C.?

"Do you know?" I asked B.C.

B.C. explained his position: He wasn't sure how I felt and wasn't comfortable speaking for me. He didn't want to push me or even seem like he was pushing me; and he understood the tour wanted me back, but that he didn't care either way whether I rejoined it or not. If I didn't feel like riding anymore, that was just fine with him.

"Let me ask you something," I told B.C. "You think Caleb would want me to quit?"

"We both know that answer," B.C. replied, fighting back tears. But what Caleb might have wanted didn't matter now. The question, B.C. said, was what did I want, given everything that had happened?

"You call them," I informed B.C., "and tell them I'm coming back to the tour."

. . .

THE FOAM pit in my parents' backyard in Krum seemed like a good place to start flipping again—ATVs, not snowmobiles. Jump there, with the foam to keep me safe. Get the feel of riding again, both mentally and physically. Then, after I've grown comfortable again, move over to the dirt landing. Right away, I struggled. Not with the jumping so much, but with the coming back down, even into the foam.

"Man, it hurts," I said.

My pelvis was still sore. Even straddling the quad left me grimacing, in pain. Maybe I was trying to come back too soon; my parents worried about that. Others—strangers, mostly—thought I should never ride again. They believed that returning to flipping wasn't just stupid; it was selfish, whispering behind my back about my decision: *"How could he do that? How could he put his family through that?"*

But my parents didn't think it selfish at all. As hard as it was for them to see me return to the foam pit in our backyard—my mother standing in the window and praying—watching me walk away would have been harder. To quit now—to dismantle the foam pit, knock down the dirt landing, sell our machines, and leave behind the life Caleb and I had pursued together all these years—seemed not only like a failure, but a rejection of the core principles that made us Moores. And, anyway, what were my other options? I didn't have a college degree. I didn't have a résumé, or relevant experience, or—really—any marketable skills whatsoever. If I weren't jumping quads or snowmobiles, I figured I'd be painting houses, or working on a landscaping crew, or just sitting around, unemployed, playing *Call of Duty* until Ashley threw me out of my own house. Riding wasn't just a job; it was part of my identity, the thing that made me me—Colten, an X Games medalist, a winner. "It's not even a question," I told skeptics. "Of course, I want to ride."

So, with Nick's help, I pulled the quad out of the foam pit after that first jump and went again. And again. And again. Aching, yes, hurting physically, but not nervous to be riding and flipping again. There were no dark visions of Darrin, and blood-soaked soil, and helicopters landing in pastures. There were no thoughts of snowstorms, and doctors, and Caleb crashing in Aspen. There was just me, and a machine, and a ramp, and a trick to pull. Out here, I realized almost right away, life was simpler, boiled down—and, in one significant way, it was better.

I could talk to Caleb at his grave site in Wheeler—and I did that. I could hang those pictures on the walls of my house—and, of course, I did that, too. I could keep his cars and his watch and wear his number everywhere, stitched into the Rockstar cap on my head. And that was fine. But nothing compared to the peace I found here—even with my banged-up pelvis, in the foam-filled backyard in Krum, with no one watching. Doing the thing we had always done together, I could feel Caleb. He was no longer far away, my brother who was gone, an abstract idea, just a memory. He was right there. He was with me.

It was time to head back out on the road, but with a few changes. B.C. asked that, on the first tour stop, I just watch the show, like a spectator—no flipping and no jumping. He trusted that everything was fine. I wouldn't tell him I was ready to go if, in fact, I wasn't ready. Still, B.C. wanted me to get used to being back in the arena, under the lights, before the crowd—or rather, he wanted to let everyone else get used to me, the new me. They could say the things they needed to say, offer their condolences. Then the following week, B.C. said, I could flip. Business as usual.

Back in Krum, my father insisted on a few things of his own. For one, he wanted Nick Hickey—our gregarious friend, the former rider, who quit because of all his injuries—to help me out around the workshop, getting my quads ride-ready. I knew more than most about how to repair a machine, but not nearly as much as Caleb had known. He loved to tinker, getting down on the floor in my parents' workshop, pulling engines apart and then putting them back together, sometimes until dawn. If we blew a gasket, Caleb could fix it. If we bent an axle, Caleb could fix that, too. And if you were just standing there watching him work, he got angry. "Go get a shovel," he said, "and dig a hole." Do something. Or better yet, get to work—with him.

Nick filled this role now. Like Caleb, he knew everything about machines, and having him around eased some of my parents' mechanical concerns. But they also wanted to make sure I had the emotional support I needed when I was out on the road—someone I could talk to, or not talk to, just be with—and for that my father had a discussion with Marco Picado.

"You need to step up," he told Marco.

Marco was twenty-four, Costa Rican by birth, and, as far as we were concerned, wealthy. In Central America, his family owned a television station and employed hired help. Marco didn't know how to cut the grass. They had people for that. Marco didn't know how to do his laundry. They had people for that, too. But Marco also knew loss. His father died when he was just a boy. And perhaps more important, he knew me. Caleb and I had taught Marco how to flip two years earlier. He hadn't just lived in our foam pit, but lived, for a while, at my parents' house, sleeping in an extra bedroom. They cared for him when he got injured, helped him find a dentist when he crashed and smashed his teeth. My father had even carried him up and down the stairs after he broke his leg. "Crazy cowboys," Marco called us. "Only in Texas." Now my father wanted something in return.

"You're a part of the family," he told him. Like another brother. No one was ever going to take Caleb's place. My father wasn't asking Marco, or Nick, or anyone else to do that. But he needed Marco's help looking after me, especially as I headed back out on the road.

My parents, after much discussion, weren't going to go to my first flip show on the Nuclear Cowboyz tour. They didn't want to put me under any extra pressure to jump just because they had traveled to be there for it. If I wanted to back out at the last minute, I could back out—that's how they wanted me to feel.

But it wasn't necessary. I traveled to New Jersey—and flipped my quad. I traveled to California—and flipped it there, too—signing autographs with the other riders after each show. And then I was off, back on the road, preparing for a big international tour across Gabon and Russia, with B.C., Marco, Ashley for a while, and one additional traveling companion. My mother wanted to come, too.

It was presented to me as a mother-and-son bonding trip, a chance for my mother to get out of Krum, for once, and travel the

world—with me. But I understood the real reason behind the idea.
She was worried about me—worried that I was depressed, that because of my depression I might spiral out of control, get reckless, and
not care if I crashed, even died. It was one thing for her to let me go
and flip my quad on the Nuclear Cowboyz circuit; I'd been doing that
tour for years. It was quite another for her to let me go to Africa and
Siberia—alone—for a month, where I'd be flipping the snowmobile
again. It wasn't really a discussion; it was the reality. My mother was
coming with me—to Gabon first, then Russia—and keeping a journal
about our travels, writing everything down.

"Day 1: June 24—Okay, the day finally got here!"

"Day 3: June 26—Everyone was laughing and having a great time."

"Day 6: June 29—It's finally show day! . . . The exhibition was impressive."

"Day 12: July 5—I am thinking I brought way too much stuff."

The trip, by riding standards, was a success—impressive, as my
mother said. We had all the usual problems that we typically face
when riding overseas: mechanical malfunctions and disorganiza-
tion, odd ramps and faulty foreign sleds. When I crashed during one
show, I got up, relatively unscathed. When the snowmobile broke
down during another—its track freezing up, not moving—I managed
to get it fixed at the last moment and ride anyway.

"For you," I told my mother.

And when the shows were over, we partied, walking back to the
hotel after daybreak on more than a few occasions. I craved a release after flipping my machine in the air—a moment to celebrate
being alive with friends, after flirting with death. Even if I didn't acknowledge it out loud, I knew that's what I was doing—we all did—
especially after what had happened to Caleb. I needed the night to
mark the fact that I had survived the day. But the parties came at
a cost, with the alcohol-fueled madness tearing off the scabs that

had grown over our emotional wounds in the months since Caleb's death.

One night, drunk on vodka in a hotel lobby in Siberia, B.C. and I argued for reasons neither of us would be able to recall—even the next morning. All I remember is, I was angry that he had mentioned Caleb's name and he was angry that I was angry. "I loved him, too," B.C. snapped at me. And before it was over, he had quit a couple of times and I had fired him a couple of times, for good measure, and we were hugging, all forgiven. "I care about you," B.C. told me, "like a son."

Another night, in a Russian town near Kazakhstan, I broke down at a bar where they served drinks called Angel Face and Monkey Nail and Kaboom. I just started crying and couldn't stop. My mother was there, along with the promoters and several other people, and no one knew what to say to me. Marco finally took me outside, where he listened and I cried some more. "I just wish Caleb was here," I told him.

We were all raw with emotions we couldn't explain. And traveling together, penned up with each other for a month, probably wasn't helping matters. At a late-night campfire on the ocean on the African coast of Gabon, my mother became angry—then panicked—when I walked off alone and disappeared for too long. While the others drank and laughed around her, warm and happy by the fire, my mother became convinced that I was drowning. I had drowned. I had gone off for a swim in the ocean at night, like an idiot, and now the only son she had left was dead, floating away. By the time I walked back to the party, unaware of her concern, my mother didn't know whether to cry or slap me in the face.

"What's the problem, Mom?" I asked her after everyone else went to bed, sensing her anger.

"Colten," she said, "you just don't understand."

It wasn't that I had walked away from the party, she explained.

It was everything else. It was not knowing where I was, or how I was, or what might happen to me today or tomorrow or the day after that. "You just don't understand what that does to me," she said. "I just can't imagine losing you, too."

I hugged my mother long and hard, for maybe the first time since the funeral, whispering as she cried, apologizing again and again, and making promises I intended to keep.

"I'm not going to leave you," I told her.

ON BOARD

THE SILENCE out of ESPN headquarters in Bristol, Connecticut, was starting to become a cause for alarm in the freestyle snowmobiling community. Months after it had promised a thorough review of the sport, we had heard nothing from the network about its plans for snowmobiles in the next X Games or beyond. Not even our most connected players—Joe Duncan or Levi LaVallee—knew anything about what the network intended to do. And the little we did know, what we had heard, didn't bode well for the future. Just weeks after Caleb's death, ESPN canceled all best trick competitions—in both the Summer X Games, for motorcyclists, and Winter X, for snowmobilers. "Nobody can eliminate risk in its entirety," the network said in a statement. But in an effort to stage events "that are as safe and organized as possible," best trick was out. ESPN also canceled a freestyle snowmobiling exhibition planned that spring for its European X Games in France.

Executives seemed anxious—and some sponsors did, too. Companies that, until now, had supported riders were pulling out of sponsorships, worried about liability and a public relations backlash against the sport. Major snowmobile organizations, not connected to ESPN, canceled events, too, following the cable network's lead. Promoters still held snocross races that winter in Michigan and Wisconsin. But gone was the flipping, canceled via press release and prepared statements.

"We're absolutely devastated . . ."

"Caleb's death has affected us all . . ."

"It is best not to move forward with the freestyle events . . ."

One reporter wrote that these events had been canceled "out of respect" for my brother—an idea that was as preposterous as it was infuriating. Caleb would have been livid about how his death was playing out, hurting the sport and the people who loved it most: the riders. Heath Frisby—who had won eight medals in the X Games before Caleb's death—lost at least one major sponsor, scared off by what had happened to Caleb. Justin Hoyer—who won the gold medal in our first year in Aspen—was soon to announce his retirement, due, at least in part, to Caleb's crash, at least according to statements he made to the press. "It's affected me probably more than most people," Hoyer told ESPN. "You try to tell yourself that all this is what you signed up for. But you really didn't." Hoyer's bronze medal in the freestyle event where Caleb crashed would be his last in the X Games. And none of us knew if we would have the chance to medal again— even if we wanted to. The sport was in crisis, with rumors flying. One said ESPN was going to ban snowmobiles. Another said the network was going to ban all motorsports—period. As Joe Duncan put it, "the worst thing that could ever happen" had happened. Anything seemed possible now.

• • •

MY GRANDMOTHER died in Wheeler that August. Brain cancer. More bad news for my family—and another funeral. We buried her in the sandy ground next to my brother in the cemetery by the electrical substation and tried to move on—again. Her death, at least, had been expected, anticipated for months. Still, it was hard being back in the cemetery, with the horned frogs hopping in the dust and the mourners gathering anew, asking how I was doing, asking lots of questions.

Most of my big trips were finished for the year. Now was the time
when we usually started thinking, at least, about the X Games, and
the tricks we might try there, and the medals we might win. And, of
course, people just had to ask about that. They wanted to know if I
was returning to Aspen.

I just shrugged. Couldn't say, for sure. All I knew was this: We had
made it clear to ESPN—through back channels and the few public
comments we did make—that I wanted to return. In the months since
my brother's crash, we never criticized the network or the X Games in
any of the hundreds of news stories written about Caleb. We didn't
hold press conferences or point fingers, assigning blame. From us,
there was no grandstanding, and no lawyers. No lawsuit, or threats
thereof. My parents didn't even consult a lawyer. Just wasn't in our
nature. We come from a place where a handshake means something,
where land and cattle can be bought and sold on a promise, where
neither men nor women are prone to whining, and where intentions
can't be reinterpreted after the fact.

Here's what we knew about intentions: Caleb wanted to flip
his snowmobile that night in Aspen. He had done so—with full,
unblinking knowledge that if he under-rotated that flip, or over-
rotated it, clipped the knuckle or flatlanded it, yardsale-ing his sled
all over the snow on national television, it could go badly for him.
He knew that he could get seriously hurt, that he could end up like
Paul Thacker, paralyzed, or like Darrin Hall, dead too young. And
he was willing to do it, anyway. "I would much rather be taken out,"
Caleb told a reporter just one year before his death, "while doing
something I love."

So, in the months after Caleb died, when major television networks
and national newspapers called, baiting us to go negative for the stories they were writing about our sport, we declined to give interviews.
No comment—again. No, thanks—again. Even though things didn't

go the way we had hoped in Aspen and Grand Junction, the reality remained the same: Caleb wanted to be there, soaring through the air. I did, too. Even knowing everything we did now—about what might happen and how it could end—we still would have jumped our sleds that night. Not because we're stupid—as the internet critics like to say—but because we accepted these sorts of risks every single day, and I was willing to accept them again, to live the life I wanted. I wanted to return to the X Games.

ESPN, the other riders, and our sport's organizer, Joe Duncan—they all knew where I stood on the matter. The fact that the network hadn't already canceled the snowmobiling events, Duncan said, was a direct result of how we had chosen to handle Caleb's death. Still, Duncan hadn't heard anything out of Bristol—until finally, late that summer, he got a phone call.

X Games officials wanted to meet—quietly, behind the scenes, with no reporters and no headlines on *SportsCenter*—at a hotel near the airport in Minneapolis. The freestyle competition wasn't out, but it wasn't in, either. Executives were only going to go forward if we could find a way to create an event that was both entertaining and safe. The question before Duncan was simple: What could we do to make the sport safer for everyone involved?

In advance of the meeting—knowing that the entire sport was potentially at stake—Duncan started reaching out to riders to get their ideas. When it came time to meet at the hotel, he showed up with a pair of important riders at his side: Levi LaVallee and Heath Frisby, two of the sport's biggest names. Unlike me, Levi and Heath could be objective, cleaving off the emotion of what had happened to focus on practical matters. But they also had something else I didn't, and never would: northern blood, with roots in Longville, Minnesota, and Middleton, Idaho. They were true snowmobilers, with a deep knowledge of the sport going back to Hetteen and

Johnson and Rippey, the early pioneers. They understood these machines better than anyone and had a lot to lose if ESPN walked away.

The meeting at the hotel in Minneapolis was casual. Everyone in attendance had known everyone for years. There was no tension to be broken or awkward introductions to be made. ESPN didn't even bother to rent a conference room for the day, holding the talks inside a regular room instead. And together, sitting around on couches and chairs, Duncan, LaVallee, and Frisby pleaded our case, making two key suggestions.

First, they recommended that the X Games require riders to wear chest protection—a Kevlar flak jacket originally manufactured for soldiers—under their jerseys. Such protection probably would not have changed the outcome for Caleb. He was wearing a chest protector—albeit a different kind—when he crashed the year before. Still, such protection had been mandated for years in snocross. And given what had happened, it seemed like a logical, if belated, requirement in freestyle, too. Second, they suggested that all riders install springs on their ski tips—springs that when the sled was in flight would pull the tips back, tuck them in closer to the sleds ever so slightly, and reduce the chances of ski tips planting into the snow, as they did in the crash that killed Caleb. LaVallee had been using such springs for years, he said. He didn't see any reason why the changes couldn't be implemented across the sport, and he left the hotel that day feeling good about our chances. He thought the sport would be back in some capacity.

Still, no one knew for sure. Even if the X Games officials wanted to go forward with the changes the riders had offered, they had bosses back in Bristol, who more than likely reported to still other bosses at the Walt Disney Company, who almost assuredly didn't know the difference between a volt and a corolla, a holy man and a flying squirrel.

Our fate now rested in the hands of businesspeople making business decisions.

. . .

B.C. ALMOST didn't care at this point. Whether freestyle returned to the X Games or not didn't keep him up at night. Perhaps more than any of us, he saw both sides of the equation. Yes, my returning to Aspen to compete again would be a great story—a redemption ride that reporters would want to cover. And yes, it was the way Caleb would have wanted it. But B.C. also knew that my return would come with great pressure to perform and win for Caleb. There was no redemption in crashing—again. Or getting injured—again. That was also the sort of story that reporters would get excited to cover. If they couldn't have the heartwarming tale of success, they'd take the devastating narrative of failure—and run with it. Perhaps more important, B.C. was still scheming to get me out of the sport altogether, hoping to keep the last of the Moore brothers safe—if not for me, then for my parents. As summer turned to fall, he didn't mention the X Games, booking me other gigs to fill my schedule and occupy my mind.

In mid-November, we flew back across the Atlantic for my second overseas tour of the year—ten stops across Sweden, Norway, Germany, England, Scotland, the Netherlands, and Belgium. For the three weeks, I was going to be flipping my quad with the Nitro Circus, a show founded by seventeen-time X Games medalist Travis Pastrana. Then it was back to the United States, and to Florida, to begin training with the Nuclear Cowboyz yet again. There were no plans to return to Aspen.

As we landed in Sweden, B.C. got word that ESPN's official decision was about to be made public. The X Games, a mere nine weeks away, were going to include freestyle once again—with some changes, but not wholesale reinvention. At the hospital in Aspen, there still wouldn't be a cardiothoracic surgeon, a costly specialty that most small hospitals do not have. But local medical officials did push for—and win—other changes to improve care and communication on the mountain. Before Caleb's crash, medical teams at the X Games communicated on four different radio channels on site. In the reconfigured X Games, medical teams—whether they worked for ESPN, ski patrol, or the hospital—would be on one radio channel. And local paramedics would have increased responsibilities. They would no longer wait for ESPN's own medical crews to assess the situation and then call for the ambulance, as they had in the past. They, too, could enter the field of play, giving immediate assessments of injured athletes, shoulder to shoulder with ESPN's crews.

None of these changes would have altered the outcome for Caleb. But the modifications—along with the ones Duncan, LaVallee, and Frisby had presented in Minnesota weeks earlier—made the competition, at least on paper, safer, a better games. In short, we were back, with some risks diminished and others not. I was going to have my chance to return to Aspen—if I wanted it.

"So what do you think about X Games?" I asked B.C.

We were jetlagged and sleepy in the middle of the day, sharing a room inside a giant white box of a hotel in Stockholm. He was lying on his bed and I was lying on mine. We were exhausted, but I needed to know: What did he think about Aspen?

"I can take it or leave it," B.C. said. He claimed he was focused on this trip, right now.

"But I'm talking to you about X Games," I persisted. "What do you think about it?"

Again, B.C. dodged the question, dancing around it and not even looking at me from across the room. "If you don't go," he said, "no big deal." But if I wanted to go, that was fine, too. "I don't really care," B.C. said, shrugging.

I just stared at him, confused and almost angry.

"Hey, man," I told him. "Look over here."

I didn't have any doubts about what I wanted to do.

"I'm taking the gold," I said, "so you better get on board."

GAMBLING

I WORRIED about the reminders in Colorado—we all did: being back at the training lodge on Electric Mountain and the rental house on North Little Texas Lane. Maybe it was best if we didn't stay at the usual house—this was a topic of conversation with my parents before going back to Aspen that January. Or maybe we should switch to a different training location, change something. My family considered everything, from every angle. But ultimately, we decided against altering our routine. There were going to be reminders everywhere.

The smell of snow.

The glare of the television lights on the mountain.

Joe Duncan standing there in his parka, counting down to the live telecast.

"One minute."

"Thirty seconds."

Three, two, one . . .

I needed to prepare myself for everything, my father told me. Friends and family were going to be there—roughly five dozen in all, far more than usual. Where did I want them? How did I want to handle the crowds? The media were going to be there, too. "A lot of media," my father said. ESPN was already calling, hoping to do a sit-down interview on camera in Krum that they could play to kick off the live telecast of the freestyle event. Was I ready for that? I had to be, my father said. "There's not going to be anything you can do about it." There were going to be questions, and requests, and autograph signings, and pressure—more pressure than I had ever faced before. For the first time at the X Games—and perhaps the first time in my entire life—I would be the center of attention, no longer the little brother in the shadows, but the main attraction, with a story to tell, a team of publicists, and a host of Twitter hashtags they had crafted for me: #RideforCaleb and #MooreGold.

I understood the reasoning behind the hashtags. I wasn't some dinosaur; I was twenty-four, and like everyone else my age, I was on social media all the time, hashtagging my life away. But that didn't mean I had to like the idea. The whole notion of #MooreGold was especially hard for me to accept. For one thing, it sounded cocky. Despite what I had told B.C. in the hotel room in Stockholm, I had my doubts about Aspen, about returning. If we had learned one thing about the X Games, it was that anything could happen—good or bad. I could win or I could end up back in the hospital, crashing again. #MooreCrashing. I worried about under-rotating my sled like Caleb had, ski tips into the snow. The newly mandated springs weren't going to change things that much. It was still risky—"gambling," one rider called it just before the competition. And the hashtag campaign didn't seem to take any of that into account, heaping still more pressure upon me. #MooreGold? What if I failed? What then? But I kept my fears to myself, doing what was requested, because if I was going back to Aspen, I wanted the world to understand why.

I agreed to the Twitter hashtags and the autograph signings. I welcomed anyone who wanted to attend. Of course, friends and family could come. "I want it to be just like it's always been," I told my father. "I want it to be the same." My only request was that my friends give me space the day of the event. No crowds in our trailer. Just family. And no talk about the past. I didn't need to sit around the house on North Little Texas Lane reliving memories, either painful or happy. There were going to be too many memories as it was. But I was willing to talk about them at least once, granting the ESPN interview in Texas and speaking into the camera, chin up and eyes focused, a Rockstar cap on my head.

"It's hard to move on," I admitted, on camera. Still, I wanted to ride.

"Why wouldn't I decide to ride again?"

⋅　⋅　⋅

HASHTAGS AND interviews were the least of my problems. I needed to get back on a snowmobile—something I had done only sparingly since Caleb's death—and I needed a mechanic, too, like right away. I offered the job to Nick Hickey—he'd been doing it unofficially for months—and Nick took it, happy to leave the air-conditioning installation work behind him. He began preparing the two sleds I was bringing to Aspen. He was there, next to the foam pit, all day as I practiced. And he had a third, if unstated, job, too: Nick became my part-time therapist, helping me focus by keeping the mood light. When I wanted to disappear after a long day in the foam pit, Nick would sit on the beanbags and play video games with me. When we drove north to Colorado—back to the mountain where Caleb crashed—he didn't let me get bogged down in my thoughts. At every gas station along the way, Nick popped out of the truck and started firing a pellet gun at me—feigning war, to stop the war within myself. And when the sleds needed tinkering once I started riding them in the snow again, Nick was calm, a socket wrench in hand. "Relax," he told me with his usual breezy demeanor. Everything was going to be fine—as long as I didn't think.

Right.

The slate of riders that winter included many of the old standards: Heath Frisby, "the golden boy of freestyle," ESPN called him; Joe Parsons, the most decorated snowmobiler in X Games history, with twelve medals to his name; and Sam Rogers, our old friend from Montana who had once helped teach us how to flip a sled. But with my brother gone, Hoyer retired, and Bodin and LaVallee out because of injury—again—the competition in Aspen was filled with X Games rookies, unknowns looking to make a name for themselves, as my brother and I once had. Cory Davis, an Alaskan, had a trick almost no one else had. He could whip his sled, making it swerve in midair like a car careening down a winding road. Willie Elam, a veteran sno-cross racer from Idaho, was looking to see if his skills might translate to freestyle. He had been riding sleds since he was thirteen. And Jack Rowe, a motocross rider from Chicago, was the talk of the mountain. He had been flipping in Longville, Minnesota, for weeks—signed to Team LaVallee and being hailed not only as Levi's protégé, but as the underdog to steal gold with Levi coaching him. "The dark horse," ESPN labeled him. *"Imagine Levi as your trainer . . ."*

To compete, I needed to go big. I was practicing a KOD flip. It was the same sort of flip that Caleb had attempted the year before when he crashed—and one I had rarely executed, despite practicing it in the foam pit back in Krum for at least a year now. The problem was, it was all or nothing. You dangled by your hands off the sled—so far away—while flipping upside down, and then swung back into the saddle at the last moment. Under-rotating, obviously, was dangerous; we'd seen how that could end. So I was focused on not coming up short. But that made me worry about over-rotating, which could end badly, too, with broken ankles on national TV.

"Calm down," I told myself once we arrived in Colorado. "Don't pull too hard. You know how to do it."

But I didn't—not really. Caleb had been doing such flips for years. I hadn't. Caleb would have known whether I should attempt the stunt off the hundred-foot ramp or the seventy-five-footer. I couldn't decide. What I needed, I told Nick, was another rider with whom I could speed-check over the big ramps, especially that one-hundred-footer, like I had always done with my brother.

"I don't know what I'm going to do," I said.

"We'll figure it out," Nick assured me.

Everyone was happy to see me back in Aspen. One year removed from a terrible X Games—the worst games ever—there was a different feeling on the course. Every snowmobiler—no matter where he came from or who he trained with—felt a new camaraderie. We were in this together: us against the mountain, against the odds, against the world. Let us know, Duncan said, if there's anything we can do. Jack Rowe, of all people, agreed to let me speed-check him, pacing his sled on the course. I crashed in practice, but only once—and not seriously. And I landed my KOD flip to snow at least ten times, giving me confidence. I could do this. The bigger problem on the eve of the event was personal, playing out in the garage at the house.

B.C. was applying sponsor decals on the sled, heating them up and smoothing them out over the red plastic body as my father and I looked on. I had requested that Caleb's name be displayed prominently across the nose of the snowmobile. "As big as I can get it," I had said. But as the decals went on, one by one, it became clear that the designer hadn't gotten my message. Caleb's name was small—too small, I thought—dwarfed by sponsors I didn't even recognize.

"What the hell do they do for me?" I asked.

B.C. started to explain. He had dozens of people to keep happy, he said. Not just me, but the companies who funded this venture, the people who paid our bills, financed this sled and even helped us afford the house we were sleeping in that night. I needed to understand that, B.C. said. This was a business. But I wasn't listening—and I wasn't giving in. I was going to stand up for what I wanted: Caleb wasn't taking a backseat to any sponsor.

"*Is this it?*" I kept saying, eyeing the tiny Caleb sticker.

I stormed off, angry and tearful, leaving B.C. and my father alone in the garage with the sled and the big decals that were all wrong. The main event was thirty-six hours away and B.C. had a new crisis on his hands: me.

"I'm going to fix it," he told my father.

• • •

NICK WOKE me the morning of the competition, bounding into my room where I was sleeping with Ashley and jumping into bed with us.

"Wake up," he told me.

"It's too early," I mumbled.

I had gone to bed at a reasonable hour the night before to be ready for the competition. Still, there were more than a dozen people staying in our rental house in Aspen, many of whom had stayed up late laughing and playing cards. And it felt cold outside the covers. I could feel winter in our room.

"I'm over it," I told Nick.

But he persisted, bouncing in the bed and pulling the covers off me.

"It's time to go," Nick said. "It's time to win gold." *Gold.*

The day was clear—no threat of snow—and a crowd was already gathering outside on the mountain. ESPN had scheduled a rack of qualifying rounds for the day in snowboard superpipe and slopestyle, but only one event was going to get wall-to-wall television coverage: mine, freestyle snowmobile, live to the world, in prime time. The course was ready. And my red-and-black Polaris snowmobile was, too—almost. As I made my way to the course that morning, B.C. was in a last-minute panic, still trying to get the replacement decal I wanted for my sled. He had it shipped overnight from our designer in Idaho. But when the decal didn't show up in time, B.C. turned to a printer in Glenwood Springs, nearly an hour away, to get the job done.

B.C. raced to pick up the decal, returned to Aspen, and then, finally, applied the decal inside our trailer at the course. Caleb Moore, the new sticker said—in big white, block letters, huge—laid over an outline of the state of Texas.

"Thank you," I told B.C. when I saw it.

"Of course," B.C. replied. It was almost time to ride.

"#MooreGold," people wrote on Twitter. One fan even baked the hashtag into cupcakes, spelling out the letters in the frosting.

"Let's get this trending," they said.

"Trending for a legend."

"Tune in now to watch."

Down by our trailer, my family formed a circle and held hands, praying. Ashley kissed me good-bye and my mother did, too, riding waves of excitement and anxiety and fear—and then peace.

"I love you," my mother said, giving me the hug she didn't get to give Caleb before he rode the year before.

"Have fun," my father told me. "Just go out there and ride."

For a long time, I just waited. Slated to go last—eighth out of eight riders—there was nothing for me to do but sit on my machine and watch, like everyone at home listening to commentators, Tes Sewell and Chris "Big Air" Burandt, doing the live telecast.

"Welcome, everyone, to snowmobile freestyle," Sewell said to kick it off. "Just check out this massive course built at the base of Buttermilk Mountain."

Cory Davis, the Alaskan, was up first, followed by a rookie from Montana, and then Willie Elam, the racer. Their runs were decent, but not great.

"A little tentative," Sewell noted.

"A little hesitant," Burandt agreed.

Both Heath Frisby and Joe Parsons—the veterans—fell short in their first runs of the night, too. It was like everyone was nervous, lost in our own heads, thinking of Caleb, or of crashing—of something. Finally, with our old friend, Sam Rogers, the feeling shifted. Sam, riding a snowmobile with angry red headlights, threw down the run of his life for a score of 85.33—and the lead. But only for a moment. In the very next run, Jack Rowe topped Sam, executing flip after flip, with Levi LaVallee cheering him on. His score: 85.66.

"So here we go," Sewell said.

The final run, in round one, had come down to me. I drove my sled to the starting line, looked down at my hands, and waited for Joe Duncan's cues. This was always the hardest part, when my heart began to race, under the lights and under pressure, just waiting. I'd go through my run, mentally hitting every ramp. And then go through it again, walling off the fear. But tonight, for once, I was relaxed—mentally going through my run, yes, as I sat there at the foot of the course, but also talking to my brother from behind my helmet.

"One minute," Duncan said.

I began to pray. I gave thanks for the opportunities that I had and the people in my life. I thanked the Lord for looking after my brother and my grandmother and Darrin and all the other riders who had passed. Keep us all safe, I asked, and help us. Help me. To my brother, I prayed for help.

"Just be with me," I said.

An ESPN camera was in my face. Eleven thousand people were on the mountain. "Going wild here," Sewell commented. And roughly a million more were watching at home as the moment approached.

"Thirty-one seconds," Duncan said.

I didn't understand.

"Thirty-one seconds," he said again.

He nodded his head and stepped away.

"Really?" I asked, confused for a moment. "Did they say that?"

But then I understood what he was saying: *31.* Duncan was

smiling—and I was gone. I finished my prayer, gave Duncan a thumbs-up, hit the throttle, and tore off across the snow, screaming toward the first ramp under the lights in Aspen.

•   •   •

THERE COMES a time in every life when you have to make a decision: between the past and the future, between the person you've always been and the person you wish you could be. These moments need not play out on national television to have meaning. Most never do. They unfold, without commentary or hashtags, in our everyday lives in the dead-end jobs we quit, the nowhere towns we leave, the people we choose to love, and the courage we summon at times just to wake up in the morning and keep going, trying to be better, as us.

I may never be as tough—or as cool—as my brother. I acknowledge that. I'll never have his cowboy swagger or that smile that the girls, and the cameras, always loved. I still don't trust myself to drive the cars that he treasured; his beloved Mustang and Ford Lightning just sit in my garage in Texas most of the time, gathering dust like old trophies. And I know, to some people, I'll always be the little brother, the kid they called Little Amigo, or Little Bud, or Shorty, the one who hardly merited a single mention in the high school yearbook back in Krum, short and thin, swimming inside my black tuxedo.

But I also know this: That night in Aspen I started rewriting the script for my own life. As I made the approach for the first ramp, my long hair flying in the wind from beneath my helmet, I was committed—fully committed—to whatever was about to happen. I was alone—and at peace with that idea—with seventy-five seconds to prove myself. Not just to the world, but to me.

Off the first ramp, I flipped seventy-five feet through the air, with no hands on the handlebars—big and smooth.

"Wow," Sewell said.

"Look at that big trick to start off this run," Burandt marveled.

Off the second ramp, I went even farther—120 feet—hanging off the sled doing a heelclicker, followed by a superman.

"A huge approach!" Sewell shouted.

"Ohhhhhh!"

"He got the combo!"

Then it was back-to-back seventy-five-footers. A seat grab, followed by another flip, and then a second seat grab. I was flying, racing to get an eighth trick into my run.

"I don't think he has time for this turnaround."

"No, time is out on this one."

But I didn't see the course officials, waving the red flags, telling me time was up, so I went for it anyway—a KOD flip off the hundred-footer, dangling from my hands beneath my upside-down sled, before pulling myself into the saddle again and landing—easy, like I'd been doing the flip my whole life.

"Look at what it was," Sewell said.

"Oh, man," Burandt replied.

"The question now: Is it good enough to take down Jack Rowe?"

I thought so, and my father thought so, too. "Nailed it!" he shouted, waiting for me at the foot of the course. And I hoped he was right.

"Let's check out this score," Sewell said. "What's it going to be?"

The judges' total: 91.33.

First place, with one round to go.

* * *

AT THE fence line around the course, Ashley and my mother, friends and family began to celebrate, telling me I was surely going to win. But I refused to listen. "Naw," I told them, shaking my head. "I ain't got it yet."

I could crash in my second run. Blow everything. Or someone else could pass me on points. B.C. was worried about time. I needed to go faster in my second effort—or at least move up my big KOD flip, the grand finale, to make sure I got the trick into the seventy-five-second window. We needed everything to count the second time around. And we were worried most of all about Jack Rowe, the motocross rider, competing for the first time on snow in Aspen. Rowe had something to prove—like Caleb and I did, four years earlier. We all knew Rowe wasn't going to hold back in his second run. There was an intensity to him, a confident focus. You could feel it. This wasn't a guy who was here to just put in a good showing, wave to the fans, sign a few ball caps, and go back to Illinois, or take a backseat to anyone. Rowe was here to win, just like the man who had been coaching him for weeks in Minnesota: Levi LaVallee, our sport's biggest icon. *"Imagine Levi as your trainer . . ."* As Rowe prepared for his second run, Levi was at his side, in his ear.

Yes, we absolutely had to be worried about Rowe. And also Frisby. And definitely Parsons, with his twelve X Games medals in his back pocket. Parsons once said that flipping a snowmobile felt like flying a unicorn over a rainbow. If that was true, Parsons had one of the fastest, toughest unicorns in the world—one badass unicorn. "Parsons knows how to do it," Sewell said on television. There couldn't be any complacency from me. Not now.

"Anything can happen," I kept saying.

And then I waited. And waited some more. The seven competitors behind me on the leader board would have their shot at a second run first. Then I'd have mine. I had the benefit of going last in the second round. I would know what I needed to do to win when it was my turn to ride, which was great. But that also meant, for the next hour, I could do nothing but watch. I was close—so close—to achieving something not just for me, but for my entire family. And yet, I couldn't allow myself to think about it. Not any of it. I couldn't get excited at all.

"Just focus," B.C. said, peppering me with advice. "Go though your run. . . . Make sure you throw your best tricks out there. . . . Do what you know how to do."

I found myself not listening. Not because B.C. was wrong; he wasn't. But because I didn't need his advice. I was already focused. I was already going through my run. I knew where I was going to improve it—and how. I knew how to save time—and when. I was calm.

"I've got it," I told B.C.

Round two began with drama—"This is going to be a battle," Sewell told television viewers at home—and, soon, Sam Rogers was up. He was sitting in third place, just six points behind me—a gap he could easily make up with a good run. And Burandt, the TV color man, thought he had it in him.

"How big is this for Sam right now?" Burandt asked. Our old friend was riding as strongly as he ever had before, gunning for me—and for gold. "I think this trick right here," Burandt said, "could separate him." He was heading into his third trick of his second run, a cordova flip, off the hundred-footer, placing his knees between the handlebars and arching backward as he floated through the night.

But Sam extended the trick too far, held that pose for too long—just a beat too long—and he crashed, landing hard and tumbling off his sled to the left as his snowmobile rolled away. He was fine, just dazed. Sam waved to the crowd as he stood up and walked away. But he was out.

Rowe was next, with his name written across the shoulders of his black-and-yellow riding gear. Jack Rowe, the dark horse. Jack Rowe, the protégé, Levi LaVallee's man. But like Sam before him, Rowe fell short. His score actually dropped in round two. If someone was going to beat me now, it was going to have to be the old guard: either Frisby or Parsons.

Frisby—wearing neon yellow and blue—was up first. "It's all up to Heath," Burandt said. "Heath, charging the course here." And nailing it. In flip after flip, the old warrior from Idaho was improving his score.

"This is going to be close," Burandt told viewers on television.

"A nail-biter," Sewell agreed.

But not close enough. The judges gave him an 86. I was still in first, with one man still to ride.

"Here we go," Sewell said. *"Parsons..."*

On my sled, at the foot of the course, I believed I was going to win. I said nothing about it to anyone—not my father and not B.C. But I felt good—still calm—as Parsons pulled away, riding his bright yellow sled into the night. In seventy-five seconds, I would know for sure.

Parsons started with a flip, then another. Then he hit the hundred-footer, following that with still another flip—big tricks. But the landings were loose. It wasn't the best run Parsons had ever put together in Aspen. When he finished his ride, he seemed to know it, shaking his head and falling to his knees in the snow as he waited for the judges' score.

I didn't have to wait any longer. And I didn't need to ride a second time. Parsons's score was an 86.33, good enough for second place but still five points lower than my score in my first run. It was over.

I had won.

Duncan chased me down to give me a hug. My parents began to cry. "I'm so proud of you," my mother told me, weeping. But for me, there would be no tears. As the final result went up on the board, I raced back out onto the course, flipping just for fun—the KOD one more time—and then scaled the landing on the hundred-foot jump to celebrate, shouting, fingers pointed at the sky.

"For you, Caleb," I said.

The cameras moved in and reporters started asking questions about how I did it, and why I did it, and what it all meant. And in that moment, I could have talked for hours about everything: about grief and loss, about love and family. I could have told them about Texas, and dirt tracks carved into dirt fields, and boys, young boys, half broke, but still dreaming big dreams on the American prairie. I could have told them about us. In my mind, standing there in the lights, I could feel Caleb—and see him, even—in memories flickering past me like slides from old family movies.

There he was, when we were just kids, teaching me how to flip on that trampoline back in Clyde. There he was on his quad, racing on ahead of me through the thistle and the dust, beckoning me to follow. And there he was smiling in the snow of Aspen. I could see him smiling—always smiling—and I could have talked to the reporters about all of it.

But my answer, for them, was simple.

"I did it for Caleb," I told them, "and with Caleb."

I felt like I was riding with my brother.

EPILOGUE

BY THE end of that night in Aspen, Caleb and I were the top two trending topics on Twitter, with the world seemingly watching, cheering, and chiming in about what they had seen transpire on television.

"Congrats and kisses from Brazil."

"So happy for the Moore family."

"Caleb was with you the whole time."

"YES!!!"

I wasn't finished. Two days later, I won the bronze in the snowmobile long jump competition—the event ESPN had chosen to replace the best trick medal. I was a distant third to Levi LaVallee and Cory Davis. Still, despite the fact that I had never competed in the long jump before, I flew more than 132 feet—farther than Frisby, Parsons, and even Chris "Big Air" Burandt, who left the telecast booth to ride with us. My father presented the gold to Levi in a special medal ceremony at sundown. For once, it wasn't just about collecting hardware: Levi's tenth medal and my fourth. It was about paying tribute. As the medals were handed out that evening, all the snowmobilers gathered to honor my brother.

My father had been tearful two nights earlier when I won gold, getting choked up just thinking about the year we had endured, the things we had survived. When a reporter grabbed him in the moment to ask what it meant to our family to see me win one year after Caleb's death, my father replied, "More than I can say." He couldn't quantify in a single sound bite the significance of the journey we had all traveled—together. "Caleb's riding with him," he told the reporter, stumbling over his emotions. "It means everything."

But at the snowmobile memorial, with a large crowd gathered and cameras rolling, up in his face, my father was much more at ease. He thanked ESPN for having the courage to continue the competition. "We're so glad that this is still here," he said, "that nothing's changed." That's the way Caleb would have wanted it. And he thanked the fans, too. "People," he said, "all across the world . . . We love all of you. We really do."

As he spoke, I stood between Ashley and my mother, their hands in mine. We observed a moment of silence, heads bowed. Then, we gave Caleb what he would have preferred: noise—a beautiful racket. We cheered and waved our Texas flags in the air and revved our snowmobile engines, dozens of riders holding their throttles wide open, as Caleb had once done. With the sun lying down and kissing the mountains in the distance, we had come full circle. The same, yet totally different. By the time I reached the state line, crossing over into New Mexico, headed home, it became clear just how much my life had changed. Strangers recognized me: at roadside restaurants and gas stations. Could I sign their hat? Could they have a moment? Aren't you that guy? *Colten Moore?*

Caleb would have known how to handle the newfound attention. I hardly knew what to say or how to reply. And my friends didn't know what to do with me, either. At one stop to adjust our trailer, in a small mountain town, my friends had to hide me from the fans, stuffing me inside the truck. They couldn't work, with all the people recognizing me, honking their horns and yelling. At a barbecue joint off Interstate 25 in the high desert, customers, noting our trucks sitting outside in the parking lot, called the restaurant wanting to know if I was still eating, if I was still there. "You're causing some commotion," the waitress noted, "with y'all's trailer parked outside." People even stopped me in the middle of the night. At three in the morning, some-where outside Amarillo, we got off the road to change a flat tire. A cold winter wind was blowing across the prairie, leaving us shivering with a lug wrench in our half-frozen hands and cursing at the busted radial. And still, two people—young women—wanted to know: Could they have a picture with me? Would that be okay? Of course, I said, amazed at all the attention.

Back home in Texas, it continued. I lived—for a while, anyway—in a gilded world of special favors and free dinners. At my bank, I got a loan to buy a new speedboat—at least in part because of who I was and what I had done. Everyone loved my story—the unlikely tale of the little brother from rural Texas who overcame tragedy to ride again. As B.C. had once told ESPN years earlier, a story can be more important than just about anything else. With a good story, you can go places, and I certainly was.

But not everything, for me, changed for the better. Ashley and I continued to argue, in part because I was still so angry about what happened to my brother. And one night that June, on tour in Austra-lia, she finally gave me what I deserved. She punched me in the face so hard that I woke up with a black eye. She moved out not long after that—and I pushed on, alone again, replaying our conversations in my head.

Her: I can't do this anymore.

Me: I love you.

Her: I'm going to move out.

Me: I don't want you to leave.

I came to a realization that didn't make any of the highlight reels. I may have a powerful story—one that TV can easily pack-age and sell, but winning, succeeding—one moment of triumph in Aspen and all the free dinners in Texas—can't wash away the grief of losing someone and make everything better. That sort of thing stays with you, long after the cameras stop rolling, and the television producers pack up and leave, and friends quit asking how they can help. Good stories don't come clean. They're messy, layered, contradictory, gray.

My life is complicated, just like everyone else's, maybe more so. Even winning the gold medal created problems for me. Some thought I didn't deserve it. One rider even said so, whispering about it behind my back in the months after my comeback at the X Games. I had collected gold, he said, only because so many other riders had been injured. The implication was that I wouldn't be so lucky in 2015—and key changes made by ESPN only made it more difficult for me. X Games officials decided to ditch freestyle for something they were calling "speed and style"—a head-to-head snowmobile race, over ramps, where we also earned points for tricks, for style. The event wasn't ideal for my abilities or experience. On quads, I had always been better at pulling tricks than reaching high speeds. If Caleb was brute force—all out to win—I was more finesse. Perhaps more troubling, I had never raced a snowmobile—anywhere. That was one area where a foam pit couldn't help me. It was time to go north again.

In January 2015, for a few days before the X Games, I trained on a snocross track in Elk River, Minnesota, learning how to drive a snowmobile for speed. It did not go particularly well. My machine—rarely driven since Caleb's crash—suffered mechanical glitches, slowing me down. And I lost time learning just the basics: how to turn, for starters. In snocross—and the new speed and style competition at the X Games—it was important to hit the turns as fast as possible, but not too fast. You didn't want to lose control or—worse yet—fall off. I worried a lot about the latter, about falling. And losing, getting smoked by the likes of LaVallee—a true northerner. He knew how to race a snowmobile. I didn't.

"Do you feel like you're ready?" B.C. asked me when I arrived in Aspen.

"I don't know," I said, listing all the problems I'd had, along with my general lack of experience, and my specific concerns about being embarrassed on national television by guys who knew what they were doing.

B.C. nodded. His expectations were low. If I didn't medal, it was going to be upsetting for my sponsors—that was for sure. But we'd survive it, B.C. thought. Obviously, worse things had happened to us at the X Games—a lot worse. He wasn't going to get stressed out over a medal, especially because no one thought I could win. Even ESPN, apparently, didn't give me much of a chance. In an online survey, asking fans to predict the winner before we hit the snow, the network initially didn't even bother to include my name on the ballot. I was the previous year's freestyle gold medalist and, already, I was irrelevant.

Still, it didn't matter. With people claiming that I didn't deserve to win the year before, and never could now in this new format, I had no choice but to prove them wrong. I went out and won gold—again.

• • •

THE BACK-TO-BACK gold medals solved one problem: No one could question my merits any longer. But the victories didn't change the fact that I was still taking incredible risks to make a living. Even with all my success, B.C. wanted to diversify. He had scrapped his taco restaurant idea. The new plan was off-road truck racing—Pro Lite trucks, midsized vehicles, on short dirt tracks. The trucks have roll cages; that's appealing, especially to B.C. and my parents. If I crash, I'm protected not only by the body of the truck, but by the industrial-grade harnesses strapping me into my seat. And just as important, the drivers don't age out, like they often do in freestyle. Many race well into their forties, even beyond. B.C. wanted me to at least give the racing a try. "I'm not sure you can make the money in off-road that you can traveling the world on these tours," he said. "But who knows where this can take us?"

I went back to school—driving school in California. I learned to read lines on a track, when to hit the gas, and when to brake. I learned that racing wasn't all about jamming the accelerator into the floorboards and hanging on tight till the finish, but about being controlled and having technique and understanding the rhythm of the road, of a race. Think of the truck, one instructor told me, like it's a pan of water. If you brake hard, the water's going to shift to one side. And if you speed up fast, it'll move to another, sloshing around, spilling over, making a mess. The goal, he said, is for that water to be as still and flat as possible. "You want to be smooth," he said, "in everything you do."

My first race was in Southern California in late February. It was just a few weeks after collecting my second consecutive gold medal at the X Games—and just days after I returned home after a lengthy tour doing flips across New Zealand. But I was ready—couldn't wait to hit the track—with B.C. in my ear, manager turned pit boss, offering driving advice from a lofty perch high up in the grandstand.

"Relax," he told me as I battled the other drivers in the dirt.

"Breathe."

"Let the car breathe."

"You've got nothing to prove out here."

B.C. was wrong: I did—as usual—have something to prove. Caleb would have loved racing the trucks, throwing dirt everywhere and fighting other drivers, wheel to wheel, bumper to bumper, for every inch of muddy ground. I wanted to represent him well. But it wasn't just about my brother anymore; it was about me. I wanted to represent myself well—and I did. I finished fourth in my first outing, beating some two dozen other drivers.

My parents were thrilled, and B.C. was, too. Maybe there was a future in the racing, after all. It was a possibility, anyway, and it felt good to be twenty-five years old—to be young and alive—and have possibilities.

• • • •

I'M STILL not the man I wish I could be. I wish I woke up earlier. I wish I were more productive, more driven, more focused on working toward the future, whatever that future might be. I know it upsets my parents sometimes. "It's up to you now," my father told me recently. "Caleb's here with you. He'll ride with you. But you need to drive yourself. Find a reason that will get you going."

Part of my problem is, I've never wanted to grow up. For as long as I can remember, I've always wanted the basic elements of my life to stay exactly the same. And whenever these elements have changed, even just a little, I've struggled to cope with the new reality. When we were boys, Caleb and I used to love watching cartoons. Our favorite was *Tom and Jerry*. We'd lie down on the living room floor, our heads in our hands and our faces aglow in the blue light of the television, as we watched the cat-and-mouse capers, laughing along with them. As far as I was concerned, we were going to watch cartoons together our whole lives—forever. But one day, Caleb decided he didn't want to watch anymore. Cartoons were for little kids, he decided, not for him—and I was furious, insulted even. How could he want to leave me watching cartoons alone? And why didn't he enjoy it anymore? I didn't understand it—and, in some ways, I still don't. I can still recall standing there and shouting at him, defiant: "I'm never going to stop watching cartoons!"

These are the things I remember now: scraps of conversation, moments in time, and bits of dreams. On at least two occasions since my brother's death, I have dreamed of Caleb. One dream was incomplete even as I awoke the next morning. All I could remember was that we were at a racetrack together, riding. He was with me again. The rest was lost—hard to see, as if obscured by fog. The other dream, however, was detailed and vivid. In it, I had a problem.

A group of menacing guys—three or four of them—wanted to fight me. I was outnumbered, outmuscled, and afraid. This wasn't going to end well; I knew it. Then, from the shadows, Caleb appeared, throwing haymakers. Suddenly, we were the ones dishing out the beating, brothers fighting side by side, until our faceless foes scattered, running away. I turned to Caleb—this was a dream I never wanted to end—but he was slipping away, slipping away, gone.

I don't cry myself to sleep at night anymore, like I did in the weeks after Caleb's death. But sometimes, I go to bed hoping that this dream will return. I want to see my brother again—even if just for a while.

• • •

AT LEAST a few things, however, remain almost exactly the same. I still practice at the foam pit that we built together at my parents' house in Krum. I still live in the home in suburban Dallas that Caleb and I bought together. And every Fourth of July, I return to Wheeler to put on a show entertaining the fans I know best. We drive up from Krum—my mother, my father, and I—crossing over the dry riverbeds, cracked like stone, passing through the tumbleweed towns of the panhandle, and gazing out the truck windows at mile after mile of hard, red dust.

My grandfather is there to meet us when we arrive, along with my aunts and uncles, my cousins, and countless others who know me, even if I don't always know them. They stop by to say hello after I ride, to request autographs, and, every so often, to give me something. At the show in July 2014, about eighteen months after Caleb's death, a small sliver of a boy—shy and quiet—found me to deliver a gift. It was a framed painting. "My son painted this for you," the boy's mother explained as she handed it to me. And it was beautiful.

"Thank you so much," I told the boy.

He hardly replied.

"This is awesome," I said.

Again, the boy was quiet. Too shy to speak.

"I can't believe you did this," I told him, marveling at what he created.

I'll stop by Caleb's grave in Wheeler whenever I'm in town, kneeling down in the dust to speak to him. On those visits, I tell him that I miss him and that I can't wait to meet up with him again. But far more often, I find myself gazing at the painting that the boy in Wheeler made for me, with his own hand. It's based on a photo he saw once of us—and I like the boy's version so much that it sits in my living room at home, right next to the fireplace, impossible to miss.

In the painting, there's a crowd in the background and two figures in the foreground, their backs turned. Caleb's on the right, wearing red. I'm on the left, in yellow. There's a swagger in our pose; you can tell, just by the way we are standing. But it's playful, it's warm, and the boy's rendering of the scene is pitch-perfect.

We've got our arms around each other. We are brothers.

ACKNOWLEDGMENTS

THIS BOOK began with questions—lots of questions posed by Keith O'Brien.

In late 2014, he began meeting with me at my home in Texas, recording our lengthy interviews that, at times, lasted all day. The work was not easy for either of us. The subject matter we were discussing and the memories these conversations dredged up inside me were often painful to discuss. And because of my general proclivity to keep things to myself, Keith had his work cut out for him. But he didn't give up. Day after day, he was back in my living room with a notepad and a digital tape recorder in hand—part reporter, part therapist, part friend. By the time it was over, he had recorded several days' worth of conversations.

But Keith didn't stop there. To give this narrative depth and richness, he also tracked down important documents, critical medical records, newspaper stories, home video recordings, personal journals, emails, and television footage supplied to us by ESPN. Equally important, if not more so, have been the interviews—lengthy and also recorded—conducted with important people, including, but not limited to: my parents, Wade and Michele Moore; my grandfather Charles Moore and grandmother Vickie Barrow; my great-aunt Shirley Jolly; my uncle Todd Moore; my indispensible manager and unwavering friend B. C. Vaught; my longtime girlfriend, Ashley Hammons; several fellow freestyle competitors, past and present, including Heath Frisby, Derek Guetter, Nick Hickey, Levi LaVallee, Scott

Murray, Marco Picado, Jim Rippey, Sam Rogers, and Austin Wilson; X Games organizers and ESPN executives, including Joe Duncan and the original X Games founder, Ron Semiao, now an executive at the NFL Network; Polaris employees, including company cofounder David Johnson and his son, Mitchell; Angie Hall, Darrin's mother; Elaine Gerson, a top administrator at Aspen Valley Hospital, where Caleb received care after his crash; independent medical experts, including a cardiothoracic surgeon and a cardiologist, who reviewed my brother's medical records; and countless other friends, relatives, and colleagues.

After many months, Keith and I had, literally, boxes of material, which he then turned into a story—the story of my life, this book. My literary agent, Jennifer Gates, at Zachary Shuster Harmsworth in New York, was the first to see the value in it. And she worked hard to find this narrative a home. Dawn Davis, our wise editor and tireless champion at 37 INK at Atria Books, saw the potential in it from day one, and Russell Lewis, a keen wordsmith and trusted editor of Keith's, offered invaluable early insights, helping to polish and improve the first and second drafts.

Without their time, input, hard work, and generosity of spirit, this book—what you're holding in your hands—never would have happened. I thank them all for helping me.

NOTES

ALL CONVERSATIONS and scenes that appear in this book have been reconstructed not only based on my memories but, when possible, with documents and lengthy interviews with others who appear, and don't appear, in these pages. No names have been changed. When necessary, efforts have been made to confirm important dialogue with the parties involved. And in the chapters where the narrative relies heavily on historical records to tell the story, I have detailed my sources in the notes below.

PART I

9 *"a region almost as vast and trackless":* Grant Foreman, *Marcy and the Gold Seekers: The Journal of Captain R. B. Marcy with an Account of the Gold Rush over the Southern Route,* University of Oklahoma Press, 1939, p. 231.

Full-Blooded

Critical to both this chapter and the next two were the archives at the Dolph Briscoe Center for American History at the University of Texas at Austin and the Cushing Memorial Library at Texas A&M University in College Station. I am especially indebted to the work of Ruby Winona Adams, William Coy Perkins, Sallie B. Harris, and Millie Jones Porter, whose on-the-ground reporting and oral-history gathering helped me rebuild the story of Wheeler County, and to J. Evetts Haley, whose well-researched biography, *Charles Goodnight: Cowman and Plainsman,* published by the University of Oklahoma Press in 1949, is required reading for anyone wanting to understand life on the trail in Texas in the nineteenth century.

19   *"the full-blooded":* J. Evetts Haley, *Charles Goodnight: Cowman and Plainsman,* University of Oklahoma Press, 1949, p. 36.

The Hardest Kind of Life

20   *shooting for a spot just behind the fore-shoulder:* Sallie B. Harris, *Hide Town in the Texas Panhandle: 100 Years in Wheeler County and the Panhandle of Texas,* Pioneer Book Publishers, 1968, pp. 28–29.

20   *"By this time," local hunter Emanuel Dubbs explained:* Ibid.

22   *J. N. Morris struck another man:* For the Morris, Holly, and Tanner murders, see Millie Jones Porter, *Memory Cups,* Clarendon Press, 1945, pp. 274–76.

22   *"wild for water":* J. Evetts Haley, *Charles Goodnight: Cowman and Plainsman,* University of Oklahoma Press, 1949, p. 132.

23   *"dirty, greasy, and the toughest-looking men":* P. C. Welburn, as told to J. Evetts Haley, January 21, 1932, in Fort Worth, Texas, in "Buffalo Hunting," Earl Van Dale Papers, Dolph Briscoe Center for American History.

23   *Jesus loves me—this I know:* Porter, *Memory Cups,* p. 515.

23   *"the hardest kind of life":* Tom Burgess, as told to C. A. Crudington, in "Forty Years a Cowpuncher," Earl Van Dale Papers, Dolph Briscoe Center for American History.

24   *The Palmer baby died:* Harris, *Hide Town,* p. 45.

Honky-Tonk Savior

25   *"the fighting kind":* Ruby Winona Adams, "Social Behavior in a Drought Stricken Texas Panhandle," thesis presented to the Graduate School of the University of Texas, August 28, 1938, p. 21.

PART II

91   *"There have been risk-takers since the beginning of time":* Carolyn Thornton, "Extreme Games find an audience," *Providence Journal,* July 3, 1995.

This Darn Contraption

For the historical scenes in this chapter—in particular the narrative of Edgar Hetteen's work to invent, build, and market the snowmobile by driving it across Alaska in 1960—I relied on multiple sources, including interviews with Hetteen's only surviving business partner, David Johnson; historical records, namely newspaper and magazine articles, most of which were gathered at the Roseau County Historical Society and Museum in Roseau, Minnesota; and other historical documents provided by Polaris. Especially critical to this chapter were six sources in particular: the biography of Betty Hetteen in *Mothers of Achievement in American History, 1776–1976,* published by the C.E. Tuttle Co., in 1976; Jerry Bassett's history of Polaris Industries, *Polaris Pioneers: A Star Is Born*; Lawrence A. Ingham's book, *As the Snow Flies: The History of the Snowmobile in North America,* published by Snowmobile Research Publishing in 2000; Bill Vint's book, *Warriors of Winter,* published by Market Communications in 1977; Rudolf G. Billberg's written journal, which he called "1960 Log of Trek Across Alaska by Polaris Sno-Traveler," and Hetteen's autobiography, *Breaking Trail,* written with journalist Jay Lemke in 1998 and published by Focus Publishing. It is through Billberg and Hetteen's own memories and written words that I was able to rebuild, in detail, the events of the past—especially the events in Alaska in the winter of 1960.

95   *"a motorized sled with a thousand uses":* Lawrence A. Ingham, *As the Snow Flies: The History of the Snowmobile in North America,* 2000, p. 256.

95   *"all men whose daily life":* Ibid., p. 257.

95   *"from the best quality solid oak":* Ibid., p. 523.

95   *"The Motorized Dog Team":* Ibid., p. 522.

96　*"A STILT-MOBILE has many useful purposes"*: Ibid., p. 212.

96　*"this darn contraption"*: Jerry Bassett, *Polaris Pioneers: A Star Is Born*, 1989, p. 19.

97　*"We've got two weeks"*: Interview with David Johnson, October 29, 2014.

97　*"monotonous recurrence"* . . . *"perpetual rainfall"*: Earl V. Chapin, "Early History of the Roseau Valley," *Minnesota History*, vol. 24, p. 321.

98　*"a factual nightmare"*: Ibid.

98　*"We will not raise dunces"*: American Mothers Committee, *Mothers of Achievement in American History, 1776–1976*, C. E. Tuttle Co., 1976, pp. 289–90.

99　*"I'll take it"*: Edgar Hetteen and Jay Lemke, *Breaking Trail*, Focus Publishing, 1998, p. 102.

99　*"AUTOBOGGAN . . . NEW!"*: Bassett, *Polaris Pioneers*, p. 27.

100　*"unless you were going downhill with a tailwind"*: Hetteen and Lemke, *Breaking Trail*, p. 125.

100　*"that didn't really work to people who didn't really want it"*: Ibid.

100　*"I gave them a little break on price"*: Bassett, *Polaris Pioneers*, p. 37.

101　*"we were alone with our thoughts"*: Rudolf G. Billberg, "1960 Log of Trek Across Alaska by Polaris Sno-Traveler," journal, p. 2.

101　*A Winnipeg man won*: Bill Vint, *Warriors of Winter*, Market Communication, 1977, p. 20.

102　*"Pat has big blue eyes"*: The (Beausejour) Beaver, February 16, 1965, sec. 2, p. 3.

102　*"This baby can do 38 mph"*: Ibid., p. 6.

102　*"Take it easy"*: Jerry Montgomery, *St. Paul Pioneer Press*, sec. 1, January 24, 1965.

102　*"There was a time you found a beautiful, unbroken expanse"*: Gerry Nelson, *Grand Forks Herald*, February 12, 1968.

Adrenaline Era

For this chapter, I relied not only on archival news stories about the X Games, their inception, and their growth, but also on interviews with current and former ESPN employees. Especially critical to this chapter were an interview with the godfather of the X Games, Ron Semiao, and the lengthy stories that *New York Times* sports television critic Richard Sandomir wrote about ESPN over the years.

106 *"Let's put it this way":* Interview with Ron Semiao, November 12, 2014.

107 *"Is silence hip?":* Richard Sandomir, "Is ESPN Reaching for the Young or Just Reaching Too Far?," *New York Times,* October 3, 1993.

107 *"ESPN2 has a new deal":* Richard Sandomir, "The Couch Potato Has All the Answers: Yes. And No. Maybe," *New York Times,* November 30, 1993.

107 *"Welcome to the end":* Richard Sandomir, "Coverage of the US Open Left Some Gaps," *New York Times,* July 25, 1995.

107 *"how much does it cannibalize ESPN?":* Sandomir, "ESPN Adding Channel and Attitude," *New York Times,* June 26, 1993.

107 *"Viewers keep asking":* Richard Sandomir, "ESPN Going into Overtime," *New York Times,* June 8, 1993.

107 *"This is what the affiliates want":* Sandomir, "ESPN Adding Channel and Attitude."

109 *"The events I watched":* Mike Holtzclaw, "Extreme Games Didn't Translate," *Newport News Daily Press,* July 7, 1995.

109 *"We'd be happy to get a 1.0":* Michael Hiestand, "Extreme Games Give Lesson in Marketing," *USA Today,* June 22, 1995.

109 *"To cite a common industry explanation":* Ibid.

109 *"some poor sap":* *Newport News Daily Press,* July 7, 1995.

109 *"trash sports":* Ibid.

109 *"Its stunts might kill":* Hiestand, "Extreme Games Give Lesson in Marketing."

109 *"a weeklong psycho Olympics":* Richard Sandomir, "Most Exciting Part of Extreme Games Is Extreme Coverage," *New York Times,* June 30, 1995.

109 *"it's become a franchise for us":* Carolyn Thornton, "Extreme Games Find an Audience," *Providence Journal,* July 3, 1995.

109 *"Are they thrill-seekers?":* Associated Press, "X Marks the Spot for Extreme Games," June 25, 1995.

110 *"we have two of them"*: Thornton, "Extreme Games Find an Audience."

110 *"When he finally made land"*: Ben McGrath, "Big Air," *New Yorker*, July 21, 2014.

111 *"Not only are we an action sport"*: Matt Higgins, "Hoping that X Games Can Turn White into Green," *New York Times*, January 28, 2007.

111 *television ratings for the X Games soared:* "X-treme Economics," *Forbes Magazine*, February 2, 2004.

112 *"We come from the adrenaline era"*: Barbara Lloyd, "At the Winter X Games, No Limit to Excitement," *New York Times*, January 15, 1998.

Seven Hundred Pounds

For this chapter, I relied, in part, on multiple interviews with former snowboarding great and snowmobiling freestyle pioneer Jim Rippey; the recorded footage, produced by Slednecks, in which Rippey becomes the first person to ever flip a snowmobile; and a visit to Polaris's snowmobile factory in Roseau, Minnesota, in the fall of 2014.

116 *"You like to ride the big bumps?"*: Jerry Bassett, "Big Bump Sled for 2008," Snowmobile.com, October 31, 2007.

118 *"The man, the myth, the legend"*: Sylas Wright, "Snowboarding's Jim Rippey: The Man, the Myth, the Legend," *Tahoe Daily News*, November 25, 2011.

Follow Me

In retelling the story of Levi LaVallee's double backflip in Aspen, I relied on a few key sources: ESPN's coverage of the event; Associated Press reporter Pat Graham's interviews with LaVallee at the time; and my own interviews with LaVallee a few years later. Also helpful—both in this chapter and in all other chapters related to the X Games—was the detailed reporting of *Denver Post* writer Jason Blevins.

130 *"coin flip's"*: Pat Graham, "Snowmobiler Scrubs Double Back Flip Attempt at Winter X," Associated Press, January 29, 2010.

130 *"I hope I don't wind up"*: Pat Graham, "LaVallee Set to Try Double Back Flip on Snowmobile," Associated Press, January 22, 2009.

131 *"God was on my side"*: Jason Blevins, "LaVallee Completes Double Back-flip," *Denver Post*, January 23, 2009.

131 *"Way more than the next closest athlete"*: Jon Nowacki, "High-Flying La-Vallee Will Play It Straight in Snocross Race at Spirit Mountain," *Duluth News Tribune*, December 11, 2009.

Cruel

156 *I love our sport:* "Injuries Sideline Polaris Freestyle Champs Levi La-Vallee & Daniel Bodin; Both Will Miss 2012 Winter X Games," Polaris press release, January 19, 2012.

156 *"Jeez Louise, that's scary stuff"*: Tim Mutrie, "X Games Snowmobilers Shrug Off Injury Concerns," *New York Times*, January 25, 2012.

As the Snow Falls

In recounting Caleb's crash, his care in Aspen, transport to Grand Junction, his surgery there, and ultimate death, I relied on several sources: ESPN's footage of the crash; air traffic control records in Rifle, Colorado; multiple interviews with my parents; and lengthy interviews with two medical officials in Aspen, Elaine Gerson, the general counsel and chief clinical officer at Aspen Valley Hospital, and Gabe Muething, director of the Aspen Ambulance District and the town's medical group leader for X Games preparation.

Most important, I relied on official hospital medical records, documenting, in gritty, blow-by-blow detail, the medical care my brother received in Colorado between January 24 and January 31, 2013. These voluminous records number more than 200 pages in total, including 57 pages from Aspen Valley Hospital and 148 pages from St. Mary's Hospital & Medical Center in Grand Junction, with handwritten nurses' notes, dictated radiological reports, and every other detail related to Caleb's care, including his vital signs, doctors' orders and opinions, and the timeline of events, especially in the first seven hours after Caleb's crash.

Any medical detail, or doctor's statement, that appears in quotation marks in the narrative comes directly from these records.

Twenty Minutes

173   *"Got knocked out"*: Jason Blevins, "Texas Brothers Caleb and Colten Moore Ready for Winter X Games Snowmobile Showdown," *Denver Post*, January 25, 2013.

173   *"'Pinch me!'"*: Keith Hamm, "Levi LaVallee Rallies for Gold," ESPN .com, January 24, 2013.

177   *"Caleb is not doing good at all"*: Jason Blevins, "Caleb Moore in Desperate Condition After X Games Snowmobile Crash," *Denver Post*, January 28, 2013.

Streets of Gold

The lengthy and detailed quotes from the eulogies at Caleb's funeral don't come from memory, but from video of his funeral that recorded the eulogies in their entirety. When quoting from the messages my family received, the same standards apply. These are verbatim quotes of actual messages.

Stakeholders

193   *"irreversible brain damage"*: "Sarah Burke Dies from Injuries," ESPN .com, January 20, 2012.

193   *"I have done everything except slow down"*: Tes Sewell, "Thacker Returns to Snowmobile Racing Roots," ESPN.com, January 24, 2013.

194   *"that rocketed toward spectators"*: Joe Drape, "Dizzying Heights, with Risks," *New York Times*, January 18, 2014.

194   *"Thousands have tweeted #prayforCaleb"*: David Whitley, "X Games Snowmobile Crash Shows Extreme Sports Are Extremely Dangerous," *Sporting News*, January 30, 2013.

194   *"ESPN has a choice"*: Jake Simpson, "ESPN Should Remove Snowmobile Flipping from the X Games," *The Atlantic*, February 15, 2013.

194   *"What a dumb way to die"*: In comment board on cbsnews.com story

related to Caleb's crash, "Caleb Moore Dies After Winter X Games Snowmobile Crash in Colo.," January 31, 2013.

195 *"My god . . . you're asking for death":* In comment board on theguardian.com story related to Caleb's crash, "X Games Safety in Spotlight After Snowmobiler Caleb Moore's Death," January 31, 2013.

195 *"When is enough enough?":* Jason Blevins, "Caleb Moore Crash and Rising Injuries Lead to X Games Safety Questions," *Denver Post*, January 30, 2013.

195 *"We're modern-day explorers":* Ibid.

Mental Lists

199 *"For reasons that are not totally clear":* Dr. James Narrod's medical report, p. 31, Caleb Moore's personal medical records, St. Mary's Hospital and Medical Center.

Some People Have It

211 *"Okay, the day finally got here!":* Michele Moore's personal journal.

On Board

214 *"Nobody can eliminate risk in its entirety":* Colin Bane, "X Games Best Trick Competitions Canceled," ESPN.com, March 12, 2013.

215 *"We're absolutely devastated":* "Snowmobile Freestyle Events Canceled," ESPN.com, February 5, 2013.

215 *"It's affected me probably more than most people":* Justin Hoyer, on ESPN telecast, January 23, 2014.

216 *"I would much rather be taken out":* Brian Gomez, "Winter X Progression Not Stalled by Burke's Death," *Colorado Springs Gazette*, January 28, 2012.

ABOUT THE AUTHORS

COLTEN MOORE is a six-time X Games medalist, a Texas native, and a death-defying pioneer in the world of extreme sports. He has competed and performed around the world, but will always consider Texas home. He lives in suburban Dallas.

KEITH O'BRIEN is an award-winning journalist and author. His work has appeared in the *New York Times Magazine*, *Slate*, and on National Public Radio. He is the author of *Outside Shot*, a book chronicling the power and meaning of basketball in rural Kentucky.